HORATIO PARKER

Da Capo Press Music Reprint Series

GENERAL EDITOR

FREDERICK FREEDMAN

VASSAR COLLEGE

HORATIO PARKER

*A Memoir for His Grandchildren Compiled from
Letters and Papers*

By **ISABEL PARKER SEMLER**

In Collaboration with PIERSON UNDERWOOD

DA CAPO PRESS • NEW YORK • 1973

Library of Congress Cataloging in Publication Data

Semler, Isabel (Parker)
  Horatio Parker; a memoir for his grandchildren.

  (Da Capo Press music reprint series)
  1. Parker, Horatio William, 1863-1919.
I. Underwood, Pierson, joint author.
ML410.P163S3   1973   780'.92'4 [B]   72-8291
ISBN 0-306-70538-9

This Da Capo Press edition of
Horatio Parker is an unabridged republication
of the first edition published in New York in 1942.
It is reprinted with permission from a copy
in the Library of Miami University, Miami, Ohio.

Published by Da Capo Press, Inc.
A Subsidiary of Plenum Publishing Corporation
227 West 17th Street, New York, New York 10011

Manufactured in the United States of America

HORATIO PARKER

HORATIO PARKER

(Courtesy of Pirie McDonald)

HORATIO PARKER

*A Memoir for his Grandchildren compiled from
Letters and Papers*

By

ISABEL PARKER SEMLER

In Collaboration with

PIERSON UNDERWOOD

ILLUSTRATED

G·P·PUTNAM'S SONS

NEW YORK

PRINTED IN THE UNITED STATES OF AMERICA

Van Rees Press, New York

TO

MY MOTHER

In all his works he praised the Holy One most high with words of glory; with his whole heart he sung songs, and loved him that made him.

ECCLESIASTICUS 47:8.

FOREWORD

IT MAY be the tragedy of this year 1940 which so urgently impels me, while there is time, to assemble for you the following picture of your grandfather's life. It was a way of life which was primarily simple, honest, gracious and free. This way of life seems threatened to-day. Changes of every sort, unhappy for many, doubtful for us all, may be destined to carry away much that was formerly known and cared for. As I write, the current of change that is moving in all lands, so quickly that it is difficult to follow it, seems like the wind that shakes shutters and doors in the pause before a thunderstorm. Things may grow worse or, someday, better (when the storm goes over), but they may never again be quite the same. Yet nothing is really lost while there are those who can remember it. It is for this reason that I have felt such a special sense of urgency about gathering together, while I could, the fugitive things that concern your grandfather—from the memories of those who knew him—from papers, diary-notes and letters (all that have been saved)—lest, waiting to collect them, they should be scattered and lost to remembrance. Years ago, when

you were babies, Mother quite naturally re-counted to
me many incidents in Father's life which, even then,
seemed so remote from our conditions for living that I
felt they must be passed on to you. Then came the dis-
covery of a faded old pink diary with its avowed con-
fession of faith in eighteen eighty-one.

Necessarily, this simple record, set down hurriedly
and in affection, is unpretending of literary 'style'; except as this often gleams in the wisdom, the revealing
humor, even the frequent delightful absurdity of his letters or papers themselves. I have tried as far as possible
to give you his own words, though his words were always
few and he is best expressed in his own art—music. But
since the letters are not complete, nor even always self-
explanatory (especially when New England reticence
steps in the way), I have found necessary some background of story and explanation. This I have drawn
from three chief sources: first, of course, from Mother,
whose memory, prompted by affection, is truly wonderful; then, from press-clippings or letters where these
show by indirection something about his character or
views, or else contribute to the picture of his life; and
lastly, as time moves on to the period I recall myself,
from my own memories of Father—what he said to me,
or in my presence—what we did as a family together.
But it remains a background only, kept as simple as I
can make it. This account, after all, as I have pieced it
together, is intended mainly as a thread on which to
string the letters themselves; or perhaps, better, as a
small display case in which Father's writings are only so
separated as to keep them from being jumbled together,

and to allow the individual charm of each to show to its own best advantage.

This, at least, is what I hope. Reading the letters from Father (or others) you should see a picture not only of a time and a way of living, but of a vivid, exciting and, as I think, rare personality. Not an *easy* person. Not a person to be taken lightly. If he did not like people (or their works) they generally knew it. His students regarded him with a mixture of admiration and terror. No man of high ambition, driven as Father always was, by a double devotion to music and to his family (under the less than abundant circumstances of a University dean) could be a really easy person. Yet he was a person of special delight to those who knew him well, who could be as gay and merry as a child whenever —which was often—the strain was lifted. Above all, he was always and everywhere *consistent*—all of one piece— one thing through and through. That one thing was perhaps the best New England had to offer—character. His devotion to duty, as he saw it, never wavered. But it was mellowed by contact with the old (and enduring) Germany of music, friendliness, philosophy; and the pre-war England of the University and Cathedral towns, of pleasant living as well as scholarship; and always kindled and kept alive by the vision of an artist. If such a picture emerges from the letters and papers here brought together, this simple account will have served its purpose.

ACKNOWLEDGMENTS

FOR VARIOUS quotations I am gratefully indebted to the Yale University Press for permission to reprint parts of "Horatio Parker—A Commemorative Tribute" by George W. Chadwick (delivered before the Academy of Arts and Letters in 1920) also the poem "A. D. 1919" by Brian Hooker—to the *Musical Quarterly* (courtesy of G. Schirmer, Incorporated), and to David Stanley Smith, personally, for his article "A Study of Horatio Parker," published in the issue of April 1930—to *Musical America* and to Walter Cramer, personally, for his article in their issue of December 25, 1929.

I acknowledge with sincere thanks and appreciation the friendly reminiscences of William Lyon Phelps, Wallace C. Goodrich, David Stanley Smith, Frances McCollin, John C. Adams, Douglas Moore, Bruce Simonds, and Mr. and Mrs. Sidney Homer.

To Pierson Underwood my gratitude for his tireless interest, enthusiasm, his valuable advice and work in this collaboration.

I. P. S.

CONTENTS

xv

CONTENTS

ILLUSTRATIONS

HORATIO PARKER

DIARY

January 1, 1882—Age 18.

I have not any intention at all of turning over a new leaf—but if the leaf aforesaid should get blown over or even half over no one would be better pleased than I myself. I think life offers two objectives. First pleasure —then glory. I do not think that the pursuit of one is incompatible with the attainment of the other, though I think that the man who selects the sterner more lasting and wholly insatiable one of the two would better not have too much to do with the first one, the less the better. I have nothing but contempt for such people as come into the world—stay in it a short time and then leave it without making an impression on humanity (which is the world to me). Every man should contribute to the advancement of the human race, should train himself carefully for work, should do something better than it has ever been done before, and above all, should raise such children, and in such a manner, that their standard of excellence should be higher than that of their progenitors. I wish that I might live to see this policy carried out by all men of the earth and to its utmost extent.

Everyone would be according to my thought ambitious, intensely, yet I think nothing so admirable or so beneficial as an overwhelming ambition if it is supported by sufficient forcefulness of character. Of course, I mean an ambition which may be commended by a right thinking man.

I find I have not strength of character sufficient to carry out my great ambition, which is to be pure in mind and body, and to be the first American in my profession.

I

NEW ENGLAND BOYHOOD

The Quiet Town of Auburndale

I HAVE set out to sketch a picture of your grandfather's personal life. I might say his normal, routine existence; but his life was neither normal nor routine, ever. It was, instead, hard, exciting, gay and tragic—in other words, vital. Yet its beginnings were placid enough.

Auburndale, near Boston, was a quiet New England town. The Parker family lived a very simple life. The elders of the family were three: your great grandfather, Charles Edward Parker, an architect of considerable reputation, superintendent of construction for all government buildings in New England under Grover Cleveland; your great grandmother, Isabella Graham Jennings, poetess, scholar and teacher of music; and her sister, your great-aunt, Miss Alice Jennings. The children, in that day of large families, were eight in all. There were your grandfather's brother and two sisters, Edward, Cornelia and Mary; and his four older stepbrothers, Grandfather Parker's sons by an earlier marriage.

Their home was a small Victorian house, surrounded by a high arborvitae hedge and beautiful elm trees.

There were flower gardens, an apple orchard and a barn. There was a cow, a goat, dogs and cats. To the duties of each child was added the care of these animals as part of his or her daily chores.*

The house within had a peaceful, austere quality. (I remember the parlor, which was always cold, stiff and dark.) Arriving for our visits, years later, Grandmother Parker was to be found reading by the lamp in the sitting room. We were told she read the Bible in many languages, mainly Latin and Greek. Aunt Alice Jennings, Grandmother's sister, whom I have already mentioned as a member of the household, was always bustling about. She was deaf and dumb, having had scarlet fever as a child, and therefore did not realize how much noise she made in that otherwise tranquil atmosphere.

It was Aunt Nellie who, when she grew old enough, attended to keeping the house, Grandmother being utterly impractical. Greek hexameters or problems from her other world of music generally occupied her mind to the exclusion of such mundane matters as clothes, meals, and the ordering of a house. Life was stern and vigorous. It was not particularly pleasant, nor was it meant to be. Stress was laid on the develop-

* The Parkers owned a goat that added a whole lot to the gayety of the neighborhood, and was really a circus all by himself. He had a commodious goat house to live in that I am told is still standing. It was a funny sight to see him climb out the window of his house and plant himself in triumph on the roof. His favorite article of diet was paper, and he did not care what the color or texture was, it was all the same to him, and newspapers, labels of tomato cans and the tar paper covering his house, were devoured by this remarkable animal with equal gusto and dispatch.

AUBURNDALE, MASS.

ment of the mind through industry and discipline. For Grandmother and Grandfather Parker were unusual parents, remarkably well educated, even for a time and place especially devoted to education. The basic pattern of their thought, underlying their attitude to life, was the old New England ideal of "plain living and high thinking."

[*As witness the following letter to your grandfather—age 12—from his father.*]

October, 1875.
Dear William:

You are left at Keene alone, and I beg you to remember you have the honor of the family in your keeping.

Be faithful and diligent, learn all you can and be very considerate and obedient to Patty. . . .

Act reverently at church, and remember that you are watched very closely by others, and above all remember the eye of God is ever on you. Don't neglect to pray to Him and ever ask His help in the smallest things. He is your Father ever faithful, kind and always able to do what you need as I cannot. . . . Remember people will judge your Mother and me by your conduct. Above all *act* right because it *is* right.

Affectionately,
Your Father.

In this, of course, they resembled their neighbors in that green, though stony little region where, two centuries earlier, in the snows and hardships of a Puritan winter, the Pilgrims from England had built their settlements in the wilderness. Some of those who crossed the sea in order to worship God as they chose—and incidentally to face the dangers of cold, hunger and marauding Indians—were your earliest American ancestors, forerunners of the Jennings and the Parkers of Auburndale. You can learn their names and the ships they came by (the tiny ships of that time) in the Genealogical Table in the Appendix. By 1863, when your Grandfather was born, all this was far in the past. Life in New England was settled and secure—yet its keynote was still earnestness. Someone has said that New England is not so much a place as a state of mind. It is as if New England thought had taken the shape of the New England Meeting House, sober and staid at ground level, to suit its practical view of the world, but lifting a slender, and often graceful spire that aims toward Heaven.

The mention of the Meeting House seems especially appropriate to the Parker family since it was your great grandfather, Charles Edward Parker, who was the architect and designer of the first "Congregational Meeting House" (so-called in the original deeds) erected in Auburndale in 1856. This was belated for New England, whose meeting houses—known by that name—were most of them built in the eighteenth century. Yet despite certain details that might betray to later eyes the Victorian date of its erection (it was painted brown, I remember, a color that even to me as a child seemed rather drab and unexciting!) it was, as I recall it, a well-proportioned and sound little building, thoroughly worthy, in the view of its own congregation, of the tradition of the older builders. Its spire was especially admired, an old

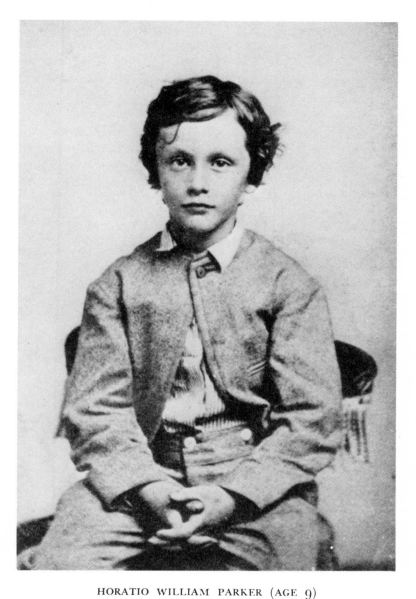

HORATIO WILLIAM PARKER (AGE 9)

(This picture was taken and made into a paper weight by father
—as a gift to his father—with the first money earned
by tending a neighbor's cow.)

account stating that: "On the night of March 24, 1862, during a violent storm, 'the graceful spire of the church was blown down upon the roof', causing serious damage to the building. . . . The steeple in falling struck the slant of the roof, and the bell, cutting a hole in the roof, fell to the ground. Strange to say the bell was not injured in its fall, and it still summons to praise and prayer." *

By a pleasant coincidence which I cannot forbear to mention, though it has no direct significance in the life of your grandfather himself, this same little meeting house, with the charming spire and durable bell, has yet another link to connect it with your grandparents; this time joining their two families together. For it was here in 1857 that the graduating class of Lasell Female Seminary—of which your then still youthful great grandmother, Isabella Jennings, was Class Poet—held their Class Day Exercises for the first time in Auburndale. Before this year they had been held in Newton, there being no church in Auburndale. Ordinary services (twice a Sunday) had been held in the Village Hall over Auburndale's only grocery store. To quote another old account: "During my schooldays we bought apples and pickles and other schoolgirl dainties of that sort, and Sundays received spiritual nourishment in the room above, where ordinary settees served for sittings, and a half dozen or so at the side of the

* The account quaintly continues that this same bell served as the Fire Alarm Bell for some time, but that the "community rejoiced when it was no longer used in that capacity"!

Reading Desk were occupied by Lasell girls in full sight of the whole congregation." *

I have quoted this account because it gives a picture of the time and place, as seen through the eyes of a contemporary. The "exemplary young women" seated on stiff wooden settees in the plain little village hall (over the grocery store)—all this must have been suggestive of the rest of Auburndale. The date, after all, is only six years before your grandfather was born. Time moved slowly then. Manners and customs did not change quickly. Add another eight or ten years, till the time when your grandfather was a small boy growing up in Auburndale, and the aspect of life must have been very much the same: unpaved, quiet roads, over which horses or one's own shoe-leather were the chief methods of conveyance; lamplit or gas-lit houses; a placid existence, with few excitements beyond church festivals or village meetings and, of course, for small boys the delights of the swimming-hole, fishing or exploring the woods and fields—all set in the surroundings of a decent, God-fearing, earnest community—this must have been what Auburndale was like.

Stiffness, and a kind of formality, of course, were part of it. Nothing was done casually, informally, as people do things now. Your great grandmother, as a piano teacher, had her pupils come to the house, and nineteenth century decorum was strictly preserved, as is evident in this invitation to a pupils' recital (an old card, yellowed with age, among Grandmother's papers):

* Quoted from "Early Days in Auburndale, A Village Chronicle of Two Centuries 1665-1870," containing Reminiscences of Early Settlers.

DAGUERREOTYPE OF ISABELLA GRAHAM JENNINGS

NEW ENGLAND BOYHOOD

Mrs. Charles Edward Parker

Requests the pleasure of your company at a

PARLOR CONCERT

*Given for the Pleasure and Instruction of her Pupils
at seven o'clock*

SOLOISTS

*Mr. John Orth, Mr. Wulf Tries,
Miss Bessie Gordon*

Pine Cottage, Auburn Place, Auburndale.

It may seem late in this account to introduce the subject of *music*—considering that your grandfather's whole life was later bound up in it. The fact is that at first he was not interested. He began as a pupil of his mother's at the age of 14, and was a most uninterested boy. Suddenly quite by accident one day he heard one of the other students having a lesson at the house. Without warning a spark was kindled—a sense of *competition* (always a driving force in his character) was aroused in him. He was determined, with a small boy's grimness, to play as well as the student he had heard. Thenceforth he worked relentlessly at his music. It became his absorbing interest. It had certainly always been his mother's hope that he would become a musician, and she made every effort, and many sacrifices, that he might hear and learn to know music. She had organ pedals put in the back room. His Diary shows how engrossed he was. He went to as many concerts as possible, and was exposed particularly to the music of the Episcopal Church, with which the family had close affiliations. At the age of 15 he set fifty Kate Greenaway verses to music in two days.* At 16 he secured an organ position in a small Episcopal church at Dedham, and would walk to church and home again, a distance of ten miles, there being no train. He was very pleased to have this position and worked hard to keep it—usually (since his musicianship was still faulty and he could read music only with difficulty) learning the hymns at home by heart. Occasionally, to his horror, the minister would ask for the wrong hymn. What happened then we are left to guess for ourselves!

It is at this point that the first comment by one of his earliest teachers, George W. Chadwick, is recorded. Mr. Chadwick says: "It was at this time that my acquaintance with him began. He had already acquired remarkable facility in harmony and modulation, to which he added a fertile vein of lyric melody, and both his melodies and his harmonies had a distinct and individual character of their own. As my pupil he was far from docile. In fact he was impatient of the restrictions of musical form and rather rebellious of counterpoint and fugues. But he was very industrious and did his work well. His lessons usually ended with his swallowing his medicine, but with many a wry grimace. It was quite natural—he concludes—that before long our relation should develop from that of teacher and pupil into a warm and sincere friendship, as it ever after-

* "Under the Window."

FACSIMILE OF "UNDER THE WINDOW" (FIRST MANUSCRIPT—1878)

ward remained." There will be many evidences of their friendship later on in this account.

Aside from his work he was a perfectly normal boy, much interested in the woods and in nature. His father was an ardent naturalist, and often took the children on long rambles in the fields, pointing out trees, flowers, birds—all the world of outdoors. Your grandfather inherited this love of nature and, as a small boy, would lie for hours on the roof to watch the stars on summer nights, charting their courses for his own amusement, trying to learn and remember their names. This early knowledge he later imparted to us children with regularity. I remember often being dragged from my warm bed to witness an eclipse, Northern Lights or other celestial phenomena. It also seems to have been accepted that if father had not become a musician he would have been a naturalist. In small boy fashion he cherished a particular fondness for snakes. These he often carried in his pockets, no doubt greatly disconcerting his elders!

He was, as he has testified himself, a normally naughty child, as well. There is one story he was very fond of telling, of an occasion when, passing to the tempting rear of the family laundress (a virtuous but ample lady) he was irresistibly impelled to push her forward into her washtub. He was only saved from a just retribution by a particularly timely nosebleed. Another tale (more creditable, but not told by himself) is reported by his teacher, who remembers that during the lunch-hour she would give him Latin sentences to translate. Upon her return, instead of classical literary efforts, she would receive bits of music which he had written for his own pleasure. One of the most romantic happenings of his boyhood has to do with a sea voyage. There was a grizzled old Sea Captain, one Ranlett by name, who lived near and was a friend of the family. He invited and finally took your grandfather on a great coast-wise schooner to Portland, Maine—your grandfather meeting him at the wharf in Boston, his stick and bundle over his shoulder like a youthful Robinson Crusoe. This was a memorable and an exciting experience for a young boy.

Yet these were sidelines, the fringes of his life. It is just at this time that his Diary begins. (If I have not before quoted his own words it is only because there have been none to quote.) The Diary entries show how completely absorbed in his work he was at the age of seventeen and a half.*

February 8
Arose 12 noon. Wrote on Rondo for Trio. Rec'd from Schmidt copies of my songs† out today for the first time. Nearly finished 1st Movement for Trio. Bed at 1:30. Wrote some on Scherzo for Trio. *Promised to pay for new rubbers for Nell.*
February 9
Arose at 8 A.M. Wrote on Rondo for Trio. In afternoon went to Methodist church to see organ—*miserable old thing.* Made a new slow movement for Trio. *Shaved myself.* Played in evening at the Methodist church (3 organ pieces of Lemmon). Went home with

---

* Italics mine throughout.
† "Slumber Song," "Wedding Song," "Goldilocks"—Boston—A. P. Schmidt. Copyright 1882.

mother. Completely finished a sketch of a new slow movement for Trio at 11:45.

February 11

Arose at 8:00 A.M. *Put my feet on stove and slept until 12.* Rec'd note from C. C. Briggs with dance job in town for 17th. Cannot take it, was engaged for another dance that eve. Lesson to Jennie and Miss Gaffney. To Mrs. Kingsbury's to supper. Saw Mrs. K. Mrs. Rose was there. Gave Mary K. copies of my two songs, "Slumber Song" and "Goldilocks." Lou Weathers is to play at an entertainment in Chapel at St. Johns on the 10th. *Must go, Amen.* Bed 12:45.

February 13

Arose 8:30. Carried Chadwick at 10:00 A.M. (the) First movement, slow movement, Scherzo and as much of Rondo as I had done. He liked first three but not last. Did not go to Orth. Home at 3:10. In the evening worked on accompaniment of slow movement. Bought four blank books and score of Beethoven ninth symphony. *Decided to begin to number my "opera."* Trio op. 6 will be what? Bed at 12.

February 16

Mother conceived idea of borrowing from Mr. Carter —plan for me to go to Europe. I think it is feasible, and hope sincerely that it both may and will be carried out next fall. *Went to a fire at 2.* Bed at 4.

March 9

Arose at 12:50. Finished copying Scherzo and copied Adagio of Op. 5. *Mother asked Mr. Burr to lend the money for me to go to Europe. He said he would.** Bed at one.

March 10

Arose at 12. Went to Boston at 1:26 to hear public rehearsal of 9th symphony under Henschel. Got very

* The Diary is always laconic. No expression of pleasure at the prospect of going to Europe is anywhere recorded in its pages.

tired indeed. *Saw Chad about going to Germany.*
Home at 9.

April 12

Arose at 1:30. Practised Bach all day. Went to
Boston, but could not go to Philharmonic because I left
my "zettel" at home. Home at 4:05. Bed at 5.

June 3

Began sonata for fiddle.

June 6

Mr. Burr called on mother in eve and offered to let
her have $150 at any time. Shall sail on July 1st.

June 7

Rec'd check from Mr. Abbott. Went in town in A.M.
Met Preston and Chad. Preston invited me to meet Lang
on next Sunday. Saw Orth. Home at 10. In town
again at 1:25.

Paid $25   —Passage money
  "   7   —For passport
  "   30   —To Orth
  "   5.50—For new pants.

June 14

Borrowed $150. Paid my passage in full.

June 25

Last Sunday at St. Johns.

June 30

Left Boston at 6 P.M. by Fall River Line. Giteau
hung today.* Played large organ in Mechanics Building
today.

---

* Giteau had shot President Garfield.

MR. AND MRS. CHARLES EDWARD PARKER AND THEIR FAMILY—1885

II

STUDENT DAYS IN GERMANY

THE ENTRY of June 30th, which marks in a way the
end of his boyhood, was the last made in this year on
American soil: on the next afternoon he set sail from
New York bound for the very different world of Germany. This had not, I am sure, been accomplished
without much earnest thought and discussion. There
must have been many conferences round the family table
in the little house in Auburndale following that February evening, so briefly noted in the Diary, when the
plan was first proposed. Somehow the money had to
be scraped together or borrowed—to be repaid later by
careful planning and sacrifice on the part of the family
at home.

Why the plan of appealing to the Carters was later
abandoned, or who was the "Mr. Burr" who finally
gave his assistance, I do not know. In any case, it made
possible a step whose importance to Father can hardly be
overestimated. It meant that his music, already reaching toward maturity, would ever afterward be grounded
in the scholarly, thorough musicianship of the old Germany. And there is a more personal reason. If the

money had not been forthcoming at this particular time, when Joachim Raff, the composer with whom Father had meant to study, had just died at Frankfort-on-the-Main, necessitating a change to Joseph Rheinberger and the "Hochschule für Musik" at Munich,* Father and Mother might never have met. In which case, I need not point out, this little record would be very different—would have to be set down by other hands than mine, to be read by other eyes than yours, his present grandchildren.

But it is probably idle to wonder about it. In one way or in another, I am sure, a means would have been found, when once the wisdom of the step seemed clear. It was Mr. Chadwick who first felt, and pointed out to the family, that he was dealing with real "talent." In these circumstances, it was agreed, America did not have enough to offer. As with all gifted students of any of the arts, Europe was thought of as the only place in which to complete an artist's education. It was not only a question of teaching, but of atmosphere or background. Only in surroundings of an older culture—mellower than America in 1880—could a young talent properly mature. So art students from all the world drifted naturally to Paris (it was the period later celebrated so nostalgically in the novel "Trilby"), and music students, equally naturally, to the Conservatories of France and Germany.

In the few remaining pages of the Diary of this year (before Father abandoned it in the excitement of his

* Where, some time before, thirteen-year-old Anna Ploessl had been admitted as the youngest student ever taken by the Conservatory.

new experiences) one can see between the lines the picture of a vanished world—a world of peace and friendly interest among the people of the different nations.

July 1

Sailed today at 4 P.M. . . . Passed Sandy Hook light ship at 7:00. Met "Nederland" going in and "City of Rome" going out. . . . 465 ft. long—47 ft. beam. Slight thunder storm about dusk.

July 2

First day out—found a stowaway . . . P. was a little sick—ate only half a dinner—saw a whale.

July 3

Second day out. Saw a nautilus . . . saw a school of porpoise . . . saw one barque.

July 12

Sighted land.

July 13

Woke up and saw the lighthouse of Penzance within two miles . . . built of red and light sandstone . . . the whole coast is very rugged and interesting . . . a great many reefs, and red, wicked looking rocks . . . passed Dover at noon . . . magnificent chalk cliffs . . . passed Ostend . . . came to the mouth of the Scheldt at 5 P.M. . . . Flushing at 6:00 . . . walled town older than the hills . . . glorious Holland sunset over the literally glassy *"zee"* . . . anchored forty miles above Flüssingen.

July 14

Anchor up at 9:30 . . . Antwerp at 12.00 . . . Cathedral chimes go by clockwork and like piano . . . pictures painted in 1812 . . . Rubens' house, Murillos, Van Dyck . . . Concert in evening.

July 16

Off at 6:00 for Cologne . . . beautiful country . . . every inch of land cultivated . . . old thatched and tiled

roofs . . . poppies and wild and blue things growing
. . . Liège beautiful on the Meuse . . . change of scenery, very wild and picturesque. . . .

By good luck, on the very day this Diary stops, we have a letter to his mother, filled with the excitement, the enthusiasm of his new experiences.

Bonn, July 16th, 1882.

Dear Mother,

I am writing in a room in the Rheinbeck Hotel which commands a view of about five miles of the beautiful Rhine. There has just been a splendid display of fireworks in the Boulevard in front of the hotel. A steamer has been going up and down in the middle of the river with red and blue and green, etc., lights on both sides, besides firing rockets, roman candles, pinwheels, etc. On the shore the display has been even more extensive. It was the finest I ever saw. They have been firing two cannon, and the reverberation from the hills around (among which is the famous Drachenfels) was perfectly terrifying.

I left Brussels at five this morning. There is so much to say about Brussels that I am afraid I shall say nothing. The Palais de Justice (unfinished, begun in 1850 and carried on incessantly ever since) is the most magnificent building I ever saw, except the six Cathedrals (Antwerp, Brussels, Liège, Aix-la-Chapelle, Cologne and Bonn). It is much larger, though, than some of them. The Bourse, Hotel de Ville, Poste Restante, Exposition, etc., etc., etc., are finer than anything in America.

I went to Mass at the Cathedral, got introduced to the organist and spoke French to him for more than an hour.

The ride from Brussels to Cologne is wonderfully interesting and varied. As far as Liège, where they have a

— 46 —

(I have got out of strong adjectives) Cathedral, is through flat country, every square inch of which is cultivated.

The cottages (always in stone), with their thatched and tiled roofs, green with age, are beautifully picturesque. There is not a *shingle* in all Europe, I have been told, and I am glad of it. The view of Liège as one comes down into the valley (it is built in a valley and on two hills; Brussels on a hill and two valleys) is simply indescribable. After passing Liège the scenery is very wild and formidable. A good deal through a mining district. Tunnels, and long ones, by the dozens.

Aix-la-Chapelle—beautiful place, beautiful cathedral, beautiful park, beautiful Rathhouse, beautiful everything.

As to Cologne—scenery unflaggingly interesting, beautiful landscapes.

Verviers on German frontier, stopped for Customs House inspection.

Duren, beautiful place, etc., eight miles from here. I had the first view of the Cologne Cathedral. It grew larger and larger, until we stopped right under it. It cost me nearly 10 francs to see the Cathedral before I got through. I did not regret them. I could write 100 pages about that Cathedral. I did not attempt to describe the one at Brussels. It was more beautiful than Antwerp, though not so large.

The Cologne Cathedral is 532 ft. high and exactly as long. There are three towers. The little one is over the dome, the others in front. I had a perfect view of the Cathedral from each of the four sides at a distance, and I also ascended the spire, which is the best way to get an accurate idea of a city before going around very much.

There are two bridges over the Rhine here, one of stone—*magnifique!*—the other a draw-bridge for boats.

Antwerp is much older than Brussels, but Cologne is older than both together. It is a very filthy, old, beautiful, puzzling, disgusting, charming, wonderful place. It used to have an enormous wall of brick all around it. Now it is strongly fortified in the modern style, but now and then an old dungeon remains—awfully romantic. Castle on the Rhine, too, between it and Bonn. Write more another time. Have seen most of Liège, Verviers, Aix-la-Chapelle, Cologne and Brüll today!! Know the way around each of them and am tired to death. Traveled 3rd Class all day. Bonn is *beautiful*. Statue of Beethoven, his house. Rathhouse, etc., etc. Ascend the Drachenfels tomorrow. Tired to death and awfully homesick. Have not spoken one English word since Preston left me. Love to all at home.

Your loving boy,
Will.

N.B. I visited the field of Waterloo when in Brussels. 'Twant much. Relics made in June, 1882, etc.

The next letter came two weeks later, after he was settled in a boarding house in Munich (where his friend Carter, already installed, seemed, as he says, very snug and comfortable). He had not yet begun his work, for the Conservatory had not yet opened, and his letter is chiefly descriptive of his travels. But there is a word about his *Gasthaus* with its view of the English Garden—descriptions of the sort of meals it afforded, the probable costs of lodging and food (all carefully accounted for, for the sake of those at home), and in general more than a picture of the sort of life he would live, as a music student in Munich, in these years just ahead.

— 48 —

STUDENT DAYS IN GERMANY

Munich, July 29th, 1882.

Dear Mother,

I have just come back from a trip in the Bavarian Alps. We (Carter and I) left here last Sunday, and rode to Murnau, about 65 miles. From there we walked to Partenkirchen, about 20 miles, through the wildest and most beautiful scenery I had ever imagined. At Partenkirchen we hired a guide, and ascended the Zugspitze, a mountain with a top about two miles above the sea. From Partenkirchen to the summit it was about 20 miles of the hardest mountain climbing I ever saw. The scenery all the way up was magnificent.

Near Partenkirchen (within three miles) there was what they called the Klamm, a ravine with a mountain stream running through it; walls of rock rising up straight 300 and more ft. At one place a cascade fell over the rocks and floated down at least 250 ft. (A stone fell the distance in 7 seconds.) At the bottom it was only mist. Two or three hours after the Klamm we entered an enormous valley 5 or 6 miles long, and ¾ miles wide. It is almost inaccessible excepting at the two ends. Surrounded on each side by tremendous mountains, each nearly as high as Monadnock and wholly inaccessible, it was a view to be remembered. The mountains on one side were solid rock without vegetation and filled with caves in which the chamois sleep, and which man never entered. On the other side they are nearly as steep but covered with a very ancient forest growth nearly to the top. The valley is filled with lovely flowers, Alpine roses, forget-me-nots, bluebells, and hundreds that I never saw before. It is too high for the Edelweiss which is found lower in great plenty.

Near the middle of the valley is a lake of the deepest blue color, really deeper than blueing water that you wash in. It is very beautiful. A little higher is a very much larger lake, the color of soapsuds with a blue tint.

— 49 —

The stream which supplies them has also a very perceptible blue color throughout. Farther up, the stream falls from a hole in the rock a distance of about 80 ft. into another vertical hole in the rock, with a noise and force which is perfectly terrifying. At the top of the valley we had a wonderful view of all that we had passed through.

Three hours more to the Knorrhüette where we passed the night. At 3 A.M. we got up and in 4 hours were on the Zugspitze. We crossed a glacier which took us at least an hour and nearly froze us. Our expectations of a view had naturally been raised pretty high, but they were surpassed. I am not foolish enough to try to describe it. The situation at the top was appalling. It was a real jumping-off place. Tremendous precipices on each side so if we missed a step or slipped in the snow we wouldn't have been fit to make tooth-picks of. We enjoyed, or rather suffered, the novelty of a snow storm in July. Etc., etc., etc.

When I first got to Munich I went for Carter and found him living in the most convenient place imaginable and immediately engaged a room side of his. We are in a regular Dutch Gasthaus. It is a long way from anywhere but more healthy and cheap for that reason. My room looks out into the beautiful English Garden. Downstairs there is a Beer Lager and restaurant so we have our meals in our rooms at cheap prices. Today I had for dinner (1) soup, (2) roast goose with (3) potatoes (fried), (4) sauerkraut, (5) bread, (6) beautiful butter, (7) pudding, (8) 1 liter of beer—for which princely repast I paid the enormous sum of 60 Pf.—15 cents. My breakfast costs 30 Pf. and my supper whatever I have a mind to pay.

My room costs 20 M. per month and my food about 1 M. 50 Pf. per day. My piano will cost about 20 M.

more. I have bought an overcoat, nearly new, of Carter, for 20 M. and must soon buy a new suit of clothes for which I shall pay about 60-80 M. My overcoat was stolen from me on the ship.

I don't know yet what my tuition will cost, probably about 300 or 400 Marks per annum. Munich is a very beautiful place indeed, which I will describe when I have more time than I have now. I feel quite at home here. Some conveniences besides what I have mentioned regarding my room are a baker's shop, a washer woman and a grocery store, a barber and a shoe store, all small and low priced, and all within 10 seconds walk of the door.

The houses here are all built of stone, very little wood is used in building anywhere in Germany. The door knobs are incomprehensibly inconvenient. The keys, of which I have to carry three whenever I leave the house, weigh about a pound each. The water to wash in is kept in a bottle instead of a pitcher, the wash-bowls are oblong pudding dishes. I sleep between two feather beds, etc., etc., etc.

If I were not homesick I should be as happy as a king.

But I have not written any description at all of my travels since I left Bonn, where I stayed two days and drank beer in the house in which Beethoven was born.

I have visited since then Konigswinter, Koblenz, Stolzenfelz, Boppard, Kaub, Bingen, Rüdesheim, Mainz, Frankfurt, Wiesbaden, Würzburg, Mannheim, Heidelberg, Stuttgart, Strasbourg, Worms, Ulm, Augsburg and many other places.

I climbed each one of the Siebengebirge and visited Castles, Churches and Museums innumerable. From Bonn I took a trip to Düsseldorf.

I could write an enormously long letter about any one place I have seen, but what am I to do? I cannot now.

I recommend you to Mr. Baedeker who has been a very good friend to me.

Next week I am going down into Switzerland with Carter on account of the very cheap excursion rates just at present.

Please do not fail to send me $50 so that I shall have it on the 1st of September, when I shall have to pay my tuition and shall have become quite settled for this year, and shall have become quite impecunious. I have made my money go twice as far as I had hoped, and shall continue to do everything as economically as possible. I have left about 100 Marks, which I could make last me till the middle of September if it were not for this trip to Switzerland, but it is so cheap that it is wicked to miss it.

I can live on what I have until Sept. 1st, but if I have to depend on my present resources after that I shall have to get into debt, which is both very hard and very disagreeable.

I was very much pleased at finding your long letter here, but I had hoped to find one from Father, too. Write lots more, longer than that, and make Father, too. Tell the young ones I shall be delighted to open a correspondence with any of them.

With much love to everyone at home, I remain,

Yours respectfully,

H. W. P.

The exact date of the next letter is not given—it is only dated "1882." But it must have been written this same summer, before the Conservatory opened, for it is clear that he does not know Rheinberger well—perhaps is meeting him for the first time at his summer home in the Bavarian Mountains:

STUDENT DAYS IN GERMANY

Dear Father,

I will try to give you a short account of my trip in the Tyrol.

Chadwick was anxious to see old Rheinberger and Whiting and I went with him. We rode from Munich to Gmund Third Class and walked from there to Tegernsee, a very beautiful lake in the Bavarian Mountains, which I think I must have described to you (I have been there twice before). The next day we walked to Kreuth where old R. spends his summers.

He received us very politely and pleasantly and was glad to see Chad and very kind to me. We stayed only two hours and went on the same day to Achenkirchen, a little village not far from the beautiful Achensee. The next day we went on the Achensee. It is a very long, very romantic lake completely shut in by great mountains. We rowed down the lake in a flat-bottomed row-boat, about four or five miles, for a Gulden.

We were now in Austria. We walked on to an uninteresting little peasant *dorf* called Jenbach, and from there took the cars to Innsbruck. You know probably about the Hofkirche there with the famous bronze statues of the Austrian Imperial family, among which is one of King Arthur of England. The Innsthal is very beautiful, very large, and completely shut in by giant mountains that seem really to have no end. In fact, the northern outlet is easy enough, but southward it has to go over the famous Brenner Pass, which I shall write to you about in the course of the day, for I am going over it. From Innsbruck we went back to Kufstein, on the border between Bavaria and Austria.

Kufstein is principally a great old fortification, now not in use, but formerly having belonged to Bavaria and of very great importance as the entrance to the rich Innsthal and the beautiful land of Tyrol. In olden

times I suspect the country was pretty well guarded
about here, for on nearly every hill I can see the remains
of an old fort or castle.

From Kufstein we went back to Munich. I was out
four days and had traveled more than 100 miles away
from Munich, and it had cost little more than 25
Marks.* I am now going down to Venice, Venedig,
Venise, Venezia. My money has not yet come, and in
fact I have had no letter for a month at all. When it
comes I have left word to have it sent to me in Italy. In
the meantime, Chad has lent me the money which I shall
need until it comes.

I am writing in the cars and just now have to go to
Kufstein and must open my baggage for inspection by the
customs house officials. On a door is painted "Visita-
tion of baggages." If I had two cigarettes in my bag
they would both be taxed. I came down to Rosenheim
from Munich last night and started at 5:30 this morning.

It is beautiful weather but I shall not get to Verona,
where I stop tonight, until 10:05 P.M., and Third Class
seats are awfully hard. I began this letter in Germany,
am continuing it in Austria, and after my next "Visita-
tion of baggages" on the Italian frontier at Ala, shall
finish it in Italy. I think I can struggle very well with
the language of musicians and monkey leaders, probably
better than with French, but that remains to be seen.

As I am now traveling through Tyrol, I would like to
tell you something about the costumes and customs of
the Tyrolese, they are so very picturesque; but they are
so entirely unlike anything you ever saw that I am afraid
I should make pretty bad work of it. The dialect, the
further south one gets, grows more and more musical,
until about Trento, or Trient, or Trent, it becomes entirely Italian. It is a most wonderful contrast to the
hard and ugly North German dialects, but although so

* Six Dollars.

beautiful it is nearly impossible to understand for one not perfectly familiar with it. Chad had an awful struggle with it and, when spoken to by the peasants, could scarcely make out one word in ten. Fortunately I knew the language thoroughly or we should have fared badly sometimes.

The old Bavarian dialect I know perfectly and can speak it pretty well. Chad can't understand the genuine sort more than half, and swears that I have the most abominable dialect he ever heard. That is not true. When I speak with common people, I use their language and speak as they do; otherwise they would think me intolerably affected, as I haven't the slightest bit of North German accent as Chad has; but when I speak with Rheinberger I speak just as High German as Chad can.

There have got some Austrian soldiers of a very peculiar description into the car. I never saw more jolly or gentlemanly fellows in my life, which wonders me, for soldiers in this country are generally cattle. These are all very handsome, too.

Already past Innsbruck. The road ascends very sharply upwards as the Germans say. Two tunnels already, one full grown and another little one; magnificent scenery, etc., etc.

We are climbing right up a steep hill all the time. Another tunnel, a young one, but dreadfully crooked, and just ahead a little baby one. The first time I ever climbed a mountain in a railroad wagon. I find it much easier than walking, but wish the seats were not quite so hard. Another tunnel. The Inn valley here is very narrow, and the Inn is a mere brook. Another tunnel, a level stretch and a little station, Patsch. Another tunnel, long, very crooked, and fearfully tipped up sideways and endways. Another tunnel. I don't get at all used to this idea of a railroad train going wandering off in the mountains all alone by itself—I don't much like it, either. I don't think anyway that a respectable, sober-minded train should do that sort of thing.

On the Rigi in Switzerland they used to tie the cars to a string, or have cogwheels or something, but here they have only rails, and very smooth ones at that. I want to make this trip with you some time and get your opinion on the propriety of the thing. They never have any accidents here, but they ought to. We go up the hill at the rate of 1 kilometer in 4 or 5 minutes. Another tunnel, a small affair, with a castle on top of it. Another station, with a little village to it, exceedingly pictur-esque—Mattei, name.

A dirty old Italian laborer has got in side of me and he smells like a trombone solo with big drums and cymbals.

There is a word over the door of the car which I think will drive me mad eventually. It is "Velhoehely." I don't know what language it belongs to, although I have asked everyone for several miles. Look for it in Web-ster's Unabridged.

The part of the road we passed over half an hour ago is now within 200 yards of us on the other side of the valley, and we have been going down hill a long time since then.

Brenner and ten minutes for dinner—three sandwiches and a bottle of wine. I shall have no more good beer now till I get back to Munich. Four other tunnels. At one place I got out and walked downhill about ten min-utes, and in a little while the train came along and I got in again. The journey after we got into the valley of the Adige was wonderfully beautiful. The many castles, the great mountains and other beautiful, natural and artificial, made the Tyrolese entirely right in speaking of their "Schones Land Tyrol."

After Ala the moon came out and made the land still

more beautiful. There are the most fearful traces all around of the inundation of last year. The amount of destruction can only be faintly imagined by one who has seen it now. Will write more tomorrow about Verona. I have no more courage now. Love to all at home.

Your affectionate son,

H. W. P.

The problem of money, as hinted in the letters, was a somewhat frequent anxiety; and I should think it might well have been. After the Conservatory opened, Mother has told me, he endeavored to live and to pay his tuition on twenty-five dollars a month. Under these circumstances, it is hardly surprising that his name was often posted for non-payment of Conservatory dues; or that his excuse, invariably resorted to, was that the "boat from America had not come!" Yet in spite of minor worries, it must have been a happy time—one of the happiest of his life. Especially pleasant were these first months, before work at the "Hochschule" began, when he had time to idle and relax (as he never had at home). Many odd hours were spent in such congenial occupations as learning the unknown German tongue, (from such people as waiters, street-car conductors, Pachträger, and the like); * walking, cycling or climbing in the Bavarian Alps, which he ever afterwards loved; or simply wandering in the town. Among other things, he bought a dog, a large white Collie named "Jack" (dogs were a passion of Father's, and move in regular succession through our family history!). Jack

* Note his cheerful superiority to "Chad" in the matter of the Bavarian dialect in the preceding letter!

accompanied him everywhere, even to places "forbidden to animals," such as the "English Garden" with its skating rink, near Father's boarding house. And there were innumerable small and cheerful inns; the excellent Bavarian beer; casual talk and pleasant companionship. It was a kind of life Father had not known, and I have imagined he loved it particularly because of its contrast to Auburndale. Not that he did not love that, too, but in a very different way.

Yet Auburndale could relax its earnestness and be pleasant and *gemütlich,* too, in its own plainer and simpler fashion; as is proved by a letter from his mother. Father kept it for many years—an instance of the deep attachment that remained with him all his life—to his mother, his family and his New England home.

Auburndale, Sept. 1, 1882.

My dear Boy,

It is still very hot and muggy and I have taken my writing-desk out on the porch where there is a breath of cool air now and then passing. The sun is behind the clouds, so it is comparatively agreeable out here.

Two little half-grown roosters are attempting to crow and making such ludicrous sounds as no other creature can. Mrs. Haskell's cockatoo whistles and chatters over the way. A host of squirrels are scolding and swearing and running up and down the trees. Nell appears now and then and tries to imitate the cockatoo's whistle. Here come five little bantams about as large as robins. They are right cunning with their pert little ways. I think I wrote you that I had sixty-three chickens.

Ted has gone down the harbor with Charlie Cole. He went early with your Father and is to stay and see the fireworks tonight. Rare fun for Ted.

STUDENT DAYS IN GERMANY

You say nothing of your health, from which I conclude you are well. Let me always feel that "no news is good news" in this respect. This letter will reach you not long before your birthday. I wish I could send you something beside love and hope for a successful year of study. But, alas, I am poorer than poverty and I cannot make anything which would be of any use just now. Before winter I will knit you some silk mittens which I am sure you will like when the cold weather comes.

We have had a present of a beautiful Altar made according to your Father's design of ash and black walnut. . . . There is some inlaid lettering on the front: "Pasci Agnos Meos.". . . There is also a Credence Table. The whole, with hangings for the seasons, has cost nearly two hundred dollars and is given by a Mrs. Dons, a friend of Miss Newell. . . .

These things you know are such a gratification to your Father, whose heart has been so fixed on the complete adornment of that Chapel. I think there was a certain justice in the fact that you were the first person confirmed in that chapel. It was meet and right that it should be so.

I hope you have the photographs. Let me know if you have received all my letters. I have written every week. Let me hear from you also, often, and remember your most affectionate

Mother, every day.

P.S. Here comes Bruin* with a wistful enquiring look on his face. He comes every day. The other day he was lying by the piano really crying with the tears rolling down his face. It is touching to see his devotion.

The next letter from Father is dated nearly a year later, in June of 1883. In this, for the first .time, the work with Rheinberger is mentioned, and a picture

* A Newfoundland dog—affectionate and sentimental.

drawn of his life as a student. I know from Mother and others how hard he was working. Only a hint of it is given in the letter, but he was, I know, a passionate student, capable of work at high pressure in such a fever of concentration that it amazed even his fellow pupils. Often he was given, for example, the theme of a fugue; and after stern criticism and correction of his original sketch, would return in the morning triumphant, with the entire assignment redone, having stayed up all night to do it (to the astonishment of the other students).

When he first went to Munich Father was a thoroughly "independent" student, inclined to question theories and rules as propounded by his elders and teachers. But in the Hochschule, this changed. Mr. Chadwick * has written of this period:

> Resistance to the dictates of musical law and order could not last under the stern rule of Joseph Rheinberger; so when Parker found himself enrolled in the classes of the eminent director of the Hochschule für Musik in Munich in 1882, his rebellion collapsed. In practice and criticism, from that time on, he showed the greatest respect for fineness of detail and the keenest appreciation of the niceties. Parker captured the admiration of Rheinberger. It is said that the teacher regarded him as the best organist among his pupils. On his side,

* Referring to Father's earlier rebelliousness as a student, David Stanley Smith says: "Mr. Chadwick bears witness to Parker's impatience with things academic and restrictive. Those who knew Parker in later years can well believe that absolute docility on the part of the young pupil was hardly to be expected. Parker himself did a little teaching, but as he afterwards said, 'not enough to do any harm!' "

Parker saw the fine series of organ sonatas by Rheinberger unfold, as the master would bring in new
manuscripts. His love for these perfect and varied compositions was based not only on his healthy admiration
of a good job, but on a sentiment not unlike the devotion
that gripped the students of César Franck.

It was at this time that he began to attend service
in the old Catholic churches, becoming always more
familiar with the essence and form of the old Masses,
which he loved. The choral music of Palestrino, Or-
lando di Lasso, Bach and Handel, soaring through the
mystic twilight of those great churches made a profound impression. The sound of the human voice is
the foundation-stone of this lovely and ancient melodic
architecture. It was the stone on which his best and
finest later works were to be constructed. No instrument ever approximated the sound of the human voice
in Father's estimation.

[*To Charles E. Parker.*]

Munich, June 5th, 1883.

Dear Father,
    At length I have time to write. I have been so very
busy with the different examinations for the year and the
preparation for them that for the last three weeks I have
had scarcely a minute.
    I am in splendid health and circumstances generally.
I have not a single debt in the world except to you and
Mother, and am in possession of 40 M. to last till the
15th when I hope to receive another remittance. You
have been so generous lately that my mind is quite at
ease. With the extra money which you sent me I have
bought myself some new music and a new suit of clothes,

and made a wonderfully beautiful trip into the Bavarian highlands. Last Saturday, Sunday and Monday I was away. I did a tremendous amount of mountain climbing and came back as fresh as an oyster, and am at present in a perfect fury of work at 40 different things. Mother wrote me something about my traveling with John Orth, when he comes. I don't think I shall be able to do that without a little extra money. My allowance of 200 M. suffices for my living simply but well enough. So soon as I have any extra expenses such as traveling, etc., I use more. If I buy music or clothes I have to live sparingly, but on the whole it is amply sufficient for my ordinary wants. I go to the opera about twice a week which costs sometimes 6 M. (when I have a standing place by the orchestra), or sometimes 1 M. 50 Pf. (when I go into the gallery). That is for both times. For other expenses I have 2 M. per week to pay for my organ practice.

I smoke now less than half as much as I did at home and tobacco is very cheap here (there is not a tax upon it, I believe), so that this is a very small item. I have to smoke cigars, for the smoking tobacco here (for a pipe) is really not bearable unless it is American, and then it costs too much. These items, and an occasional extra meal in a Wirthshaus, or cup of coffee in a Kaffeehaus, together with my daily living, room-rent, beer, etc., for servants and music-paper (of which I use a perfectly enormous amount) swallow up my 200 M. pretty completely every month.

At the present date I am exactly 40 M. ahead of nothing. When my money comes again I shall have about 80 M. extra money to live on during the month. My school is out on the 15th of July and I would like to go to Vienna and Salzburg for a couple of weeks if you can send me the necessary funds on the 1st. I should not use so very much more than usually except for carfares and living in Vienna—which is very dear.

STUDENT DAYS IN GERMANY

I should like to make some money myself but see no earthly way in which it is to be done. This summer I shall write every day in a newspaper letter and send the result to you or mother for polishing up and see if I can't earn something in that way. I think I could give lessons here but I really have no time for it. I use every hour that I have out of the school for myself. Mother said she had a musical newspaper which she could send me. I should be very thankful for it indeed. Can't you send me a "True Flag," * too, once in a while, to liven me up? The Dutch newspapers are so ponderously elephantine in everything (but particularly in their playfulness and jokes) that an American newspaper is like a glass of champagne on a hot day.

I wish you could see this town of Munich and, in fact, all Bavaria. The architectural beauties here. The many Palaces of the King and his multitudinous relations. The many and beautiful Churches, the Statues, the Paintings, the National Buildings, etc., etc. You would go mad if you only had a week to stay. You could learn the taste of real beer in the Hofbrauhaus where one gets the King's own beer at 6 cts. per liter (more than a quart). You could make a trip into the mountains and learn what old goat's cheese is like, and how cheaply it is possible to sustain existence on the face of the earth. Henceforth, I shall try my best to write to you and Mother oftener—at the very least I shall write once a week. Goodness knows I have enough to write about but no time to write it in. Our examination in Counterpoint consisted in writing a Fugue for string quartette in one day. I used only 4 hours and made a Double-Fugue which pleased old Rheinberger immensely. It tickled me, too, that mine was the only Double-Fugue in the whole batch.

* An Auburndale publication.

I append the theme which R. gave me and which is really a most miserable one.

I have written some songs for a mixed chorus which will be produced very soon at one of the closing concerts of the school. Shall direct myself, naturally.

How are the children getting along? Are they all well and industrious? How is Mother? Does she have as much as ever to do? Dave sent me a Boylston Club program the other day. (Tell him I gave it to Rheinberger). Please thank him for it and say I will write him as soon as I can.

I shall write again on Monday. (Today is Friday). Why don't some of the young ones write to me?

I have got to make and play at the Schluss concert a Double-Fugue with a Prelude for the Organ. I have got it half done, and have already begun to practice it. It is awfully hard to play. I'll send it to Mother, together with the program, when the concert comes off.

I have no more time now but lots more to write.

Your affectionate son,

H. W. Parker.

Give my love to the whole family.

P.S. I think I have received all the money you have sent but as I have kept no memorandum I must enquire at the Bankers. In the last five months there has been no mistake.

It was some time in these early days of study at the Conservatory—exactly when I do not know—that Father and Mother first met. Nor can I give many details of the courtship—though I am sure it was both charming and romantic. Mother was still very young, (she was thirteen, as I have said, when she entered the Conservatory, the youngest student ever admitted). Father, also very young, a tall, dark-haired, good-looking American. What Mother looked like in those days I can only guess, though I am certain she was very pretty. But as to Father's appearance I have Mother's own testimony that his American-cut clothes could hardly have been more unbecoming! Their homeliness and lack of style (by 1880 standards in Munich) were only surpassed by the new German clothes he bought with his first allowance check from home. He must have made a great contrast to the elegant Münchener young men, so careful of dress and appearance, as all of them were at that time. Father had been diligently picking up the German tongue, but Mother, even when she came to New York as a bride, had only small and limited English at her command.

It was not an easy courtship. Mother's family had serious objections, and indeed one can hardly blame them. The Ploessls were old-fashioned, very conservative people. America was far away, an unknown and dangerous country, populated (so far as they knew) by feathered Indians and colored people. The novels of James Fenimore Cooper, always extraordinarily popular in Germany, must have helped in this misconception. At any rate, they did not help the courtship. When Father sent Mother anonymously a small gold ring, which she rashly wore, Grandfather Ploessl irately forbade her to keep it. She wore it, however, at School, no doubt to the pleasure of the donor, and, in spite of the ring, by the next year, on Mother's sixteenth birthday, Father had so far advanced in favor as to be invited to dinner at the Ploessl home.

Yet I do not suppose that the romance could ever have flowered in marriage, except for one circumstance —that your great-grandmother Parker, bringing two of the younger children, made the long voyage from America and took up residence in Munich. Here, little by little, she conquered the Ploessl family, who recognized her rare quality as that of a kindred spirit. The end, of course, was a happy wedding—but not quite yet. Father had still to complete his courses at the Hochschule, and to write the work expected of every student before graduation. In Father's case this was "King Trojan," his first major composition.

I shall close this chapter with your great-grandmother's letter to Aunt Alice Jennings—sent in 1885; and with the newspaper criticism of "King Trojan" which was published at that time:

Munich, April 11th, 1885.

My dear Alice,

Your very interesting letters, I mean yours and Mother's, were a great pleasure to me and should have been earlier answered but that we are in a state of turmoil, as we are obliged to move, and I have had to spend a good deal of time in hunting for a new place to live. After all, we have decided to go, with the two old maids and the five dogs, to a house in Maximilian Strasse which is in many respects even pleasanter than this, looking out over a beautiful square on the finest street in the city. This house is being remodelled entirely and the two lower stories are virtually taken out and one suspended in mid air by three steps. It is only necessary now to take off the roof to complete our comfort. Really, the house is no longer habitable.

I was much interested in your account of all your goings and doings, delighted that Lornie has returned, and sorry you had so much trouble about the bill. The birthday card was most welcome I can assure you, and in its fresh New England look reminds me of home every time I look at it. Thank you for your congratulations. I wish you had been here to offer them in person, for you would have seen some very pleasant German people who came to congratulate me in their own hearty fashion; wishing long life, happiness, prosperity and the best of everything, in their inimitable courteous fashion, and every one bringing some small gift.

The poem in the "Watchman" is very good, though I know how much better it would have been if you had had more time to "lick it into shape." I am going through that sort of a struggle in translating the Poem for which Will has written music for chorus and orchestra, his latest and largest work.* It is in two parts, the first in 16 and the other in 15 divisions. It will require over an hour to perform it. English translation is necessary in order to produce it in America—you may think there's some work in it. It is an exquisite poem— in I don't know how many kinds of meter, all of which must be exactly reproduced in order to suit the music which has been written for the German text. Only those who have tried it know how much work it is, and after doing my best I shall feel like the German writer of whom I read a day or so since who, after translating Homer into German with infinite labor and care, threw down his pen saying—"Reader, learn Greek, and burn my translation."

I am as thankful as possible that Mother is again able

* "King Trojan."

to use her hand and foot, and it seems to me that with her wonderful vitality and recuperative energy she must soon be comparatively comfOrtable. I hope to be able to do something for her comfort before long.

Always your loving sister
Bella.

[*Criticism.*]
From the Munich "Allgemeine Zeitung."

The second part of the program was entirely taken up with the performance of Mr. William Parker's Ballade for solo, chorus and orchestra—"King Trojan," words by F. A. Muth. Mr. Parker is a pupil of Rheinberger, and is the most versatile and talented of the English-American colony in the Munich music school. "King Trojan" is the most important work which Parker has yet composed, although it is not quite free from faults, on the whole it is worthy of the highest recognition, and indeed we enjoyed it very much. In the treatment of vocal as well as of instrumental material, the talented composer has already made great progress; and in both he understands how to produce the most touching as well as the most powerful effects. The performance, which Mr. Parker carefully directed himself, was all that could be wished. With this highly promising composition, which secured for its author repeated recalls from the numerous audience gathered in the hall and gallery, the performance of the music school for this year closed in the most effective manner.

This is the end of the Munich episode, and Father's life in Germany. Though he conducted "King Trojan" he did not linger after its performance, but, without waiting like the rest to graduate with his class, hurried back instead to seek work in America.

III

EARLY PROFESSIONAL
STRUGGLES

New York: Garden City: Boston

I HAVE said that Father did not wait to graduate with
his class.   Indeed, as Mother has often told me, he
never received the actual diploma to which his work at
the Hochschule entitled him.   Instead he hurried to
America, on fire to find employment and to begin his
professional career.   Unfortunately at first this was
easier to plan than to accomplish.   Work for young
musicians was not plentiful; and, for a while, he and
Arthur Whiting hung out a hopeful shingle on Tre-
mont Street in Boston waiting and looking for pupils.
In this period of enforced idleness the two young musicians laid more firmly the foundations of a lifelong friendship.   It was perhaps, too, from this time when he first
lived in Boston that his affection for its people, its
brick-built streets, its pleasant air of a large quiet
town, dates its beginning.   In later years no American
city ever took, in Father's affections, the place that
Boston had always held.   Yet it must have been an
anxious, impatient period of waiting until, for Father,
luck turned.   On the suggestion of his friend, Mr. J. B.

Whitney, organist of the Church of the Advent in Boston, he was offered a position to teach music at St. Paul's School in Garden City, Long Island, at a salary of $1200 a year.

An offer of $1200, plus "living expenses" was, of course, not one that Father could afford to refuse. And presently he was fortunate enough to secure an additional position, at a yearly salary of six hundred dollars, as organist of St. Luke's Church in Brooklyn. He was now, at last, able to save, putting by with faithful regularity a portion of every check with such good effect that by July of 1886, accompanied by his sister, Nellie, he sailed once more for Germany to marry your Grandmother.

They were married in Munich on August 9, 1886, in the lovely Cathedral, the "Frauenkirche." A wedding breakfast followed, German in its lavishness, German, too, in the warmth, the friendliness and simple gaiety of family and guests. The gala festivities were only marred by the thought of the departure of the young couple to so far distant a land. Their wedding trip took them to Salzburg and Berchtesgaden, then back to Gmund on the Tegernsee, to say goodbye to Mother's family.

They left for America in September, taking ship, *The Gellert,* from Hamburg—a little party of three, Father, Mother and Father's sister Nellie. It was a stormy crossing, twelve days of rough weather on the gray September Atlantic. Mother has told me that they were seasick most of the way, but that they recovered in time to celebrate their journey, rashly treating themselves to champagne, and managing (none of them quite knew how) to spend most of their small funds before arriving in New York. After going through the Customs and paying duty on wedding presents, Father found himself with no money at all. He turned to his sister Nellie, saying: "Where can I get some money?" Luckily there happened to be an old friend of the Parker family in Brooklyn. Leaving his bride and sister perched on the luggage at City Hall, Father went to Brooklyn, via horse-car, and succeeded in borrowing sufficient funds to get home to Auburndale.

They reached Auburndale early on a Sunday morning. Mother has described this "homecoming." No one was up and about. The streets were dark and deserted. Equally dark and inhospitable appeared the windows of the Parker house itself under their Victorian gables, beyond the arbor-vitae hedge. Whether through a mistake as to the time of arrival of the young couple from Europe, or simply in New England fashion, not thinking such a gesture necessary, no one had "waited up" to greet them. For the young bride in a strange land, so many miles from home, it must have been a sad contrast to the pleasant commotion, the innumerable greetings, the warm stir and confusion that always heralded arrivals or departures of friends or family in distant Munich. However, by dint of climbing in a kitchen window, the family was aroused, and the new daughter welcomed formally, and, I am sure, warmly as well, to life in her new home.

In October, 1886, they moved to St. Paul's School in Garden City where a new life began in earnest. This was a hard move for Mother. Beside being taken, for the first time, from her home, she knew little of the language or customs of the country, and was alone most of the day, and very homesick. One can imagine how life in an American boy's school must have seemed to a young wife, hardly more than a girl, whose childhood had all been passed in Munich. Father spent his days in writing and teaching; Saturday there was choir rehearsal, and Sunday services necessitated his being away all day. There were a number of kind people who helped to fill the long hours, but many were the days of loneliness.

They moved next to New York where Father had an organ position in St. Andrew's Church, Harlem.

Father continued going to Garden City twice a week to give piano lessons. But in the midst of numerous duties, often dull and laborious, he never abandoned the constant effort of musical composition. It was during this period that he composed much of his music for practical use in the Church—anthems, services and hymns. His genuine feeling for the Church, as deep and abiding as his reverence for music, is always evident in his writing.*

Of their value from a musical point of view Mr. Chadwick has written:

> No choirmaster can fail to be grateful for these compositions. They combine in a curious way respect for tradition (Parker was always a faithful communicant of the Episcopal Church) with an escape from the dullness that is the distinguishing mark of much of the older

* Sermon by Rev. Winfred Douglas—Appendix.

music of this type. It is English, but with an ingratiating admixture of New World buoyancy. A loss of sternness is compensated for by original touches of harmony and pleasantness of melody. Parker, even in these simple compositions, never allowed himself to merge with a "school" of composers, but in every piece is unmistakably Parker.

In this connection it is interesting to note what Father himself had to say on the subject of music for the Church, particularly hymns, as set down in a paper which he read in 1899 before the Episcopal Club of Massachusetts. It is the earliest of Father's addresses (later so familiar a feature of his life in musical and academic circles) of which the text now remains; yet, in many ways, it is of a piece with all the later ones; in its honesty and directness, its quality of never mincing words—even though some of his words must have seemed very critical to the audience who heard him. Not intended for publication, and only existing in a manuscript copy, now yellowed and brittle with age, it is too long to quote entirely. But some sentences and paragraphs are so clearly and saltily phrased, and sound, moreover, so much like Father—with the whole accent of his speech and personality—it seems worth while to copy them here in the hope of saving them from oblivion: *

Music is the art which comes nearest to the people and the one to which they can get nearest themselves—This

* It is evident that his hearers took with respectful attention the criticism of this young man whose own eventual contribution was to bulk so large, for he was chosen as sole editor of the Revised Hymnal of 1903. In 1916 again he was a member of the Committee for revision of "The Hymnal" now in regular use in the Episcopal Church.

art has been the faithful handmaid of the Church from the beginning of the Church's history, and has shown itself worthy of care and respect at the hands of the Church authorities—but the Church has recently treated the art something like a stepchild, or, perhaps, rather like a pretty stranger—nice to have in the house, but to be sternly suppressed at the first sign of independence. . . .

Partly as a result of this attitude, he says—Musicians look upon the making of hymn tunes as an amusement rather than a serious occupation. The setting of conventional words has not appealed strongly as a task to the great living composers, and on the whole Church music is regarded as a field in which it is expected that they shall gain their daily bread rather than immortality. . . .

However, the simple nature of the Hymn Tune is nothing against it. There must be all kinds of musical as well as natural creations! A hymn *must* be simple. It may be very simple without great harm—many of them are—but it ought not to be didactic, if it is for common use. What is true of hymns as poetry or literature is true in greater measure of tunes as music. They must be simple in rhythm, melody and harmony, not merely on account of the difficulty of things not simple, but rather because nothing other than simplicity will serve as a vehicle of expression for the feelings of a mass of people.

Later in this same early paper he sets down one of the main tenets of his own deeply-felt musical faith: *

I want to advance the proposition that we can get used to anything. If we give people weak music they will accept it and love it. *Likewise will they accept strong*

* Italics mine.

music, and love it infinitely better in the end, for they can also respect it. . . . I want you to consider our Hymnal in the light of this statement. We are entrusted with the task of forming the taste of the next generation whether we will or no. They ought to begin where we leave off. It is possible for us, with care and devotion, to find out what is best for them, what they can respect as well as like, *and it is our duty to do so. . . .* There must be some good poetry and some decent tunes, outside the ennervating atmosphere of complacent platitudes, musical and literary, which permeates our present books. . . . *I think the moral effect of bad music much worse than that of foolish verses for I feel sure that it makes a deeper impression, especially on the young. . . .*

To revert to the tunes—some of those which have worn best are the minor ones of our great-grandfathers, like "Windsor," a splendid type that will flourish long after the last vanilla-flavored tune has vanished from human recollection. Most of these have been carefully omitted from the present collection, but they will be in the next. I acknowledge that the hymns of our ancestors were dry, but they had something in them which preserved them. The modern tunes are the reverse of dry, but they surely lack something which will keep them from spoiling. In fact they carry in themselves the . . . seeds of decay. To show that I am not afraid to take my own medicine, I call your attention to Hymn 23. The tune is by a young person (Horatio Parker) brought up under the enfeebling influence of the Anglican School. The tune is not without its redeeming features, but it carries its sting in its tail . . . I have heard this ending characterized as "measly," and I have agreed. . . .

I have given you what I venture to think an honest, expert opinion regarding one phase of our Church music. I plead for higher standards of artistic morality. . . . Music has developed magnificently . . . and has fulfilled to the utmost her duties and offices toward the Church. Shall not the Church now through her clergy and those of her laity who are in authority acknowledge and perform those duties which she owes to music, by refusing and repudiating that which is common? By encouraging and sustaining . . . that only which is entirely worthy? . . . In this way, and only thus can the Church purify and elevate the Art which has served her longest and best. . . .

From all that I have been told these first years in New York were hard. There was very little money. Worry, combined with almost overwhelming domestic grief accentuated Father's already poor state of health and nerves. Yet there were helpful and alleviating circumstances—aside from the growing recognition of his work. In the winter of 1898 some of Father's work was performed by the "Manuscript Society" in Chickering Hall—a society founded by Frank van der Stucken for the performance of American manuscripts. Father and Mr. van der Stucken became great friends. Both taught in the National Conservatory of Music, of which, for the three years 1892-5, Antonin Dvorák was director. The black-bearded, dynamic Bohemian composer—son of a butcher of Prague—whose E Minor Symphony, No. 9 (known as the "New World Symphony") swept Europe and America in 1893, was one of the great figures in music whom Father knew personally.

Brief and hurried jottings in Father's Diary of these years give some idea of the course of his existence. These little diaries were carefully preserved by Mother through the years and date from 1890 to 1919.

EARLY PROFESSIONAL STRUGGLES

March, 1890
Wrote "Service in E."
April, 1890
Finished piano pieces. Saw Van der Stucken—Stubbs.
May, 1890
Anthem.
June, 1890
Dined with Chad and Whiting.

Apparently in this summer of 1890 he took a brief holiday abroad; but, as usual, even in the course of what may have been intended chiefly as a vacation interlude, continued writing. I do not know Father's reason at this time for visiting the succession of English Cathedral towns listed. Possibly it was to study choral methods as then in use in the great English choirs. Perhaps it was then, too, that he and his work first became known to that group of English musicians, ever afterward among his closest friends.

The Diary continues:

July, 1890
Arrived Antwerp—Munich—Rehearsal—Rheinberger.
August, 1890
Finished Anthem. Sketched and finished "Kobold." Oxford — Leamington — Warwick — Stratford-on-Avon —Worcester—Hereford—Gloucester—Bristol, etc. Dreadful gout. Sailed from Liverpool (10:30). Wrote on "Kobold." Very rough.
February 4, 1891
Grandmother Jennings died. Resigned Garden City.
April 13, 1891
Wrote a little on "Hora Novissima." * "Harold Harfager" from Schirmer.

* The first mention of this work.

May, 1891

Finished "Ballade in F Minor." Sketched "Jubilate."

July, 1891

Played for Chad. Mary died.* Played for Mother—P.M.

September, 1891

Wrote on "Dream King."

March, 1893

Letter from Mrs. Thurber about prize. Sent "Hora Novissima" to Thomas (Theodore Thomas).

May, 1893

Bicycled.

July, 1893

Finished Cantata "Holy Child."

The brief notation in the Diary of April 13, 1891, indicating merely that he had begun work on a new composition, is the first mention of a work which has been called "by far the most important of his early period, and one of the most important in the whole range of American music." It was the work which was to bring him his first measure of fame, carrying his name out of America to England, and ultimately to Cambridge University, and to put an end to the comparative obscurity of the young writer for the Church. However later criticism may deal with it (and the words quoted were written long after its composition), it seems fair to think that of all Father's extended and more ambitious works this is the one most likely, with the passage of years, to lose none of its power and beauty, but to seem as fresh and vigorous as the day it was written: and so, perhaps—though one can only

* Father's sister.

guess—to keep his music and memory alive for future generations.

Begun, as Father notes, in the spring of 1891, it was carried forward with labor and devotion for the next twelve months; until, in April, 1892, exactly a year after he began writing, he sets down in the Diary; "Scored 'Hora Novissima.' " It had been a year of great physical and mental strain; and also, as already mentioned, of almost intolerable domestic grief. His father, to whom it is dedicated, died before its completion. So, too, did his younger sister, Mary. In this same tragic year Mother and Father suffered the loss of a baby boy. Under the stress of grief and suffering—perhaps born of it—"Hora Novissima" was written. I feel sure that the profound courage and spiritual sympathy of the two people closest to him sustained and encouraged him through this period of sad bereavement. Highly sensitive as Father always was, these sorrows profoundly affected him. He was intensely nervous for years to come, and only Mother's patient assistance and unobtrusive comfort and cheer enabled him to carry on his work. Almost equal in its support in this particularly difficult time was the companionship and inspiration of his own mother. It was she who had made the English translation (admittedly fine, though it is seldom sung) of the great Latin hymn of Bernard, known as "The Rhythm of Bernard de Morlaix on the Celestial Country" on which the work is based.

Of the work itself, many commentators—friends, colleagues, impartial critics—have written. For many years it was in the field of choral writing—on subjects usually,

but not always, of religious inspiration—that Father's
work was to find expression. In this group, looking
backward, "Hora Novissima" stands at the top.

The poem, a favorite of his father's,* begins in the
Latin in which it is usually sung:

Hora novissima Tempora pessima Sunt vigilemus!
Ecce minaciter Imminet arbiter Ille supremus;

Keeping faithfully, as was necessary to the rhythms
of the original (since the music was written to fit the
Latin) Grandmother's translation opens:

> Cometh earth's latest hour,
> Evil hath mighty power;
> Now watch we ever—
> *Keep we vigil!*
> Lo, the great Judge appears!
> O'er the unfolding years:
> Watching for ever.

Writing of it, years later,† one of the best-known and
respected of American critics and writers on music,
Mr. H. E. Krehbiel, sets down, after a brief description
of the poem and the scheme of the oratorio, his own
opinion of its musical worth:

> "The poem," he says, "is of the twelfth century, and
> was written by Bernard of Cluny.‡ It lives in the ad-
> miration of most English-speaking people who know of
> it today chiefly because it supplied the original of Dr.
> Neale's beautiful hymn, "Jerusalem the Golden." It is
> a marvelously beautiful composition, and as Professor

---

* Father made a beginning on another Latin poem, "Vita nostra
plena bellis" but abandoned it on account of the monotonous rhythm.
† 1910.
‡ Bernard de Morlaix was a monk of Cluny.

Parker has shown, excellently adapted for musical setting, being full of varied and lofty imagery and noble
sentiment. Professor Parker's music is fascinating from
beginning to end to lovers of sound, dignified and earnest music. The work is divided into eleven numbers,
including solos for soprano, contralto, tenor and bass, a
quartet for the same voices, an unaccompanied chorus in
the old style, a capital fugue, a double chorus and four
unaccompanied choruses. At the bottom of the composition lies a finely conceived and very pregnant phrase,
in the development of which Professor Parker has dis-
played a degree of learning, a skill, a fluency of musical
utterance, both vocal and instrumental, a sense of
euphony and depth of feeling which redound to the
credit, not only of him as an individual, but also of the
American school. . . ."

It was for mother and son, in a truer sense than usual,
a labor of love; a happy renewal of early days when, as
teacher and student, they had worked at the beginnings of music in Auburndale.

Father had left, at this time, his organ position at St.
Andrews and gone to the Church of the Holy Trinity
(which he called, with characteristic absurdity, the
Church of the Holy Oilcloth, because of its gaily-colored
and variegated roof-tiles) where he had a most genial
relationship with the Rector, the Reverend Walpole
Warren. Here "Hora Novissima" had its first public
performance by the Church Choral Society of New York
on May 2nd, 1893, under the direction of Richard
Henry Warren. The Handel and Haydn Society performed it in 1894, and the Cincinnati Festival the same
year, with Theodore Thomas conducting. It has been
given, since then, many times and in many places, most

notably at the great Three Choirs Festival at Worcester, England, and in Hereford. Indeed it still is sung frequently by church choirs and oratorio societies. Its moving climaxes (whether of pure, unaccompanied voices—the effect Father always so loved—or of full orchestra and chorus together) have not lost their power to stir singers and audiences. As I write a notice has reached me of a performance of "Hora Novissima" to be given within a few months by the Long Island Choral Society at the Cathedral of the Incarnation, in Garden City, Long Island, and at a concert of the Juilliard School of Music.

Considering it in retrospect, many years after its first performance, David Stanley Smith has written:

> And yet the world comes back again and again to "Hora Novissima," possibly because in this work Parker's distinctive style is for the first time fully developed. His originality—and "Hora Novissima" is very original —is the more striking in that repetition of treatment has not yet set in. The melody and part-writing are particularly fascinating, and the sentiment, which lies midway between the celestial and human, responds naturally to the feeling of the thoughtful listener.

In the same vein, but considering also Father's many works for the Church, Mr. Wallace Goodrich, head of the New England Conservatory, has written to me in a letter this year:

> As a composer your father achieved success in many fields, but it is particularly as a choral writer that he was surely pre-eminent. His early training in music, following the strict and splendid training of Rheinberger in vocal part-writing which he received in Munich, en-

abled him to produce in "Hora Novissima" a noble work of which I know no equal in American choral literature. And his position as a leader in the creative field of church music has neither been challeneged nor filled in this country; for it has been all too rare to find musicians of distinguished attainment in other musical fields who have labored with so much earnestness in the service of the church. Your father left the church richer because of what he wrote for her.

In 1893 Father became organist and choirmaster of Trinity Church in Boston. Mother and Father moved to Boston where life was much happier. They were near Grandmother Parker and many of the family, as well as Father's old teacher and friend, Mr. Chadwick, Arthur Foote, Philip Hale, William Blake and others. The Kneisels and Adamowkis made a most sympathetic and congenial group. As one who knew him recalls: "Here he found his old friends, Chadwick, Foote and Whiting, and spent many happily contentious hours in their company." . . . "He once described the criticism," the reminiscence continues, "that these young men made of one another's music as 'characterized by candor rather than courtesy.'" Knowing Father, I can well believe it.

Boston had begun to reach out of its essential Puritanism to acknowledge and encourage the arts of music and painting; Father and Mother both enjoyed their life there.

Letters from Mr. Chadwick and others, written to Father at about this time, and giving an indirect picture of this genial existence, are included here in default of any letters of Father's own—none of which, if they existed, have been saved from these early days.

[*George Chadwick to Father.*]
THE ST. BOTOLPH CLUB
April 8, 1886
Feast Day.

My dear Parker:

Being a holiday I find time to answer your profane and characteristic epistle. In the first place, Kneisel gave me for an excuse for not playing your Quartet that so many people wanted to hear the Brahms Sextette that he was obliged to put it on the programme to the exclusion of the great American work! And in the second, Bro. Gericke told the astute critic of the Transcript that he was so exhausted by his arduous labors with the flute and oboe player that he could not longer read a score, in which the as. critic doubtless sympathized with him! . . . That, however, he saw no reason why he could not play it next season and also that he could do it *early* in the season.

This, I think, will be much better for you than to have it *half* played at the M.T.N.A. For that I would select the Allegro in B flat which you can easily call "Venetian Overture"—which is not only a good tune but a good name also (which is rather to be chosen than great riches).

I saw your Father and Sister this morning at the Requiem Mass at the Cathedral, (Cherubini in C minor) and I hope to see your smiling countenance at Easter, when we will punish several "Bocks" * if it lasts till then. I have made some new songs for one and four male voices, scored my Dedication Ode, and am at present at work on a string quartet in D maj. which I hope to show you completed when you come. Whiting

---

* "Bock Beer," of course, only available in early spring.

— 84 —

MOTHER AND FATHER, standing, AND MR. AND MRS.
GEORGE W. CHADWICK, MUNICH.

has done *Nothing! Niente! Gar Nichts!!* Says he hasn't any ideas. Perhaps I haven't either, but I don't mean to forget how to make notes, etc., while I am waiting for some. I want to see that opera of yours. That it will be funny I have no doubt.

Yours aff.

Chad.

[*Chadwick to Father.*]

March 9, 1889.

My dear Parker:

I am much obliged for your offer of the Raff but I got it myself and we have concluded not to do it this season.

I have been too devilish busy to write letters, but have managed to knock out a short Ballad for ch. and orch. which I shall be glad to turn loose on you.

I heard that they played your waltz at the M.S.S. but did not hear it owing to a slight coolness in my direction from the M. S. Club.*

What do you think of Whiting's engagement? The last conundrum here is, "Does Miss Gorham put 'whiting' on her neck?"!! Gericke played "Melpomene" the other day in a style to make your hair stand up. I understand that we are all invited to Cincinnati in May to conduct our own works, and have all our expenses paid. This will be a good chance for you to see us again. I have been looking for you ever since Christmas and have not yet given up hope. . . .

Parker, if you've got any of that B&H 20 line music paper I wish you would lend me ten sheets. . . .

Sincere regards to the handsome and amiable *gnädige frau* and to the baby. Write soon.

Faithfully yours,

G. W. Chadwick.

* Manuscript Society.

HORATIO PARKER

[*Chadwick to Father.*]

William Street,
Brookline,
Nov. 24 18—?

My dear Parker:

Well the boot is on the other leg this time sure, but I have just been getting into a new house and haven't written many letters.

I am busy as the devil, have a first rate, regular, nickel-plated chorus with the Orchestra Club and I think that our season will be a great success.

I would like very much to do "King Trojan" but I am afraid of the M.S.S. parts which our girls and boys are not used to. However, if you can send me the orch. to try, I should like to make the experiment.

I have not made any music for the devil of a while, but I mean to go to work pretty soon now and see if I can't whack out something. Have you seen my Christmas anthem pub. by Schmidt? It is not very high or very hard and I should like to have you try it if you like it.

Whiting played his Concerto the other night, and was quite well received. It is a scrappy work, the material is beautiful, characteristic, original even, but I think it shows his want of sound technic in counterpoint and form very plainly.

Write soon and let me hear what you are up to.

Yours faithfully,

Chadwick.

[*Theodore Thomas to Father.*]

Felsengarten Cottage
Bethlehem, New Hampshire
July 4, 1899

My dear Mr. Parker:

Your letter of July 2nd received. I am glad that you

have written something for Orchestra,* because I like to see your name sometimes on my programme. I accept the dedication with pleasure and pride. I regret that we cannot meet this summer, but console myself with the knowledge that you will have a good time in England, and rejoice in the fact that an American goes over to conduct his own work.

Wishing you all success and health,

Believe me,

Sincerely yours,

T. Thomas.

[*Stephen A. Emory to Horatio William Parker,*
at Cathedral School of Saint Paul.]

Newton Center, Mass.

May 25th, 1888

My dear Mr. Parker:

This is the first opportunity I have had to acknowledge your kindness in sending me the Buffalo Programme containing a notice of yourself and your courteous reference to me.

Yet, while it is a pleasure to count you among my former pupils, I feel that I did very, very little toward your success. I hope you feel as Beethoven felt, as Michaelangelo felt—that when God trusts the care of a talent in the hands of any human being, it is that it may be used unselfishly, nobly, to bring one's fellow men nearer their Maker and all that is good in Heaven and on earth. They whose aim has been to become great have rarely achieved greatness; but the truly great in all times have been those who in self-forgetfulness have been so lost in the greatness of their particular mission in life, that, all unconsciously, they have grown and developed and risen into the majority of immortality. May He

* "Northern Ballade."

— 89 —

HORATIO PARKER

who has so richly endowed you keep you worthy of His Goodness.

With hearty wishes for your prosperity,
I am always,
Yours cordially,
Stephen A. Emory.

IV

YALE UNIVERSITY

In 1894 Father was called to New Haven, being asked to take the chair of Music at Yale University, Mr. Samuel S. Sanford acting as emissary. Father and Mother debated it earnestly before Father finally accepted. Desirable as such a position in one of the great Universities must have been to a young man, it was a wrench to leave Boston and their kind and comfortable circle of friends to take up life in yet another new place. Yet, in the end, Father accepted. The advantages were undoubted, both professional and otherwise; one of the lesser ones being, so I have been told, that life in a quiet University town seemed to offer a suitable environment in which to bring up a family of daughters! The appointment was confirmed by President Timothy Dwight, in a formal but friendly and courteous letter.

The move to New Haven must have been made some time in summer or early autumn, September, before the assumption of Father's new duties. We lived on the corner of Sachem and Prospect Streets in an old-fashioned, square wooden house which is still standing. It is, later, in this house that I first actually remember

Father. He came into the bathroom while my sister and I were being simultaneously scrubbed in a large tin tub, and said solemnly; "Queen Victoria has died."

His work at Yale started at once, classes being first held in the squat, old Treasury Building that stood in the middle of the Yale Campus. Here, as David Smith says; "A few students with the Professor in charge occupied a double room, with a piano and blackboard for tools." Early in this period he organized, at the instigation of Mr. Morris Steinert, a local symphony orchestra which became the "New Haven Symphony" and is still the combined possession of Yale and New Haven; also a women's chorus named "Euterpe." All this time he was writing assiduously. He still went to Boston, as Organist and Choirmaster of Trinity Church, and on these trips always found time to visit with his mother in Auburndale. In New Haven Father's association in an academic atmosphere with many of the older scholars, such as Timothy Dwight, Dr. Munger, Professors Seymour, Morris, Sumner, Dexter, Perrin, Lounsbury and Ray Palmer was immediately stimulating to one of his intellectual taste. The Seymour family became very dear friends and I can remember visiting them in their beautiful old house on Hillhouse Avenue. We children had rooms on the top floor and it was very dark and spooky, dimly lighted by low gas jets.

Another member of the Yale Faculty and a dear friend from early New Haven days was Professor William Lyon Phelps (known affectionately to generations of students, as "Billy Phelps"). He has sent me, at my request, a sheaf of delightful reminiscences of Father, of which I should like to quote part:

> He (Father), Professor Phelps writes, conducted the Yale Music School through the most difficult years, and lived to see it take its place among the best in the country; and as the First Conductor of the New Haven Symphony, his training brought it from unavoidable amateurishness to professional excellence.

But although I was a spectator of all this, for I was present at the first performance of the Orchestra in 1894 in Alumni Hall, and although I sang among the basses in the chorus of *Hora Novissima,* in other oratorios, in the *Greek Ode,* all under his direction, and although I succeeded our beloved Morris Steinert as President of the Orchestra, it is not of Dean Parker's professional work that I wish to speak; and for two excellent reasons. Not being a musician I am incompetent, and others who are musicians have given their testimony.

I have often wondered whether a remark he made to me on a certain occasion was really true. He was invariably kind and affectionate with me, though I think my ignorant enthusiasms about music must often have appalled him. We were sitting together at a concert of the Boston Symphony Orchestra. At its close he said "You *enjoy* music more than I do." I said, "Do you mean that because you can detect the slightest variation from pitch by any player and I never can, that my comparative sensitiveness is a blessing?" "No, I don't mean that at all. I mean that you listen to the thing as a whole and enjoy it; I am continually thinking of its construction from the professional point of view." I suppose many people enjoy certain *books* more than I do, because they do not read them with critical attention.

I had the honor of being one of his colleagues on the Yale Faculty; he was one of Yale's greatest assets. But I also had the privilege and pleasure of knowing him intimately; my admiration and affection for him cannot be exaggerated, it was boundless. To people who did not know him well he sometimes seemed cold and aloof. To ignoramuses who attempted to discuss music with him he was annihilating. He was severe with the Orchestra at rehearsals, but as he was always right and they knew it, they followed him as soldiers follow severe disciplinarians who lead them to victory. Over and over again I have heard him say to the Orchestra—"The only thing I know is music, but I do know that." As a matter of fact, his mind ranged over many fields of culture, but he emphasized at the proper time and place his authority.

It was refreshing when standards were slighted or ignored by the mob, to see a man adhere without any reservation or compromises to the ideal. He had a quiet irony all his own. He never raised his voice, he never became declamatory in denunciation; his ironical calmness added to the effect. He quietly asked the double basses if they thought they were sawing wood; a professor in another department said to him, "I know you do not care for the pianolas, but which one would you advise me to buy?" His reply: "You had better consult a mechanic."

There is one thing to which I *am* sensitive. That is the spoken English language. I have never heard any one speak it with more beautiful enunciation or more correctly and yet without one shade of affectation or pedantry. This made his remarks at golf all the more humorous. It was a delight to play golf with him, as it was a delight to be with him anywhere. He was the best company in the world, if one knew him well and intimately, as I did. His comments on some of his own shots were devastating, as annihilating as his remarks at an orchestra rehearsal, or after hearing in public some piece of music inadequately given. I have always regretted I was not present at a dramatic moment; but Professor Harry Jepson was, and reported it to me. He was playing in a twosome with Mr. Parker, and the latter's ball got into a sandtrap. Parker did not know that Jepson was directly behind him, an auditor as well as spectator. He thought he was alone. He made three attempts to get the ball out of the sand, without success. Then he said something to the ball. He never raised his voice, but in that same beautiful, cultivated accent came the words, "And now, you white-faced . . . ," and Jepson's laughter interrupted.

Like some other absolute masters in their chosen professions, Mr. Parker was not only without any mannerisms or affectations, he hated them. In appearance he was studiously inconspicuous. No one meeting him would have guessed he was a professional musician. He looked like a cultivated gentleman, a man of the world. His hair was cut and parted in the prevailing fashion, his clothes showed such conformity that I cannot remember what they looked like, though how distinctly I see his face: I remember him in the early nineties when he came to Yale, when he played the organ in St. John's Church at the wedding of Joe Sargent and Louise Weir, when he first conducted the orchestra. A perfectly turned out gentleman with his rather pale face and dark mustache; and when his hair became grey I can remember him equally well, but not any more distinctly.

It might seem strange to those who knew Dean Parker only officially, or to those who asked him absurd questions, that I affirm positively he was one of the most lovable, one of the most affectionate, one of the most loyal and devoted friends I ever had. My mind goes back to him constantly, for I miss him terribly.

New Haven, indeed, "made him welcome," as President Dwight had assured him it would, and as Professor Phelps' charming words of memory and appreciation testify; but life did not consist only of these pleasant scholarly and academic contacts, but behind the scenes, as always, of unremitting hard work, in a schedule that as time went on only grew more laborious. And there was another factor with which Father, and his family, too, had to reckon—a constant trial for many years of his fortitude under the exacting conditions of his life. This was the painful rheumatism which, though it may have begun earlier, seems at this time to have grown acute. No matter what Father was doing; conducting choir rehearsal, correcting proof, coming home in the evening from the Music School, any time it might strike. It is one of my earliest memories, and no one who knew him could have escaped realizing how painful it was. Yet he bore it and, in spite of its toll on his strength (and temper!) always managed to get through the work that had to be done.

Mr. Goodrich recalls this, among other things about Father. The rest of his kind letter, part of which I have already quoted, seems appropriate here, since much of it deals with this time:

> Through a friendship of thirty years or more—during most of which he lived in New Haven—I saw him only when he came to Boston, save for delightful visits with him and your dear mother in West Chop,* and even an overnight stay outside of Munich.
>
> But my recollection of him is vivid; of his keen wit,

* West Chop was the scene of early summer vacations.

MOTHER, FATHER AND BROWNIE—PROSPECT STREET,
NEW HAVEN

his ready repartee, and of his boundless store of knowledge in so many fields, which I always understood he had inherited from his father. How many times did his more than frequent reply to a statement, "I do not agree with you" precipitate interesting discussions! That he was serious in his work goes without saying. I recall when with him in West Chop that he had set himself the task of completing ten pages daily of the orchestral score of "St. Christopher"—the work which contains the marvelous *Jam Sol Recedit*—which he did while the rest of us were swimming or playing tennis, or doing something of the kind, which he so enjoyed himself.

I often substituted for him at Trinity, at special services for which he could not come up from New Haven; not forgetting the occasions when he had struggled through a morning service only to have to lie down prone on a pew in the choir gallery during the afternoon owing to the miserable and agonizing gout with which he was then afflicted. But, above all, I think of his cheerful bearing under the worries and cares of his profession, and of the warm friendship which we enjoyed for so many years; and of his devotion to your mother and you children, for do not forget that I knew you all when you were babies!

Time, and time only, proves the value of the work we all do in our careers; but my estimate of your father's place in the annals of American music has not changed in these twenty years since his death. The music school which he founded (as a complete school) at Yale testified to the soundness of that foundation upon which he built, and which influenced the many students of music in this country. Two of these students are at the Conservatory today—Quincy Porter, who is at my right hand, and Ruth Conniston Morize, and we speak of your father so often.

This letter mentions "St. Christopher," or to give it its complete title, "The Legend of Saint Christopher; A Dramatic Oratorio." This was Father's next big work, finished some time in 1897, and given in New York by the Oratorio Society in April, 1898, Walter Damrosch conducting. It contains, as Mr. Goodrich says, the lovely chorus for unaccompanied singers—"the marvelous *Jam Sol Recedit,*" as he calls it—which many think Father's most perfect single achievement. Like "Hora Novissima" it is based on a text by his mother—this time not a translation, but an original poem. Mr. Chadwick mentions here—as was the case with "Hora Novissima"—the "labor of love" it must have been for his mother to write it for him. "Working side by side," he says, "the poem and music grew at the same time." Written in this way, it was partly an expression of both. David Stanley Smith says of it:

> "St. Christopher" reaches its high moment in the religious scene. Here, in the great "Gloria in Excelsis" and the a cappella chorus, "Jam sol recedit" (probably Parker's finest and most beautiful composition), the composer accomplishes new and splendid things. American music at the turn of the century shows no passages comparable with these in originality and massiveness of structure.

Again brief notes in the Diary give a picture of the passing, and always active, days:

1895
January
   Kneisel—Rehearsal, Quintette—Tavern Club—Gout—Adamowski, Whiting played "Suite" at St. Botolph Club.

April
Lunch with Loeffler and showed him Concerto—Phelps musical.
June
Sailing for England—Oxford—Cambridge.
July
Kneisel, Roth, Svecenski, Goodrich, Nickish, Gericke. Met Brahms *—Ischl—near Salzburg.
1896
March
Handel and Haydn Society—Rheumatism—Euterpe Concert. Dined Seymour's—Kneisel concert.
June
Europe—rheumatism—rain, rain, rain.†
1897
August
Finished part I of "St. Christopher"—Rheumatism—Pneumonia.

Here—written in a quiet interval when Mother and Father had gone to Lakewood to allow Father to recover with rest from the effects of pneumonia, I record the first letter I can ever remember receiving from Father. So far as I know, it is the earliest letter sent to any of us, as children, which has been preserved. After this when he went away many and charming letters reached us, needless to say to our delight:

[*Father to Isabel.*]   Laurel House,
                                        Lakewood, N. J.
                                        March 19, 1898.

My dear little Isabel:
Mamma received your letter this morning and was

* Johannes Brahms.
† The two facts of rain and rheumatism become almost synonymous!

very glad to get it. She thought you wrote very nicely and she liked the picture very much.

I hope we can get home the day after you get this letter, but there is time for you to write once more if you will do it on Monday.

We both like to get letters from you and Lottie. You must tell Lottie to be sure to use warm water for the mice and rats and not to get soap in their poor little eyes. In teaching them to dance she must be gentle and never speak roughly for they learn much more easily if they are treated nicely.

I hope you and Gracie are both good children and that you both go to sleep in the day-time after you come home from your walk with Lizzie in the morning.

I am sure that you always stay on the sidewalk and never run out into the road and that you do not plague Gracie, for those are not nice things to do and I am sure that you are a nice child.

Now kiss Gracie and Lottie for me, and be good and have a nice time.

With many kisses for yourself, I am,

Always your affectionate and loving
Papa.

I include here, though its date is somewhat later than the others, a letter from Professor Bernadotte Perrin, because it bears so exactly upon the kind of work Father was doing in these early years.

[*Professor Perrin to Father.*]

New Haven,
March 30, 1904.

My dear Colleague:

I tried long to find you last evening, because it seemed to me that I could not sleep before I had expressed to you my personal gratitude for an exalting, uplifting evening. I felt when I heard that you were to attempt the Passion Music (*St. Matthew*) that you were too ambitious, but such success as you achieved inspires all your fellow workers to dare more nobly.

I may represent perhaps the average listener last evening, and I can honestly say that I noticed only twice that the chorus * did not attack well, but even then the sensation of incompleteness was not pronounced, and was very fleeting.

The extempore tenor was weak at the start, but increased in power and effectiveness up to the very last.

Of course you will be conscious of many imperfections, but I think you ought to feel that you have done the University and the community of New Haven an inestimably great service in bringing into the life experience of some three thousand people so fine a rendition of so great a work. And Bach! ah, what a revelation to me of his power to achieve great results by honest means! All the quaint fervor of evangelical Teutonic piety was poured out into every listener's soul!

I hope you may feel some slight reward for all your exacting and multifarious labors in the knowledge that my sense of gratitude to you, deep and keen, is shared, whether they take the trouble to tell you so or not, by many who realize more and more every year what a blessing your presence and work among us is.

I wish I could cure your rheumatism for you. As I told Mrs. George Farnam last evening, rheumatism seems to love "a shining mark." But "that too will pass."

Sincerely yours,
B. Perrin.

* The chorus in which Professor Phelps and others sang.

HORATIO PARKER

[*Oscar G. Sonneck to Father.*]

Washington, D.C.
May 10, 1908.

Dear Professor Parker:
Abul Hassah Ali Becar:

O, wie der ruich ver-Vennest (?)

The sins of my youth are heavy on me and I am doing
penance. That is why I chopped the heads off the caps
so consistently and patiently. Look at the Russian names
with the translations into impossible English and you
will see that I am really a penitent sinner and could
have adorned in olden days a tree stump, my big left
toe scratching from morning to night my right nostril.

I thank you for your kind words of appreciation and
encouragement. The fundamental idea governing my
efforts here is to build up systematically a collection that
will render it unnecessary for the American musician,
scholar, historian, conductor, critic and what not, to go
to Europe if he wants to consult and study scores. How
far we have accomplished this task the opera catalogue
proves only in part. Since its publication we have added
over one hundred scores. I wish you could see our
collection of orchestral and chamber music. That is
still more formidable and I doubt knowingly that you
will find anything like it abroad.

You see, my ambitions run high but it is so difficult to
make people understand that the Library of Congress is
our National Library in the same sense as the British
Museum is for Great Britain. One of my pet schemes is
to induce the representative American composers to de-
posit with us autographs showing them at their best.
MacDowell gave us the autograph score of his "Indian
Suite," Dudley Buck his opera "Serapis" and his Golden
Legend. We also have the autograph of Paine's "Mass in
D" and his unfinished "Lincoln" symphonic poem. *But
we do not have as yet any autograph of Horatio Parker.*

— 104 —

Though you appear to be closely related to this representative American composer, you will admit that our National Library should possess some characteristic work or works of his in autograph. Can't you induce the gentleman to see the matter in my light? Please do. It would make things so much more cheerful for

Yours sincerely

O. G. Sonneck.

V

ENGLAND

DIARY
1899
    Letter from Ivor Atkins for Worcester Festival.
"Hora Novissima!!"
    Read paper on Hymnal.*

THIS is all we have to assure us of Father's pleasure at being invited to go to England—two terse exclamation points! I believe, however, that these many visits were a source of the greatest imaginable pleasure and delight to him. He obviously felt warmly sympathetic in this environment, both musically and personally.

Sir Ivor Atkins, graduate of Queen's College, was organist of Worcester Cathedral in England. The invitation was for Father to go to Worcester and conduct a performance of "Hora Novissima." No such invitation had ever before come to an American composer. The great "Three Choirs Festival" held at Worcester was an institution with 175 years of history behind it, and conservative, as are all British institutions. How his music and his name had traveled so quickly and so far I have never quite known, though I do know that some English musicians (as Mr. Watkin Mills of Bristol, for example) had been in America and had heard

* Quoted in a preceding chapter.

FACSIMILE OF THE FIRST PAGE OF "HORA NOVISSIMA"
(Courtesy of the Library of Congress)

"Hora Novissima." Mr. Mills had returned to Bristol eager to have the Bristol Choral Society give it, but Bristol, forestalled by Worcester, had perforce to follow later with a performance of "St. Christopher." Worcester itself, enthusiastic about "Hora Novissima," invited Father later to compose a work especially for its Festival. This was the "Wanderer's Psalm" (later referred to in letters) built on the "Peregrine Tone," a theme of Gregorian chant which legend ascribes to days as early as the Last Supper of Our Lord. Another work commissioned by and composed for the musical authorities at Worcester was the "Star Song."

Speaking of this time Father says:

"Since my first visit to England I have felt very much at home in that country. It seemed at first as though I was visiting relatives of whom I had always heard, but whom I never had seen. I have had most delightful experiences of English hospitality, and feel a profound admiration for that distinctly Anglo-Saxon institution as well as gratitude for the cordial frankness and goodwill I have always met among my British colleagues.

"My first experience with an English chorus was rather amusing. I attended a rehearsal with the understanding that it was to be strictly as a listener, but the conductor was delayed by a lame locomotive somewhere in Yorkshire and I had to conduct. There were a few misunderstandings. What is called a 'pause' in England we call a 'hold' in America. I did not know what minims and breves and crotchets were—we call them half, and whole, and quarter notes. But we soon got into sympathy, and I enjoyed the practice thoroughly.

The best English choruses are quite the best choruses in the world. I have great hopes for English music. With Cowen, Elgar, Mackenzie, Parry and Stanford the nation has made great progress within my own memory. The Germans and French have made enormous strides in recent years, but I am not sure that they are in a direction in which Anglo-Saxon need strive to follow. I hope for a powerful school of Anglo-Saxon music in time—less subjective and nerve-racking than that of Continental races, more broad, reserved and self-contained, with a larger respect for that economy of resource which characterizes all true artistry, and I hope that Americans may bear their part in the development of this school."

It is impossible to disentangle Father's comings and goings at this time. Whenever he had a summer vacation he went to England, usually for the performance of one or another of his works.

For the most part the letters tell their own story, occasionally, luckily, in a very close daily sequence. And, since they are able to, I cannot do better than let them speak for themselves.

[*Chadwick to Father.*]

1900

My dear William:

I had thought to see you again either here or in Boston before you sailed, but as it is now too late, this is to send you my best wishes for a great success and a safe return. You are now a missionary, whether you will or no, of the American Board of Musicians, and I know that you will continue the conversion of the British which you began with such great results last year.* None of us could do it as well, and we are all proud of your success *"im voraus."* You deserve all and more.

Some Sunday when it rains I hope you will find time to write me a few lines about Hereford. And so goodbye and God bless you, from all the

Chadwicks.

[*Father to Isabel.*]

August 15, 1899

My dear little Isabel:

Yesterday I wrote a letter to Lottie but it was with pencil and on an old piece of paper and I think it is only fair to write one to you, too. You can ask Lottie to read this one to you and you both will be about even. I am in a very strange country called Wales. The people all speak Welsh which I cannot understand or even pronounce at all. There are two men in this room in which

---

* [*Newspaper Clipping.*]

Musical Times, London
September 1, 1899.

The "Three Choirs Festival," soon to be holden at Worcester, will be invested with unusual interest. An American composer will make his first appearance at an English Musical Festival.

At Worcester, Professor Parker will conduct (and he is an excellent conductor) his "Hora Novissima" (an analysis of which appeared in *The Musical Times* for October, 1893) a work that is eminently suited to the religious environment of an English cathedral.

Much has been said in the public press on the entente cordiale between the two English-speaking Nations of the world, the theme is one that should never cease to vibrate in the hearts of all true sons and daughters of both countries. And should not its harmony be strengthened by the internationalities of statesmanship, commerce, journalism and art? Therefore, as the oldest English musical journal, and as representing the musicians of the "Old Country," we extend a cordial welcome to an apostle of harmony from the other side of the Atlantic—the distinguished composer who is to honour us with a visit at Worcester in the person of Horatio William Parker.

I am writing and although they are talking quietly what they say sounds a good deal like firecrackers, and one of them speaks as if he had a piece of pie in his mouth, but I cannot understand a single word.

I am going to learn a few words of Welsh to scare you and Grace with when you are bad, if you ever are bad, when I come home. It would be nice for you to be so good that I should forget them before I need to use them. This is a lovely old town called Carnarvon. It is beautifully placed on an arm of the sea. I have been riding nearly all day in sight of the sea and through a very beautiful country. I will tell Mamma more about it in my next letter to her. One time I looked out of the window and saw a long line of geese walking in single line something like this . . . . . . and I thought at once of my three little chickens at home. Not that chickens are geese, but I thought I should like to have them see this long line of silly looking geese. I am sure they would have made you laugh.

The children here all wear sunbonnets when they play on the beach, and have bare legs; they are very much like West Chop children except when they speak. I am afraid some of them are rather bad, but some I can see are very good and always mind quickly and speak gently to their nurses and their mammas and their sisters. When I write to Grace I shall try to tell her a little more about them.

There is a great old castle here which I like very much. You must get Lottie or Mamma to tell you what a castle is. It looks a little like this but much finer and is built of gray granite surrounded on all sides by a deep ditch or moat to keep people out who ought not to get in. I am at the end of the paper and must stop now and go to bed, although you are probably just having your supper.

With much love and many kisses OOOOOOOOOOO

OOOOOOOOOOO which you must divide with Mamma and the two other children.

Your loving
Papa.

[*Father to Lottie.*]

August 30, 1899

My dear Lottie:

I do not feel that I ought to draw any pictures in your letters, so they will not take so long a time or so much effort as those which I write to Isabel and Grace.

I left Ilkley (not the house where Isabel was born but the place it was named for) this morning and spent the best part of the day in riding to York. Not New York where you were born but old York, one of the most famous cities in all English history. I think it was for hundreds of years the most important city in all England, excepting London.

It has one of the most beautiful churches on earth. York Minster it is called. I think it is the largest Church in England, and just now I think it the most wonderfully beautiful place I have ever seen. I walked all about it this afternoon and rode around and through the city in many ways on my bicycle to see how it looked from different points. It was completed in the 13th century and is very satisfying to look at. You may tell Mamma that I have bought a glorious photograph of it. Our part of the Cathedral, the Chapter-house it is called, was so very beautiful to see with the afternoon light streaming through its old stained glass windows that it actually made me cry. I never shall forget the overpowering effect of that beautiful white marble and windows with the most exquisite coloring I ever saw.

I hope you may see it some day when you are old enough to understand and appreciate it. You must not tell people that it made me cry, but you may remember it, and when you see the place, if you ever do, I think you will know why. Tonight I am asleep in a queer old English hotel in Durham. Durham is near Scotland and has the finest Norman church in England. The Church Cathedral is side of a great old Castle and both are built upon high rocks above the River Weir, which almost surrounds the city. I hope that I can find some photographs which will show you just what it looks like.

I wish I could go from here to the North, but I must get to Leeds the day after tomorrow, so I must turn southward again. I send you in this letter a cutting from a Worcester paper, which will show you what some people thought about your papa the first time he had anything to do with an English chorus. It was very good fun for they did sing well, and I loved to hear them. Ask Mamma to keep the cuttings to paste in our book. Last night I called on Sir Alexander MacKenzie, who is President of the Royal Academy in London. He was very nice to me and received me in his slippers and didn't have any collar on. We had a long talk, and he walked home with me, and, of course, I had to walk back with him, which was rather a task for he lives half a mile up in the air, as it seemed to me.

He is a Scotchman, and always says *wass* for worse, but he is an original character, very interesting and a splendid musician. I am glad I saw him. All the good musicians have been very kind to me, and I expect to meet a lot more of them next week.

I have been on my bicycle almost all day and am very sleepy. It is too bad that this letter is not more interesting to you. I will try to make the next one more so, but I want you to answer this letter. If you get it before the 9th of September, send your answer to Liverpool, but if later than the 8th send me a letter to the S.S. *Etruria* which will (D.V.) arrive in New York on the 23rd of September.

I hope to see you on the 24th, but want to have a letter in New York just as soon as possible.

With much love and many kisses to you, to Mamma and the two smallest chicks, I am,

Your affectionate
Father.

[*Father to Lottie.*]

Chester
July 16, 1900.

My dear Lottie:

There is really not much to write about, but I am lonesome and just a little seasick and write to you for lack of someone to talk to.

The *Etruria* reached Liverpool late Saturday night. Just late enough for me to miss the last train for Chester —by about 20 seconds. I heard the horrid thing whistle at me as it went out of the station at Birkenhead. Since there was nothing else to do I went back across the Mersey and went to bed in the Lime Street Station Hotel. The bed was very unsteady and rocked badly all night so that I was very seasick indeed in the morning.

I had my breakfast at 11:30—my watch, which still tells your time, said 6:30, so I thought it was not so very late after all.

Then I went to Chester at 2. I saw Dr. Bridge, who is very like Mr. Woodcock of Garden City. He took me to his house and gave me tea and bread-and-butter and strawberries—big ones which one must take by the stem and dip in sugar. Delicious they were in flavor—better, I think, than any we have at home in America. It was then about six, so I took out my trusty bicycle and rode till about 8:30. Lamps do not have to be lighted till 9:18. I rode out to Eaton Hall where the Duke of West-minster lives sometimes. I think I wrote about it last year. He has a front driveway more than three miles long. I went around again toward "Hawarden," which is called "Harden," a castle in which Mr. Gladstone used to live. There were the same beasts in the park which I saw last year. Hundreds of ridiculous little rabbits with white tails when they hopped, but gray all over when they were still. I think I shall try to draw one of them for Isabel in my next letter. They all look alike and they did not let me get near enough to see whether they were the same ones I saw last year, but there were many more. I think they must have relatives staying with them for the summer. There were the same splendid pheasants with brilliant feathers and proud heads and, best of all, a great herd of beautiful fallow deer—the most graceful things you can imagine. I suspect it was just their bedtime for the little ones rushed back and forth about the field as if they had been Grace and Isabel running into the hall and bathroom in New Haven. The old ones scolded a little once in a while, but it seemed to have only a slight effect on the young.

There are beautiful fawn-colored deer, as large as the largest of the calves we saw in Mt. Carmel with beautiful spots on their sides. The smallest deer were about as large as the largest rabbits and the smallest rabbits were about as large as the rubber one Grace used to have. I am tired and must get up early tomorrow so goodbye. More next time.

Best love to you all from
Your lonesome
Papa.

There is a break in the letters here naturally accounted for by the busy days of rehearsal for the first performance of "Hora Novissima," September 14, 1899.

ENGLAND

The Diary entries, however, give a bare outline of events.

1899
August
   England—Worcester Cathedral—rehearsal at 8 P.M.—Called on MacKenzie—
September 14 ...
   "Hora Novissima"—Worcester—Splendid performance.—Presentation of vase.*—Luncheon with Mayor—Dined—Picnic—Speak to the Bishop.—Sailed from Liverpool.

The letters again take up the story.

[*Atkins to Father.*]

> 8 College Yard
> Nov. 13th, 1899
> 10 P.M.

My dear Parker:
   I am just in from a choral practice and mention this, not because I want to point out my virtue in writing at this hour, but *rather to tell you that I have seen it*—after some months, after I had even forgotten all about the fact that there ever was to be such a thing—well, tonight,

---

* [*From old clippings.*]

Presentation to Professor Parker.

Today (Friday) was the anniversary of the birth of Professor Parker, and so cordial have the relations been between himself and the chorus that a suggestion to mark the event in some practical way was quite enthusiastically taken up. A very handsome potpourri Vase of Worcester porcelain was purchased. The Vase is of handsome design, stands some 18 inches high, and is a splendid example of the potter's art.

The presentation took place this (Friday) afternoon in the interval between parts I and II of the programme, outside the western door of the Cathedral. Here were assembled the members of the chorus, and in addition many admirers of Professor Parker, whose genial and kindhearted manner has secured for him many friends during his short sojourn in Worcester.

this 13th Nov., I have seen *it*—THE PEDESTAL.* Somerton might be an elemental force, he moves so slowly. About Sept. 29th I broached the subject of something in the shape of a letter mentioning the presentation, and at the time we thought a pedestal the more suitable thing, but at last, *c'est un fait accompli!!* How long it may be in reaching you I cannot say—my advice would be "Possess your soul in patience"!

You must let the letter end here if you are at work on any mediaeval subject for Hereford. We are all very much grieved not to have heard from you. I am, and so, too, is dear C.L.W., but I pass over myself. With regard to C.L.W. *verb. sat: sap!* There is a man amongst men—you know my admiration of him. Don't make us feel we are only an episode in your life.

Anyhow we are not. And in proof of this I will go on and tell you that we are both anxious for you to do brilliantly. So far as I feel myself entitled to offer advice I would say, "Let yourself go." Intellect must not entirely dominate heart. Now, Horatio, there's the rub. . . . However, as I begin to suspect that I am reaching the harmless lunatic stage, I desist. I enclose a cutting from which you will see that "St. Christopher" is to be done at Bristol. What about Worcester?

We both join in sending love. Do take what I say as

---

* The pedestal bears the following inscription:

WORCESTER MUSICAL FESTIVAL 1899

Ivor Atkins, Mus. Bac.   Conductor.

Presented to Professor Horatio W. Parker

By members of the Chorus of the Festival of the Three Choirs at Worcester, as a mark of their high appreciation of his HORA NOVISSIMA, a token of their esteem and regard for his genial friendship and kindly disposition towards them, and with every good wish on his birthday, September 15, 1899.

J. W. Somerton,
Chorus Superintendent.

the lispings of one who is only very much in earnest about your success, not only in the lighter sense of the word, but in another and more enduring sense.

Your friend
Ivor Atkins.

[Father to Mr. Somerton.]
(Acknowledgment of Pedestal)

162 Prospect Street,
New Haven,
January 17, 1900.

My dear Mr. Somerton:

When I returned last week from my Christmas holidays I found your extremely kind letter, and the pedestal with its cordial inscription, awaiting me.

I am at a loss for words to thank you and the chorus and Mr. Atkins for your kindness to me.

It was more than kind to send such a token of regard, and I value it with my vase as the most welcome gift I have ever received.

I am deeply touched at the thought that my friends in England feel toward me still the affectionate interest I shall always have in them.

The remembrance of the days I spent in Worcester is quite the most delightful in my whole store of recollections.

It has not faded at all, but remains still as bright, as clear, and as cheering as it was in September.

It will interest you to know that I brought the vase safely home, a good part of the 3,000 miles in my own hands. It stands on its pedestal on a black bracket in my study, and seems to have grown handsomer even than it looked when I first saw it near the west door of the Cathedral. It is much admired, and I am much

envied by all my friends, but they envy me the experience I had in Worcester as much as they admire the gifts
I brought home. They all want to know more than I
can tell them about our brother-musicmakers in England, and having spent a good part of my life in cultivating my imagination, I never let them go away empty
for lack of details.

But truth is pleasanter than fiction, and I confine myself (except upon extreme provocation) to authentic accounts of the hearty friendliness shown me in so many
ways by your gifted conductor, your Worshipful Mayor,
your own jolly self and your splendid chorus. I assure
you, a lot of people in these United States think better
of you all for treating a wandering American musician
so well, and wish they could get at some of you, for pur-
poses of hospitable revenge.

I look forward with unmixed pleasure to seeing you
again, and in the meantime, send you my thanks, my
love, and my warmest good wishes to all my friends of
the Worcester Festival Chorus.

With the utmost appreciation of your goodness, and
regret only that I cannot express it more adequately and
skillfully, and with cordial regards and greetings to Mr.
Atkins and yourself.

Believe me, dear Mr. Somerton,

Sincerely and gratefully yours,

Horatio Parker.

[*Atkins to Father.*]

Feb. 14, 1900

My dear Parker:

Your delightful letter and presents arrived during my
little holiday with my people, and awaited me in
phalanx on my return. Thank you very much for your

kindness in remembering me. . . . I have only had time to glance over your organ works but in that hurried peep singled out two for my next Recital. I enclose the programme and tomorrow shall be busy working them up in the Cathedral. It will please you to know that as a result of some recent unearthing in Novellos I secured H.W.P. in "E", and the Cathedral have no copies of the *complete* service. This week I lit what I hope is to be a perpetual lamp to your memory by putting the service into rehearsal with my boys. They take to it well and retain very pleasant memories of your little chat with them (or part of them). I am now going to start a campaign to introduce it elsewhere—certainly to Hereford and Gloucester.

I am almost sure they are going to do "Hora Novissima" at Chester Festival, but you very likely know more than I do. If you are going to conduct it be sure and reserve a holiday to be spent with me. I do not wish to inflict myself upon you to the inconvenience of yourself in this next visit to England, but just realize now in February, while there is yet time, that if it is in any way possible for you to spare me *many,* days it will be conferring a joy upon me. It will give me very great pleasure, dear old Horatio. . . .

Somerton read your letter to the Society last night to the accompaniment of ringing applause and cheers for H.W.P. They were much amused at the passage in which you allude to your Imagination. . . . In May we do "Hiawatha" and the "Death of Minnehaha.". . . When is our part-song coming along? * We will do it well when it *does* come.

With our love to you all
Yours ever,
Ivor Atkins.

* The "Star Song."

HORATIO PARKER

[*Jaeger to Father.*]
NOVELLO & COMPANY
Music Publishers

I Berners St.
London
July 21, 1900.

My dear Parker:

Welcome in old England, and many good wishes for yourself both at Chester and Hereford! Many thanks to you and Mrs. Parker for your kind words a propos the birth of my little girl. Both mother and cheerio are doing nicely, seem quite adorable to this proud Pa!

You have led us a nice dance over those things of yours. Why don't you *register* proofs from your benighted "star-bespangled" Fatherland?

Those last 20 pages never reached us! Now tell me please at once:—Is *"A Wanderer's Psalm"* * to remain the more or less absurd title? (I have no views myself, *I never have* in writing to a big-powerful chap like yourself, I only *quote!*). Sinclair don't like it, and his clergy don't, and nobody don't, only H. W. do!! Secondly, are we to put on the title "Composed for the Hereford Musical Festival 1900"? We don't want to, but will do so if you and Sinclair wish it. . . . You will make a big success with the work, I'm sure. Chori and

---

* In this connection Mr. David Stanley Smith has written: The immediate success it, Hora Novissima, won, inspired the managers of the Hereford Festival to order a new choral work. Parker, ever ready with ideas, and quick to put them down, responded with the "Wanderer's Psalm," Opus 50. This, and the "Star Song," Op. 54, written for the Norwich Festival in 1902, achieved only moderate success. His fame in England was strengthened by the performance at Bristol of the largest and most ambitious of his oratorios, "The Legend of St. Christopher," Op. 43, the text by the composer's mother. The third act of this work was given at Worcester the same summer. (1902) Dean Smith's opinion of the power and beauty of parts of "St. Christopher" has been already quoted.

audience will like it muchly, and of the critics only. . . .
Reminiscenter Jaeger will be "narsty."

Fine, wholesome, big, and most effective stuff. No
wonder our "readers" revelled in it. Not being a musician I don't know anything about your masterly workmanship which they rave over.

A full score of the "Hora" went to Chester yesterday.
We pasted the proof sheets together and made quite a
nice job of it, as you will see. Strongly bound, too.

I hope I shall see something of you when you come
to London. Will you stay over the B'ham * Festival?
It will be the most memorable Festival to *English* Art
since Festivals began: two *real creations, original, strong,
beautiful:* Taylor's "Hiawatha" and Elgar's extraordinary, inspired "Gerontius," the biggest thing *any* English
composer has ever done—you don't think much of E.E.,
I know, but wait till you hear this "Gerontius.". . .

Much love,

Ever yours,
A. G. Jaeger.

[*Father to Lottie.*]

London
August 2, 1900

My dear Lottie:

I am going away to Germany this evening, and just as
I came in from a visit to the Royal Academy (a picture
exhibition) with Mr. Sanford, I said to myself, I must
sit down and write a letter to Lottie before I go away.
Exactly as I was going to begin your letter was handed
to me so that I can answer it now besides.

Of course I like "Alice" † and I hope all my children

* Birmingham.
† "Alice in Wonderland."

will. It must be great fun to act in it, and I can imagine you describing your treatment of your little boy with fervent feeling. You will find that nonsense sticks in your mind much more readily than real sense. It is a family trait, and does no harm if you don't confine yourself to nonsense and exclude the other kind.

You *must* not give your books too long a vacation. They really have a good deal of rest in the winter-time (a little too much, I think, from Miss Willard's report), and you must not begin behind the others in your class. I know there is very little fun studying in the summer, but I have to do it, and you must, for I want you to cultivate your mind and your body that both may be fair and sweet, healthy, vigorous and active. Take care of both and see that both are growing all the time in size and improving in quality. Cut off your bad habits as fast as they grow out. I find there will always be fresh ones to trim, but they *must* be cut or they will grow too big and strong to cut. There is not a great deal of news to write about London. It is the same old place. The hotel is very comfortable and the servants very careful and attentive. They take my clothes and shoes away as regularly as Rosa did but they do not hang them in piles. They fold them after having brushed them, and lay them in drawers and wardrobes. Mr. Atkins is going to Germany with me, and is to take his bicycle also.

I wonder what Grandpa Ploessl will think of him—he is *so* English and knows no German. I hardly think they will be able to quarrel much but, of course, I shall encourage them to do what they can. I am glad enough at the prospect of seeing all the Germans again, Papa and Mamma first, then Tante Sophie * and her chickens and her husband.

We go to Cologne tonight, tomorrow to Bonn and

* Mother's sister.

then to Mayence, Frankfurt and Munich, I hope Sunday night.

I have been asked to dinner and luncheon, etc., several times since I have been here and have accepted the invitations. Last night Mr. Sanford and I dined with Mr. Andrew Black. It was a beautiful dinner, very good things to eat, wonderful cut glass and a lot of silver. He has a very large house with high rooms—his dining room is as large as our parlor and the furniture is old and carved and beautiful. There we played billiards and had a gay time smoking and talking until late, but I should have enjoyed a dinner in our little cottage in West Chop much more.

Mr. Black is to sing the bass part in my new work, which is a Peregrine (not Perigan) Psalm. He has already been engaged to sing it again in London next March, so we were on good terms with each other. Everyone has been kind to me and it is a delight to see old friends again and to make new ones. It is now getting late and I have other letters to write so I must stop.

With much love and many kisses to you and Mamma and the smaller chickens, I am your loving and homesick,

Papa.

[*Ivor Atkins to Father.*]

August 13th, 1900

My dear Parker:

. . . I can't tell you how much I enjoyed myself, because it would be impossible to find words in which to do so. I simply had a heavenly time. Everything paled rather after South Germany and Austria. By Jove! I don't know what the Austrian is like as a man, but there's a land to be patriotic about! I can almost imagine it making an Andreas Hofer of any decent soul.

Many evenings stand out amongst those I spent with you, none, I think, with quite the same amount of

pleasure as one evening in München—that was delightful
—quite one of the happiest evenings in my life, though
why I could hardly tell you. I found myself entering into
what I know must have been such a happy time in your
life, and there was something in your description of
everything that made me feel quite an old friend to the
Rathskeller. I look fondly at my Rathskeller Wine List
which you shall be allowed to see when you come. We
expect you on Monday, Sept. 3rd, but if you are going
to Hereford, as Sinclair says you may, do let me know.
Please remember me most kindly to all.

Yours ever,
Ivor.

[*Father to Isabel.*]

Brannenburg,
August 26, 1900.

My dear little Isabel:

I have just had a very long and very lovely letter from
Mamma with so much news about you and the other
two chicks in it. But I have written to Mamma several
times since I wrote to you, so she must wait another day
or two until I can finish this one. Perhaps you can remember Brannenburg and the great blue and black and
gray mountains on all sides. They were so beautiful last
night at sunset that I was very lonesome, and wished
that my little girls and their Mamma could have been
here to see them, or that I could have been in West
Chop to see the sunset over the water from the beach
near the Cedars.

Mamma says that you have been a very good child.
I thought you would be, and I shall try hard to find
something in London that a *very* good child would like
to have. If I find something I will bring it home with
me.

Yesterday in Tegernsee I saw three children who used

to be at Zeiserer. Lottie will remember them if you don't. Helen and Anna and Willy. They all remember you and Lottie and sent their love to you. Perhaps you will see them next year. You must learn to speak German and you must see that Gracie learns a little, too, so that you can speak it with them. I saw a pretty sight in a village in Tyrol last week. In a large house with a wide hall running through it, there was an iron bracket hanging from the middle of the ceiling to hold a lamp in winter. Well, this summer a pair of swallows, papa and mamma, had built a nest in the place where the lamp goes, and there was a whole nest full of little swallows with big, black mouths which they held wide open for bugs and such good things to eat. The big swallows flew in and out of the doors and their friends and neighbours flew in and out to call on them and talk with them. All the while people were sitting in the hall eating sausages and drinking beer. It was very amusing.

Mamma will see from the postmark that I have left Brannenburg. I am now going to Paris and from there to London. I hope to be at home with you all about three weeks after this letter reaches you. With much love and many kisses for you and Lottie and Gracie, and particularly Mamma, I am,

Your loving
Papa.

[*Father to Aunt Alice.*]

Paris,
August 30th, 1900

My dear Alice:

I feared that I might not be able to write to you, but remembering Moore's recipe

"The best of all ways
To lengthen our days
Is to snatch a few hours from the night, my dear!"

I proceed to lengthen a very long day, and sit up to write to you when I should really be in bed, snoring loudly.

Moreover I am to beat Mother over your back, as it would not be polite to do it directly. This afternoon I went to see Miss Conant, who asked, with a torrent of language I cannot, and wild horses could not force me to repeat, why in the *devil, devil, devil* . . . my Mother had never written to her since she left America. Now, as I obviously cannot put such a question myself, I must beg you to clothe the thought as you see fit, and convey it under suitable circumstances to the person for whom it was intended.

So much for business—the Exposition * is pure pleasure, and has many delights which will remain in my mind as long as memory continues its functions therein. There is a magnificent collection of pictures, which I love about as well as I do music. I really could spend a week at them if I had the time, and rather more, the money. The pictures come nearest to me. Next—the wonderful buildings, which look more like a beautiful dream than anything I ever have seen. They are terribly florid and all white and gold, and green, and red, and yellow, and blue, but *not* noisy. Rich and satisfying—to the discreet enjoyer, a feast, one however which may easily degenerate into a perfect gorge with all its unpleasant consequences. Next to looking at the pictures, I love to sit at one of the hundred cafes on the bank of the Seine and look at the marvelous forms everywhere about me in the air. I smoke and drink a modest bottle of wine, jaw the waiter in lame but active French, and feel as if I owned the whole outfit. The Eiffel Tower is a thing of beauty, if you get near enough to it, and it leads to a perfect fairyland of fountains and electric devices, all housed in the most wonderful buildings I ever saw.

* The Paris Exposition of 1900.

There is a restaurant every other step where you can have shark's fins, or fresh gray caviar from Russia, or things boiled in oil, or smothered in Paprika (Hungarian red-pepper). One can be fed as in Finland or France, as in Germany or Greece, Spain or Siam, Roumania or Russia, all of which interests me very much. The drinkables are as various as the eatables and as delightful. I read the program and run terrible risks in the search for new sensations wherewith to tickle my jaded old palate.

Surely I must be growing younger, for I would have been bored by, and superior to, all this stuff ten years ago. Now I can bask in the gayety of this charming and most beautiful city without caring to analyze my feelings. Then I would not have left one stone upon another in my efforts to discover why and when and how, etc. Old Epicurus had a very level head, and "carpe diem" is a fine motto. I only wish he had bequeathed us some sufficient remedy for homesickness. But for that, I should be happy, and I am not so very miserable as it is.

I hope to get home about two weeks after you receive this letter. In the meantime, I send love to all the dear ones, particularly to you.

Your affectionate nephew,
H. W. Parker.

From the Spring of 1901 to the autumn of 1902 was a Sabbatical year from Yale University. The family went straight to Munich, making that city their headquarters, but leaving it in the summer months for nearby Brannenburg. From Germany Father made various trips to England, and returned in October of 1901 to America for the Bi-Centennial of Yale University, for which he composed the "Greek Ode" ("Hymnos Andron"), to the text, a poem, by Professor Goodell of Yale.

HORATIO PARKER

*[Father, returning to Europe after Bi-Centennial,
to his Mother.]*

Dampfer "Kronprinz Wilhelm"
November 3, 1901.

My dear Mother:

This is the last of a long series of letters and must be brief.

We have had a wonderfully smooth and pleasant voyage so far and expect to reach Plymouth tonight. Think of going to sea in New York on Tuesday and going ashore in England the following Sunday. The average daily run of the ship has been over 537 miles. Dr. V. Martens, a great Russian authority in international law, is on board. He received a degree at the celebration in New Haven and is a most interesting and genial old duffer. Also Prof. Biles of Glasgow University is here. These two have been my chief playmates.

I hope your passes have come and that you are safely and smoothly on the way to the west by this time. Please send me Nellie's address—also the newspaper with nigger tunes in it if you can. I hope to reach Munich in three days now and to rest and get a fresh start by Nov. 20. The sea voyage always bores me. I sleep too much and not very well, and feel no impulse to any kind of activity. I hope that stagnation of liver and brain are restful. If so I have surely rested.

I am sorry I could not give you some money for immediate needs, but I did not dare to for my own resources are very narrow just now, but you will pull through I am sure, and it may be that an easier time will come for all of us soon.

With my best love to Alice, and with many sincere thanks for the good care she and you took of me and my things, I am,

Ever affectionately,
Your son
Will.

ENGLAND

[*Father to Chadwick.*]

Yale University
June 11, 1901

My dear Chad:

With the best intentions and all the interest and sympathy in the world I have not yet been able to write before. You know my letters have to be printed by hand and their name is legion, or worse.

Your directions about the tibia dolorosa were duly carried out. I have seen as much as possible of the (grass) widder and the two children. They are now in an excellent state of preservation, and I think there must be a glorious future immediately before you, for you surely have already had your share of hard luck.

In spite of your pain and distress you must have enjoyed British hospitality. It is a fine and a unique thing.

We have already discussed your state so thoroughly that further comment seems tantological. We have had extracts from your letters (concentrated essence of Chadwick) administered to us from time to time, and would have enjoyed them thoroughly, but for the pity and sadness they called forth.

You have had a jolly chance to practice five finger exercises in philosophy. It is a d— poor cloud that hasn't some kind of a light-colored lining, and I hope you have turned yours over by this time and found it pure gold at least.

We hope and expect to welcome you on your return, to condole and congratulate, though we shall probably leave the next day ourselves. Good luck and a pleasant voyage to you. Anna and the little ones send you their love and all good wishes.

Affectionately yours,
H. W. Parker.

HORATIO PARKER

[*Father to Mrs. Chadwick.*]

Brannenburg,
Aug. 20, 1901.

My dear Ida:

Anna has informed you of our movements and the state of our health and morals generally, so that this letter is to be taken rather as a spontaneous, altogether unnecessary token of good-will toward the Chadwick tribe than as a supplement to the news you have already received. We are going away tomorrow for a few days and I am trying to reduce the number of my ungiven "answers to correspondents," whether I really owe them or not.

We are very well and happy and comfortable here. One of the abiding joys and complete successes of the summer is *my sponge*. It and the rubber bag have inspired respect and sometimes enthusiasm day after day. Every morning, rain or shine, I take it out to the bathing pool—the rest I must leave to the imagination. The water comes right down from snow and ice, and is so cold that it seems to burn, but it is enormously invigorating. Even the young ones like it. The one drawback is that it stimulates the appetite to such a degree that I look forward to next winter with grave apprehension. We shall subsist chiefly on oatmeal, rindfleisch and lentils I suppose. It will be plain living and (I hope) high thinking. At any rate the first is secure.

Just now, however, we are living like fighting cocks—well fed ones. Our cook is a genius and does things so beautifully that Anna turns her nose up at the fare in the best restaurants in Munich. And it is not as well cooked as what we have at home. Every day we climb mountains or walk or ride bicycles for hours in frantic efforts to keep our belts at their springtime holes, and every day we come home and the cook spoils the results of our patient muscular endeavors. She receives $6. per month, which includes her beer.

I hope you are all in good condition and that Chad is doing well. You must be very good to him now that he can only kick verbally. Perhaps he has learned to use his crutches skillfully, but they will never quite replace a healthy toe. I hope sincerely that his disability is growing less every day, and that he will be able to dance at the next and several succeeding Bicentennials at Yale.

Let him comfort himself. There are folded rose-leaves everywhere, at least in every bed I get into.

Even I who write so cheerfully have produced more than 200 pages of orchestral score since July 19. A sad commentary upon the frailty of our human nature. But I am learning to loaf rapidly and can now be idler in two days than I could be in a week at home.

No doubt Anna has told you that we were in Bayreuth with Gray and the Goodriches. We had a jolly good time, and a still jollier though more frivolous one with the Prestons and the above mentioned lot in Nürnberg, where we thoroughly celebrated our 15th wedding anniversary. I wish you could have tasted the Bowle we had in a deep, dark cellar. We tasted it both wisely and well. It was worth the price of two tickets to see us come out again into daylight. Gray, who was sick and stayed soberly in his hotel, enjoyed it hugely, but not so much as we did.

Anna and the chickens join me heartily in sending love and all good wishes to you and to Chad and to your two imps. Our own two minor ones often speak of you all and wish they could get at some boys over here just like them.

There are six children in the house and the room on a rainy day is like a box of fish worms with their arms and legs.

Good luck to you all, and *Gute Besserrung* to Chad's leg. If wishing could cure it it would not be sore long.

Sincerely yours,
Horatio Parker.

HORATIO PARKER

[Father to Isabel.]

Hotel Dominieri
Rue Castiglione
Paris.
December 12, 1901

My dear little Isabel:

I have meant to write to you and Gracie before this many times but I have been too busy to do it, and now must hurry and write fast and send the letter away quickly or I might get home before it does. That is, I hope to get home some day next week, and it will be nearly, if not quite, next week before you get this letter.

I wonder how you would like Paris. The people cannot speak either English or German. How would you like to ask for a "bang show" and get a hot bath? And there are a lot of funnier things than that. It is a beautiful bright city, but it is raining cats and dogs just now, and I am in a house writing to you instead of going to the Opera, which I meant to do. I do hope that it will be clear tomorrow for I want to do many things, and I don't want to paddle about in the rain. I am not a duck, even if my children sometimes talk or act like geese. But in spite of that I am very anxious to get back to them.

Mamma has not said very much about your being good, I suppose she thinks I know you have been good unless she tells me something different. Now you are to be good just as hard and fast as you can until I get home again. Don't forget! And then you can be bad a little while, if you want to, just for a rest.

I must write to Gracie so I will not make this letter much longer. I could go on writing to you for a great while now, but I want to save something so that we shall have something to talk about when I get home.

Give my love to Gracie and to Lottie and to Mamma and *Schönen Gruss* to Anna and to Fraulein. I hope nothing has happened to your appetite since I came away. It used to be good and a fine, healthy appetite is one of the nicest things for chickens like you to have. Little pigs and little girls always ought to have good appetites for they grow fat and are very nice to eat.

With much love and many kisses to you all, I am,

Your very affectionate

Papa.

[*Father to Grace.*]

Hotel Dominieri
Rue Castiglione
Paris
Dec. 19, 1901.

My dear little Gracie:

I have just written a long letter to Isabel. I had to write to her first, you know, for she is older than you are.

I did not tell her very much for there are some things I want to save to talk about, but I think I will tell you a little about how I came to Paris. It was mostly on railroads. Two hours in England and then an hour and a half crossing the English Channel. And it was rough. The wind howled and great waves came up from the south and battered and banged at our poor little boat so that it trembled and shook all over. Some people were sicker in that hour and a half than all the people on the Barbarossa put together in almost two weeks. These were the usual positions of the boat, and it went from one to the other without any notice and tipped people

over who were not ready. A sailor lent me a big rubber coat and hat so that I was on deck all the time and saw it.

There were other positions but I cannot draw them. You can imagine combinations of these for variety.

And then we came to France. The train made a doleful skreek and started off as fast as it could for Paris— four hours. It had been going for about one hour when the wind blew the covering of the roof off our car and it hung and flapped holes in all the windows on one side of the car. The people were very much frightened, and one man was badly cut by the broken glass. Even the locomotive was alarmed and, I suppose, looked around to see what was the matter. At any rate, it stopped for half an hour before it could get up the courage to go on again. After that there were no more accidents.

One customs-house officer looked very carefully indeed into my bag, and poked everything over several times. But another had my trunk to examine and he hardly looked into it at all. Travelling is not all fun by any means, but I am glad to say that my travelling is now coming to an end very soon. Won't I be glad to see you and Isabel and Lottie and Mamma!

I said something in my letter to Isabel about being good. I will now write it out again for you as well as for Isabel, and I think Lottie, big as she is, had better read it. I expect to write to Mamma tomorrow and tell her about when to look for me. It will not be a week I hope before I shall be able to spank you myself if you need it. But I hope I shall not be obliged to work very hard at that for I don't like it any more than you do.

Give my best love to Isabel, Lottie and Mamma. Give them all kisses from me, too, and take as much love and as many kisses for yourself as you want.

Your very affectionate

Papa.

ENGLAND

[*Father to Mrs. Chadwick.*]

Hotel Dominieri
Rue Castiglione
Paris
December 13, 1901

My dear Ida:

In response to your indirect invitation I subjoin a short account of myself and my doings.

My visit to England was very pleasant. I banged about a lot and lunched and dined and visited more than I can catalogue.

Atkins' chorus sang two unaccompanied pieces of mine very well at a concert November 25th. It was a pleasure to hear and conduct them. They (the chorus and the audience as well) gave me a hearty welcome.

I went to Birmingham, Leeds, Glasgow, Edinburgh, Cambridge, Hereford and other places, mending fences, and roaring when called upon to do so. It was pleasant and profitable. Many people sent regards and kind messages to Chad, including Cowen, Parry, Stamford, Jaeger, Harold Bauer, Alfred Littleton (with whom I dined in Baunt) and, of course, Atkins and his wife.

Chad seems to have left a luminous trail of good-will behind him. Please have him send me without delay a few copies of his "Lovely Rosabelle" and his "Phoenix." I have promised some people copies of them and it will do no harm at all.

You will see by the heading that I am tethered in Wallace's old stamping-ground. It is a convenient place to sleep in, and I have hardly time for that. I have found so many friends and pleasant acquaintances that the temptation to devote myself to social enjoyments is almost too much for me. I have not seen Widor yet, but hope to do so next Sunday.

When I return to Munich (before Xmas) I shall regard my vacation as finished, and my sprees and my letters shall be like hen's teeth—few and far between. There is a lot of work waiting for me when I can get to it.

Please write to us from time to time and tell us what musical earthquakes are impending or have taken place. This is a fine country to visit, but Heaven preserve me from being obliged to live here more than a year at a time. It would be very easy, but I am so old that I cannot bear without disturbance the inevitable interruption of my industrious and studious habits.

Please give my love to Chad and the young-ones—to Wallace and to his mother. I will write to him shortly.

A letter turned up from the Prestons last week. They are still in status quo and waiting. They are likely to come to Munich almost any time now. The sooner the better.

With many thanks for your congratulations in the matter of the welcome Paderewski prize (Anna saw Paddy in Munich not long ago), and with love and all good wishes for a happy Christmas and New Year to you all, believe me,

Sincerely yours,
Horatio Parker.

[Father to Chadwick.]

40 Barer Street,
Munich
April 19, 1902.

My dear Chad:

Since the mountain evidently doesn't mean to write to Mahomet, I must take the initiative.

In a recent letter, a very sketchy one for such a model correspondent, Ida said that you had been haled to New Haven to save the tatters of my reputation.

Thank you very much for going. I had a letter from my lawyer about it and am sorry enough that the proceedings resulted so farcically. I hoped you would have had some legitimate fun out of the picnic and feel apologetic that things were so tame but, as a great man once said, "You can't skin a skun dog." But I am just as much indebted to you for your kindness and trouble.

Apropos—ought I not to send a bill for my valuable services in the conservatory prize matter? I am getting near the bottom of my barrel and looking about for means to keep it covered. Should I send the bill to Hadley or to Jordan? Even the Hymnal, to say nothing of the Bible, contains frequent references to Jordan's banks. It seems as though I ought to be able by systematic industry to tap one of them slightly. I will do the rest of the work uncomplainingly when the rest of the boodle is to be awarded.

I am on the eve of a two and a half days bicycle tour with Lottie and want to get my worldly matters in order before saying good-bye to Anna. *Hinc illud negotium.*

You have perhaps heard that Cambridge has offered me the degree of Mus. Doc. Whiting's idea is that it resembles wearing a crown on top of a plug hat. I have always respected and shared your prejudice against musical as well as other doctors, but there are Doctors and Universities and Cambridge has been conferring the degree for so many hundreds of years that they can probably do it by now so that it will stick. At any rate I shall be in very good company and lucky if I don't turn out the worst of the lot.

I expect to be presented to the congregation in June.

There is so much to be said about the state of music in this country, that I do not dare to begin writing about it. It must wait till we can talk until some very late hour. Generalities are so untrue, and I should hate to mislead you.

David Smith is here, is writing large and elegant pieces and taking them to ———. He is a good boy and will turn out well, unless I am dreadfully mistaken. I wish we had a larger crop of such chaps. We must have if we are to hold our heads up as a nation in the world of music.

Anna and our three chickens join me in sending love to you and Ida and the boys.

Do send us a line in time.

Ever yours,
H. W. P.

[*Father to Chadwick.*]

40 Barer Street
Munich
May 29, 1902.

My dear Chad:

Your letter of May 2 came duly and found a warm welcome.

The round-robin was much appreciated. Apt quotations are much more intelligible than absolute originality. I, too, have been rather idle since Xmas. I have worked hard enough but have not brought forth much yet. *Festina lente,* is a good motto for all the composers I know.

The organ concerto is all done and copied. Of course, it will be great fun to play it in your new hall and I will do so with great pleasure if you give me a chance. I am off to England again next week and hope to meet Whiting in Oxford a week from next Saturday. We are to spend a week-end with Hadow, I hope. It will be good fun even if not exciting. Thank you for your congratulations in the Cambridge matter. I am much pleased at the prospect, but you must not confound the Mus. Doc. *honoris causa* with those who acquire the degree by honest toil. It is frequently a very different breed of cats. I envy you the days in Auburndale. Until yesterday it has rained here every day since April 26, but things are looking better now. Anna and our chicks all join in sending love to you all.

Stick to your abhorrence of 6/4 and I will try to do the same.

Ever yours,
H. W. Parker.

[*Father to Chadwick.*]

Brannenburg
July 22, 1902.

My dear Chad:

Your last letter was welcome and much appreciated. I am sorry that I have very bad news to send in reply. Lottie has had a serious accident. She was riding last week and the horse, plagued by insects, reared and fell backwards with her and on her. The exact injury is a broken pelvis. There are no complications, and she is now as comfortable as is possible under the circumstances.

She suffered a great deal at first but has now no pain which is not to be borne with comparative comfort.

She was in splendid physical condition and has borne the shock magnificently. She has a fund of youth, strength and courage which are unusual and will help her to get through as quickly and easily as possible. It is now merely a question of lying on her back till the great bone has knit together. Our own relief from the terrible anxiety which we felt until it could be definitely known just what had happeend is indescribable. It might so easily have been so much worse that we are more thankful than I can possibly say. The problem now is to make the weeks of lying on her back as short and pleasant as may be. Please write to her cheerfully and ask Ida to do so, too, and Mrs. Preston. I am not in the right mood to give you much news. The Whitings are here and are well. Every other member of our household is well and all join me in sending love to you and yours.

Ever yours,
Horatio Parker.

[*Father to Lottie.*]

Cox's Hotel
Jermyn Street,
London, S. W.
September 15, 1902.

My dear Lottie:

Your letter reached us this morning on the anniversary of my birth and gave us much pleasure.

Your congratulations are not unimportant, but are among the sweetest things which have come to me in my life. Don't forget this, as you may in a few years.

Mamma left me this evening bluer than indigo, with tears in her brown eyes, and a lurking suspicion that the boat would go down in the Channel. I am sitting with Sammy Sanford and trying to cheer him up. He has not been well but is now better.

We have made two very nice visits in England, one to the Festival and the Atkins, and the other to Mr. Augustus Littleton. You must make Mamma tell you about them both. I think she had a good time; if not, it was not because I had not tried to make it pleasant and easy for her. Now I am in much anxiety to learn just how much you have improved in walking since we left you. Please write me a few details. Tell me how much you have to support yourself and whether or not you feel pain or local weakness. Now that Mamma is gone I am going into the country for rest and quiet and shall be able to write more frequently to you and the chicks.

Excuse the dullness of this letter, I am very tired. The next shall be brighter. With much love and many kisses to you, to Isabel and Gracie, I am,

Your loving
Papa.

ENGLAND

[*Father to Lottie.*]

Commercial Temperance Hotel
Exe Bridge
Exeter
Sept. 21, 1902.

My dear Ducky:

I dare write to no one but my own relations on this paper, so I lay aside all hopes of business and shall try to tell you a little about my day's ride. I awoke at 7:30 in Wadebridge on the north coast of Cornwall. It was drizzling and looked as if it would rain a week. It was my first bit of bad weather since leaving Bristol last Wednesday. So I made friends with the chamber maid and had a private sitting room and set out to write letters, which I did. Sometimes it drizzled and sometimes it rained, but about twelve it grew brighter and was only drizzling so I started. It is all uphill everywhere in Cornwall, or it is dangerously downhill; and by the time I got to the top of the hill toward Camelford it had stopped drizzling, a little further on the road was quite dry. The roads are wonderful. On the moors, twenty miles from anything but villages, they are as good as the best of our own town streets. I went on briskly up and down and in time came to Tintagel where King Arthur's castle was.

Now there are merely ruins there but the situation is one of the most wild and romantic I ever saw. The castle is enormously big, covering more ground, I should think, than the Tower of London. It is on a jagged peak or cliff of most forbidding-looking brownish-black stone with sides absolutely precipitous and falling into the Atlantic on three sides. It was Sunday, so there was no means of getting photographs, but I hope to find some here tomorrow. After Tintagel, which impressed me more than anything has for years, I went on to Boscastle which was at one time the house, and I believe, the birthplace, of King Arthur. It is a most fascinating place, more interesting as to cliffs than Tintagel, but I did not dare to take time to climb them and looked at them only from below. From Boscastle I rode to Launceston, first up a hill a good three miles long, utterly unrideable in spite of a perfect road, then twenty miles over the moors.

From Launceston (which I saw spelled on a stone signpost "Lauson" as it is pronounced) to Okehampton—more steep hills and moorland. I have become very fond indeed of the moors. From O. to Exeter I had to take a train for it was dark and I will not ride about in moor country except in the broadest of daylight. It is too late to go on tonight so I will send the continuation tomorrow. Be a good child and get well as soon as you can. Write to me sometimes and give my very best love to Mamma and the two smaller children. I send a great deal of love and many kisses to you.

Your affectionate
Papa.

DIARY

1902
    June 10th.
    Hadow's—Oxford.
    Cambridge—Conferring of Degree at three.

It is evident that this was a busy and happy time, not only of new friendships but of growing accomplishment and recognition. But certainly the climax was reached on this date just noted (June 10, 1902), when Cambridge University, in a colorful and ancient ceremony, conferred on Father the degree of Doctor of Music. Quoting Mr. Chadwick:

HORATIO PARKER—1902

Doctor of Music, Cambridge University
England

ENGLAND

The cordiality of the English people toward the music of Parker found ceremonious expression in the award of the degree of Doctor of Music by Cambridge University in 1902. If we consider the conservatism of English musical taste, especially in Cathedral towns, we must admit that this is rather a remarkable record for a young American in his thirties. The prophet is not without honor in England at any rate.

I do wish that Father might have expressed more comment on this occasion; at least some is contained in the following letter. All that we have is the memory of his gown representing this degree. It was made of heavy, cream-colored satin brocade, with a cherry-colored hood; and on his head a black velvet cap such as you see in Holbein portraits of the time of King Henry VIII. As small children we gazed in awe at this most regal attire, so conspicuous amid the traditional black gowns and mortar boards of the faculty at Yale Commencements. Later, we looked upon Father with pride and admiration in his Cambridge robe.

The Diary, as we have seen, makes only the barest mention, not even stating that the "conferring of degrees" included one for himself! Yet it must have been impressive. English Universities have given the degree of Doctor of Music (Mus.D.) since 1475. At that time the New World was still undiscovered, the Armada was a hundred years distant in the future, ladies wore pointed headdresses, and Edward IV was King of England. To stand in that ancient place and receive an honor so old—for the first time given to an American —must have been a deeply thrilling experience.

HORATIO PARKER

[Father to Mrs. Chadwick.]

40 Barer Street,
June 23, 1902

My dear Ida:

I am just back from England where I had the time of my life in a decorative and ceremonial sense. The doctoring was well done. There were two Indian Kings, gorgeous in silks and jewels, two Ambassadors and the Duke of Argyll, all being doctored at the same time I was.

Arthur and Grace Whiting were there and now are here in Munich with us. The weather is and has been vile. We all go to Brannenburg next week where we sincerely hope for better things. I need winter flannels and arctics all the time. It will snow in B. but below the snow line it is warmer and much milder than in the city and, of course, we do not have the limestone dust in the country.

The one advantage in the rain is that one does not have to breathe such loads of lime. The water is so hard that after one has been without tooth-powder for twenty-four hours the taste of lime is perceptible to the meanest intellect. This is not my oriental imagination but actual fact.

We are now coming to the end of our year and are rather in the habit of summing up. I do not think we have lost anything by being away, but I am sure that I at least have gained a lot in repose of judgment and in freshness. I have not been idle at all, nor have I been composing all the time. I have made sketches and have done the obvious drudgery which does not interfere with intellectual processes when it offered itself, and feel that I have really a better objective view of music than ever before. This is not horn-blowing nor is it for other than private use—it is merely what I have to offer in excuse for having run away from home and country a year.

I am glad to have done it and glad that it is soon to be behind me, for my appetite for work and for home is growing rapidly. Anna and the children have gained, too. Lottie has a good deal of fluency in French, which would have been hard to get at home, and a considerable command of German.

The chickens have lost all their English, but it is not far off and easily recovered. In return they have a lot of the most idiomatic German ever heard. And they have a certain taste in language, too. They select better and reject inferior expressions not merely because they are told about them, but partly by instinct. They are a queer lot, but not bad. Their tendencies are rather upward than otherwise, and I hope they may have children who will be better than their grandparents. This is a rather dry return for your long letter, but you did not ask any questions—with the usual result.

We, Anna and I, leave Brannenberg August 20th to go to Paris and England. Do send us a line before then.

With love to Chad and the boys, as well as yourself, from all of us, I am,

Sincerely yours,

Horatio Parker.

[*Father to Lottie.*]

The Close
Hereford
Thursday, Sept. 25, 1902.

My dearest Lottie:

I am writing just a few lines before dinner. When one is visiting there is not much time for anything else. I got back to Bristol safely on Tuesday after a horrid rainy time in beautiful Cheddar.

Had a fine rehearsal with the chorus Tuesday night after a very nice dinner in my honor at which the festival committee were present. Wednesday morning I

read proof and wrote letters. Wednesday afternoon I
went bicycling with Riseley and his daughter. We went
to Almondsbury which they pronounce "Amesbury."
Had a beautiful ride, some tea, a gorgeous view and
scorched back. In the evening I read proof and wrote
letters, and this morning I took a train through the
Severn tunnel and rode through Clufstown to Tintern,
where there is a beautiful ruined Abbey, and on to
Monmouth-Ross where I had my luncheon. After that
I rode on to Hereford. Dr. Sinclair rode to meet me
and we met a little outside of Ross. It was a beautiful
day and the scenery all the way up the valley of the
Wye is beautiful.

In Bristol on Tuesday I found two welcome letters
from Mamma and one very nice one from you. I will
think about a rug, but cannot promise to buy one. My
funds are low and going down, but we will see.

Much love and many kisses to all of you from Mamma
to Gracie. Love to the others as well.

Your loving

Papa.

[*Father to Lottie.*]

3 Priory Road
Tyndall's Park
Bristol
Thursday, Oct. 2, 1902.

My dear Lottie:

I had a very nice letter from you yesterday and am
snatching a few minutes before breakfast to answer it. I
have not yet heard from Mamma and cannot imagine
why she has gone to Prof. K. I hope she will write to
me again some day. One week from today is the performance of "St. Christopher" for which I have been
waiting so long, and I leave Bristol twenty minutes
after the performance, and I hope to leave England the

same night and meet you the next morning in Antwerp. I am not quite sure that I can do this, but shall try. You must make rapid progress with your leg so that we can get about in Antwerp and see things a little.

I am glad you amuse the small fry. It is one of the best and surest ways of amusing yourself, and I know how much they admire their older sister and appreciate any attention from her. I have now had my breakfast and am off on my bicycle to Gloucester. I am to stay there over night and go to Worcester, also "per Rad," * tomorrow to stay till Sunday, when I return hither. I shall try to write a few postcards. That is easy when I am in hotels and have my evenings free, but when I am with people there are not so many opportunities of being undisturbed.

With love and many kisses to you all, I am,

Your loving

Papa.

Be a good child and tell the others to be good. Love to the Brannenburgers all!

[*Philip Hale to Father.*]

1087 Boylston Street,
Dec. 16, 1902.

Dear Horatio:

I have read of your triumphs in wretched England, that bloated monarchy, and also of the football game with Harvard, and my heart was thrilled. I am sorry not to have seen you since your return.

Your organ piece will be played Dec. 26, Mr. Gericke tells me. Would you not like to write your own synopsis? If you do not have time, please give me sufficient data, so that I can make an article; but I should much prefer to have your own version for the Program Book,

* Bicycle.

inasmuch as I believe a composer knows better his intentions than any outsider can guess (them).

Please mention date and place of composition, and what orchestra you use.

We have been having the devil's own time, moving into the new *Journal* building and getting out the new *Journal*.

Under Munsy all the boys are well, and I am glad I can say this of myself.

With best wishes,

Yours sincerely

Philip Hale.

[Mrs. Atkins to Father.]

Dec. 7th, 1904.

My dear Professor:

I expect you and Mrs. Parker have called us both by a good many bad names for never writing, but though we do not write we often talk and think about you. Now this is to tell you a piece of news and to make a request. The news is, we are the proud possessors of a son who arrived on November 24th. The request is, will you be one of his Godfathers? We are both very anxious you should be, and we promise we will try and bring him up in quite a correct manner so as to save you any anxiety in the matter. If you will be a Godpapa will you send us a wire at our expense saying so? The Christening is to be on the 21st of December. I am afraid you won't be present, but if you feel inclined to run over, a warm welcome will await you, and if you don't we will get someone to represent you.

With our love to you and Mrs. Parker. We hope you are both coming to the Festival next year. You really must.

Believe me,

Yours affectionately,

Dora Atkins.

We are asking Professor Sanford to be the other Godfather. Please wire in any case, but we hope it will be, yes.

I have included letters of later date, because they have to do with this phase of Father's life. Yet, in many ways, the year 1902 marks the climax of this period. For this reason it is especially fortunate that I have Father's words (in a talk to "The Club") given in New Haven on his return from his Sabbatical Year in Europe—the first he had from his duties at Yale University:

[*Address*, 1902. *Read to The Club*.]

Impressions of a Year in Europe.

I expect to follow the example of my colleague, Professor Weir, although I have no hope of being able to put things so clearly and well as he. That is, I shall try to give impressions and opinions. If I am betrayed into dogmatic utterance on any point, please lay it to inadvertence and do not think it necessarily true. I must apologize also in advance for the shower of first personal pronouns to which you must be subjected. I do not know of any way to produce autobiography without them.

I went to Europe early in July of 1901 with my family and left them in the Bavarian Mountains till it was time for the children to go to school in September, when they all moved into the city of Munich. I spent a large part of that summer in scoring and finishing the details of the *Greek Ode* which was sung at the Bicentennial Celebration, for which I returned to this country. I came back on the new ship *Kron Prinz Wilhelm*, the first voyage she had made; the worst sea voyage that I can remember, and went back at the end of October in the same ship and had a wonderfully pleasant voyage—very fast. Passengers who had breakfast Tuesday in New York had breakfast the following Monday in London; that is, we left Tuesday at nine and got to Plymouth Sunday night. There was a small but very pleasant ship's company, including Professor Byles of Glasgow and his Excellency Dr. Martens of St. Petersburg.

I went to Europe for a change of Occupation, not because I needed rest, and not for the purpose of taking lessons, but to study the condition of musical culture in various countries, to be near the head of things and to find out what was really going forward and the direction in which it was progressing. I had not been in Europe in the Winter for seventeen years. I had been there in the summer, but musical life in the summer is hibernating, if you will excuse a Hibernianism.

A note is inserted at this point, "three functions to the making of music: studied all three."

I got to Munich early in November and left for England about ten days later to see to some publishing business and to be present at the performance in Worcester of a choral piece which I had composed expressly for the Society in Worcester. I began to make careful observations in England. It was produced at a concert in the shire hall by a chorus and orchestra. The chorus was excellent and did very fine work. I had met the chorus twice before, in 1899, when they sang my "Hora Novissima," and in 1900 when they formed the chorus which sang my "Wanderer's Psalm" at Hereford. I had many friends among them and met with a very pleasant reception; more hospitality than I could accept in London and in the country as well. Although Worcester is a provincial town, the chorus is as good as our best ones. It is a remarkable and very significant fact that the best choral singing in England is done in the provinces, the worst in London. The provincial Societies go to London from time to time, apparently to show the Londoners how to do it. When Edward Elgar was commanded to write an Ode for the Coronation last summer he was permitted to select the best chorus that he knew of to sing it at the Coronation. He selected a chorus from Sheffield which was brought bodily to London.

From Worcester I went to Leeds to visit some friends and hear a choral concert. On the way I stopped at Birmingham and heard a rehearsal of the Birmingham Festival Choral Society, and went to a chamber music concert which interested me considerably. There were all kinds of people in the audience, men and women in evening clothes and some particularly rough looking specimens as well. It was a classical program, well given, but I found six people in the audience who wore their hats throughout the entire performance, and it was evidently not absent-mindedness but a habit of theirs; yet I could not discover that they took any less interest in the music than the people in evening clothes. . . .

From Leeds I went up to Glasgow in a perfectly unheated train and with the thermometer considerably below zero. I stayed in Glasgow with Professor Byles, who is known to some of you. I met a number of Glasgow musicians and heard one concert of a series of orchestra concerts which were given there during the winter in St. Andrews Hall. . . . The conductor introduced me to the orchestra after the concert in a club house for musicians. I said that I was surprised at the excellence of the orchestra, whereupon they seemed amused, and said they had been pegging at it for twenty-five years. I said I wished we had as good orchestras in similar cities in the United States, whereupon the conductor asked me about Boston, New York, Chicago. I was obliged to explain that I meant cities like Philadelphia, which now has an orchestra, although it had none at that time; St. Louis, which has a very imperfect one; Pittsburgh, which has a young one; Buffalo, which also has a young one, rather bad I imagine . . . etc.

Of course, the number of positions which will yield a living for the oboeist or the bassoon player is small, but many young men are able to secure favorable conditions of service in the army by cultivating these instruments and they frequently become efficient and valuable. . . . And there is another source of supply in the wind instrument problem, which is always the most serious in the development of an orchestra of small means. In the manufacturing districts of England different factories often have excellent bands. Proprietors of manufacturing undertakings encourage and take pride in their bands . . . and one frequently sees such advertisments as this: "Wanted: *a good weaver who can play E flat clarinet*" or "*Hand for foundry work who can play piccolo*"—this is very interesting to me, and I was told that manufacturers encourage such undertakings partly, and I imagine, mainly, for the benefit which results to them through the higher moral tone of those communities in which a taste for music is cultivated as compared with those in which it is not present. My authority for this matter of manufacturers' bands is Sir Alexander MacKenzie, Director of the Royal Academy of Music. . . .

I went back to Munich by way of Paris and heard some interesting concerts in Paris, orchestral music and chamber music as well as opera. One incident impressed me; that was the advertised final rehearsal of "Siegfried" at the Opera with Jean de Reszké. The cheap seats were thirty francs. I did not go to it. I got back to my family for a German Christmas, which we spent very pleasantly in the country. I climbed mountains for the first time in winter. On New Year's Day I had my din-

ner out-of-doors in the open air at an elevation of 6,000
feet, and the same day the smallest of my children found
a marguerite in the open field in blossom, although it
was not a particularly open winter.

Immediately after the Christmas holidays I engaged a
studio, had a good piano put into it and went to work.
I never worked under such pleasant conditions. It was
a large room with a fine north light and a big drawing
table. There was an American stove, a self-feeding one
which ate anthracite coal. I think it used to get up in
the night and feed itself, because the coal cost just
about as much as the studio. I usually worked in the
morning and afternoon, and went to a concert, opera or
theater in the evening when I wanted to. There were a
great many interesting concerts in Munich. For instance, in one week there was the performance of "Ekker-
hard," *A kaim* concert with Liszt's Faust Symphony under
Weingartner, and a concert by the Bohemian Quartette.
One of the most interesting concerts of the season was
one of his own compositions by Richard Strauss. A concert, by a Spanish conductor, of Russian music, which
showed the provincialism of the Germans, their inability
to appreciate music which is laid out on lines unfamiliar
to them! They seem quite unable to understand Tschaikowsky. The personal element enters very largely into
the German's enjoyment of music. If one is well known
and popular it makes little difference how well or badly
things are done. For instance, I heard a performance
under Zumpe of Tschaikowsky's B minor Symphony
about as bad as possible. It would have left a New York
or Boston audience perfectly cold, but the Germans became almost frantically excited because Zumpe conducted. But there is great interest and enthusiasm about
music generally, not merely about opera. I felt sorry
sometimes that the enthusiasm was so indiscriminate.
It rather laid the judgment of the people open to some

doubt, but they certainly do their duty in the matter of encouragement and interest.

It interested me to contrast the condition of opera in Germany with the opera in New York. Opera in Germany is surely a boon; in New York it is frequently a bane! Bad as it is, in Germany, it is local; in New York there is nothing local about it. No one is American excepting a high-priced soloist here and there. In Germany it is always a permanent organization; in New York everything is kaleidoscopic. One gets dissolving views of singers, players, conductors. The one constant factor is the Jewish impresario; everyone else is a visitor, living in a trunk or in a hotel, sometimes in a flat, never in a house. Things are sometimes well done in New York, often in fact, but one always has a feeling it is on account of the money that is coming in. Opera in New York costs several times as much as anywhere else on earth and is a purely exotic growth. Singers in Europe are usually in touch with the audience personally. They are singing to their parents, their children, often to their grandchildren. To show the personal element, take the episode of Morena, who was a nice girl with a fog-horn voice, such as the Germans love. She had just been jilted by a lieutenant, and everybody knew it, and she had to sing a part about a faithless lover, which put a great deal of interest and life into her work and elicited tremendous applause and sympathy. In New York such things are the work of the press agent; in Germany it was the result of gossip. A *gast,* or guest, comes once or twice a month to the large German theaters. In New York everyone is a guest all the time. You seldom or never hear a French singer in German opera. Why not? Because they do not know the language of the country. We seldom hear a singer in opera who does know our language. One is tempted to say that a knowledge of our language is a hindrance rather than a help in gain-ing admission to the opera here. I think all American singers who have appeared in New York have come in from the European agencies in one way or another, and the rank and file of chorus and orchestra have to know other languages, but do not need to know English. This, I think, is distinctly humiliating to us. Opera singers on the continent of Europe must know the language of the country thoroughly.

The same conditions as in New York obtain in great measure in London. I think this indicates that opera is not at home among the Anglo-Saxons. From time to time a movement is begun in England for opera in English. A fine theater was built several years ago as the home of English opera. Sullivan's "Ivanhoe" was given there successfully, and other operas, but the venture languished and now the theater is a music hall. I am not complaining because continentals sing and play opera better than Anglo-Saxons. All honor to anyone who does anything well; but I do think it is fair to express regret that so much money and interest which are needed for the support of native endeavor should run out into the sand of quixotic undertakings which we do not try to imitate or to initiate on our own account. New York is the place more than any other which gives excuse for such regret. The opera there is certainly an incubus brooding over the music of the place. It monopolizes interest and attention and, more serious, more impersonal and, I think, more valuable musical activities are supported in but luke warm fashion.

We had some very pleasant social life in Munich. One very charming family with which we came in rather frequent contact was that of Professor Prinxheim, the mathematician, at whose house we met a number of very interesting people. On the first of March my pupil, David Smith, turned up in Munich to study. I introduced him to suitable teachers and left for Paris on the fourth of March. In Paris I heard a number of orchestra concerts, Lamoureux and Colombo orchestras.

It (the French) is an older civilization, superficially rather better bred than the German, and apparently much more discriminating. The German music is rather a hard pill for the French to swallow and they seldom do swallow operas, excepting Wagner, whom they find long and dull, but beautiful; but they take German chamber music and orchestra music in large quantities. I saw a number of interesting men in Paris—Professors Hardanard, Widor, Gabriel Fauré, and some painters, and the large colony of Yale men; and received a letter offering me the honorary degree of Doctor of Music from Cambridge. I went to London about some business, and then went from London to Berlin. I stopped over a day in Düsseldorf. I heard a performance of Bach's "B Minor Mass" under Prof. Buths and compared German and English choruses. I spent the week in Berlin; heard orchestras and chamber music but no choruses—some Strauss and Gernsheim. I then went to Munich by way of Nüremberg and Rothebourg.

I found my studio in Munich still vacant, engaged it again, and went to work at once. Early in May I received a telegram saying that my "Star Song" was to be performed at the Norwich festival. I left Munich for London early in June, met Elgar in Düsseldorf. Went to Cambridge June 5th with Stanford and heard a concert in King's Chapel. I went to Oxford June 7th to stay with Hadow. Saw Richmond of the "Times" and Allen of New College (he was a grandson of Mendelssohn). Went from Oxford to Cambridge (again) where I stayed with Sedley Taylor. The conferring of degrees took place on the 10th of June. We had luncheon at Peter House at one, the degrees were conferred at 3, and there was a banquet at 7:30.

I went back to Munich for the summer which we

spent together in Brannenbourg. I had a sad lot of proof to read; a new batch came every day. I had to read the "Star Song," Hymnal and an Organ Concerto. I could not work at anything because there was so much drudgery. September 1st I went back to England and heard rehearsals in London, Worcester, Norwich and Birmingham. Three of my works were done at English festivals last autumn. I spent the time between rehearsals in long bicycle rides down into the West; and in visits to friends in different cities and country places.

I gained a most interesting and apparently valuable insight of musical conditions in European countries, although I did not depart from the beaten track in the least. The tendency of the new music in Germany and in France seems to be a natural reaction from the intense paternalism under which the Germans live. It made on me the impression of a continual effort in the direction of individualism and protest on the part of the composer against being confounded with his fellow men. The music of Strauss is a shriek for the recognition of his own personality. It is plainly removed as far as he can get it from the impersonal, abstract serenity of the great classic masters. In the "Heldenleben" and the Symphonic "Poems," Strauss is in the van of musical progress in Germany. He is going in a perfectly definite direction and after him there is a long vacant space and then a great number of other composers, all going apparently in his direction. I have great doubts as to whether Anglo-Saxons can ever adopt this tendency. It seems to me anti-pathetic to our character, and I think there is a better direction in which music can be guided. We profit enormously in technical details from Strauss and his long train of followers, but I do not think that we, the Anglo-Saxon race, need be among them. We can admire but we need not imitate them.

HORATIO PARKER

(Added in pencil.) . . .

Met Strauss again at Prinxheim's. Had known him nearly twenty years ago but had never seen him in the meantime. My recollection was a very tall, thin, consumptive-looking chap. I found him big and broad, very healthy and very sane. A fine conductor and in spite of all the spoiling he has had, a fine fellow and a splendidly honest musician. His figure occupies the largest part of the musical horizon of the present day in Europe. Not in comparison with composers who are not living, but of living ones, none receives one quarter the attention given to him—(Three magazine articles within the last week). He is thoroughly educated, naturally most gifted, and original to a degree which is sometimes positively painful. He has succeeded in convincing the public and the musicians that he is the factor to be reckoned with in the future of our music. He seems the logical outcome of the Wagner movement, and therein is to be found, I believe, the weak point in his work, if there is one. Beethoven based on Bach—Bach on his predecessors—but Strauss always takes a point of departure outside of music itself . . . always tries to express something other than music: philosophy, religion, jokes, definite ideas, sometimes even physical happenings. I don't think music can make that an end. It may be that the art of absolute music is exhausted. Strauss thinks so, but I am loath to believe it. On the whole, I am inclined to think that music among the Anglo-Saxons is built upon a more solid foundation, one better calculated to sustain the weight of an imposing superstructure, than the music of the Germans. The music of the Germans is now so colored by externals that it has hardly a separate existence. That of the French seems not to come from deep enough, not to go deep enough—superficial. That of the Italians is opera—a form with such manifest limitations that one may almost regard it as outside the sphere of reasonable activity among Anglo-Saxons. For the present English and American music is surely as a whole more impersonal, more abstract than thin, and if it remains untainted by these (qualities) seems sure to bring forth results of great beauty and value. German, French and Italians unite in one grand scramble to dodge the obvious ways of putting things. They are all trying to create an entirely new vocabulary. So much so that they frequently lose sight of form and substance. The old vocabulary will do very well if one has but new ideas to express. Not that I object to addition to our means of expression—but the new vocabulary must always remain a means, and never become an end of expression.

Had much encouragement and profit from a year's absence, but was glad to come home again. Quite convinced that this is the only country for a self-respecting American to live in permanently.

VI

FAMILY LIFE—NORFOLK—
SUMMERS

WITH THE steady growth of the Department of Music, there was always more detail work to which Father, of necessity, added still more and more responsibilities. Traveling, being slower and more tedious than at the present time, was, of course, wearing. He was no longer able to spare the time to go to Boston and assumed the position of Organist of the Church of St. Nicholas on Fifth Avenue in New York City.

In about 1907 or 1908 Father was invited to conduct two choruses, first the Orpheus, a men's chorus, and then the Eurydice, a women's chorus. These engagements entailed still more traveling, but they were among his most enjoyable associations. He appreciated the companionship of many of the members, their generous hospitality, and above all, their musical intelligence. It was for the Eurydice Chorus that he wrote the seven "Greek Pastorales" and they are dedicated to that group. As a treat I can remember going to Philadelphia with Father to stay at the home of Mr. and Mrs. Louis F. Benson, who entertained us most royally.

Typical of his Philadelphia friendships was that for

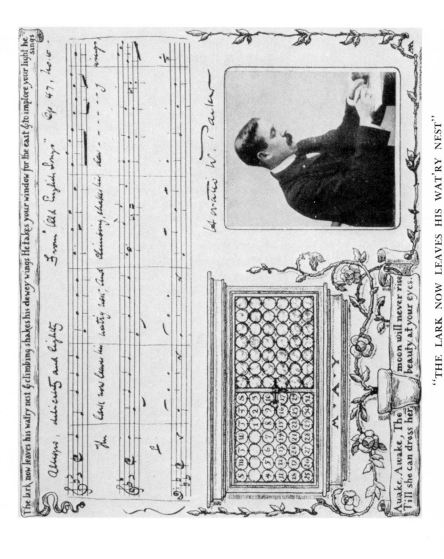

"THE LARK NOW LEAVES HIS WAT'RY NEST"

Edward Garrett McCollin, one of the members of the Orpheus Club, and for his daughter, Frances McCollin, then a young girl, but since a successful composer in her own right.* Father, always fond of young people, was particularly fond of Frances. She has sent me some of her memories of this time, of which I should like to quote all but only have space for a letter.

[*Father to Frances McCollin.*]

Yale University
Department of Music
126 College Street
New Haven, Conn.

January 3, 1908.

My dear Frances:

It gave me great pleasure to learn of the successful adventure of your "Agnus Dei" into the land of the publishers, and still more to see it and read it myself.

It is a very sweet and reasonable setting of the beautiful old text—and ought to be widely useful, for the voice-leading is just right, and the harmony effective and appropriate.

I showed it to my children, who are fond of singing, and of church music in particular. I told them where I had seen you and how old you are.

They were delighted at your success, and hope to hear the choir of Christ Church sing the "Agnus Dei" before long. We all join in wishing you a Happy New Year.

With kindest regards,

Sincerely yours,

Horatio Parker.

---

* Frances McCollin had been blind from birth, but never allowed it to daunt her courage or interfere with her career.

HORATIO PARKER

When in New York Father stayed at the Century Club where he felt happy and at home. I am sure he enjoyed his membership in the Academy of Arts and Letters, of which he became, in 1904, one of the two musical members, the other being Edward MacDowell. Other members of the Academy at that time were William Dean Howells, President; Mr. Augustus St. Gaudens; John La Forge; Samuel Clemens; John Hay and Henry Adams.

Father was often not well, suffering periodically from the familiar severe and painful attacks of rheumatism. I can see him now, coming home from Philadelphia or New York and getting out of a cab on crutches, having had to conduct, or play the organ with one leg on a stool and only one left for those innumerable pedals.

There was often a soloist for lunch on the days of concerts—beautiful Louise Homer, Alma Gluck, Maude Powell or Harold Bauer. I remember rushing home from school to find the atmosphere electric—Father strained, exhausted and cross, and Mother always cheerful, doing her best. (Father was a firm believer in public schooling—perhaps from necessity, but I believe from conviction. We all went to public schools, except for some time at Les Fougères, Lausanne, Switzerland, where we were sent to learn French, and to know and understand foreign children.)

David Stanley Smith has described the ordinary course of Father's life at this time (as I well remember it myself). He says:

It may be of interest to follow Parker through a week, typical of the weeks through which he passed for many years. Late Saturday afternoon, choir rehearsal in New York; Sunday, service morning and evening; Monday afternoon and evening in Philadelphia for rehearsals of the Eurydice and Orpheus Clubs; night train to New York, thence to New Haven for two classes on Tuesday; Tuesday evening by trolley to Derby for a rehearsal of the Derby Choral Club, arriving in New Haven at midnight; Wednesday, a lecture on the History of Music and a class in composition; Thursday, again two classes; Thursday evening, rehearsal of the New Haven Symphony Orchestra; Saturday, off again for New York. Naturally these rehearsals culminated in frequent concerts. Then there was the inevitable grind of the Dean's office, with conferences and letter-writing.

One can see from this schedule that Father had little time to be at home. He was always away on Sundays, and generally on Christmas Day, so that our celebrations were held on Christmas Eve, and great mystery and excitement attached themselves to the occasion. The door of the living room was locked for days in advance, this act in itself heightening our anticipation. Each Christmas over a period of years Father wrote a trio for the Toedt * family—one of whom sang, another played the violin, while their mother accompanied them.

* Mr. and Mrs. Toedt were old and dear friends of Father and Mother, the friendship dating possibly from the time when Mrs. Toedt sang the soprano role in "Hora Novissima" at its initial performance by the Church Choral Society in 1893. Together Mr. and Mrs. Toedt taught singing and, after the death of her husband, Mrs. Toedt, gallant soul that she was, continued her work with her own pupils, and at the Institute of Musical Art, where she taught for thirty-four years, until her death a few years ago. It is a privilege and inspiration to have known her and to pay her here my own tribute of admiration and affection.

Father never failed to complete the Trio so that they might have it on Christmas Day. And then—about six o'clock on Christmas Eve, by which time our house resembled a beehive, with everyone sewing on last-minute gifts (which we always made), Father would come to the door and say to us all, "Which one of you will help me buy your Mother an umbrella?" This meant dropping whatever we were doing and walking downtown—it was dark by then, and generally snowing—to streets crowded with other last minute shoppers.

At home again we would have our Christmas dinner, and later—at long last, heralded by the tinkling of a small silver bell (I can still hear it) the doors were thrown open and there stood the great Christmas tree, lighted by many candles, and around the room small piles of gifts for each member of the family, not excluding Alexander Freckles, our most dignified, somber, but wayward dog, a Llewelyn setter, commonly called Sandy.

Not long ago, listening to the Brahms' D Major Symphony, Mother remarked, "You remember, Papa and I used to play that four hands." I do remember so well! They played "four hands" often—Mother was far more adept at the piano than Father but, in her eagerness to please him, would play steadily faster and faster, and Father would then roar—"*DON'T* hurry!"

For any family occasion, generally to surprise Mother for her *Namenstag,* Father would write a simple song in three parts and expect us to make the correct sounds (one could hardly say sing) at sight from the manuscript. I can still hear my youngest sister, Grace, droning her "B" throughout a certain piece for fear of forgetting her note. I can never remember when we didn't read music—we all had piano and singing lessons from an early age. In the same offhand manner I asked Father to write a hymn for my own wedding; I had no sooner made the request than it was done—presto—ready.

During all of our childhood in New Haven there were the Kneisel Quartette concerts, and Mr. Arthur Whiting with his delightfully illustrated musical lectures (Loraine Wyman usually singing), so popular in all of the universities to which he went. There was John Philip Sousa, with his great band, a favorite concert with us. One year when they came Mr. Sousa became seriously ill of malaria and had to be taken to the New Haven Hospital, where he remained for weeks, while his family, summoned in haste, stayed with us.

One could not pass over the subject of these many concerts without mention of Mother's and Father's hospitality to all of these artists—most of whom were, of course, warm friends. As Mr. David Smith has recently reminded me, "Few musicians came to town without being dined and 'beered' at 420 Temple Street. Doubtless Mr. Kneisel and his colleagues never left New Haven after their many concerts without sitting down to a post-concert supper. I, at that time, not being a married man, did not realize what this must have meant to your mother." The "suppers" for the Kneisels consisted of beefsteak, potatoes, mushrooms, beer, and so forth, at ten-thirty at night. Now this is a meal hardly to be taken lightly at any time! Pro-

— 173 —

fessor John C. Adams, of the English Department of Yale, continues in the same vein: "In later years my wife and I had the great pleasure and privilege of close friendship with the Parker family—we were often at their house (especially after a concert by the Kneisels or some other musical occasion). Mr. Parker was altogether delightful in his functions as host, husband and father. Mrs. Parker—the perfect wife for him—played up to him with charming banter. Sometimes Yale undergraduates joined the group and Mr. Parker was always amused by their cublike cavortings around his three attractive daughters. . . ."

There were symphony concerts, and each year an oratorio in which we sang from about the age of ten. Thus, every side of music was a perfectly natural part of our life at home. Father's views are well expressed in the following talk entitled: "The Art of Listening," which, characteristically begins—

> You will understand that it is not the *keyhole* variety of which I am to speak to you. . . .
>
> It is, therefore, at home that one can most quickly and most certainly gain the best part of a skillful listener's equipment. Especially in the smaller cities, public performances are not frequent enough to afford the continuous, constant training which a skillful listener needs. A volume of Beethoven's sonatas, another of Bach's instrumental works, a collection of arrangements of orchestral scores within easy reach will help a listener wonderfully to train himself.
>
> While it is possible to spend an enormous sum for music, on the other hand, an investment of ten dollars in good popular editions will furnish a listener with

material which will take him some years to digest. And I believe there is a particular virtue in owning and seeing music even if one's executive powers are very modest. Stevenson, in one of his letters, speaks jocosely of arranging the Beethoven Symphonies for one finger. One finger can accomplish a great deal. More useful still would be the habit of reading music silently. This is not so difficult as it appears. . . .

But the very best way of familiarizing children with music is to have it at home where it is restful, stimulating and elevating, if it be good music. I recall clearly what I owe to home influence. My Mother taught me to play, but not until after I was fourten. She corrected my ideas of good and bad and was a very constant inspiration and influence throughout my childhood and youth; an influence which I never can value or appreciate too highly. It may be that by encouraging natural aptitude for music in your children, the great American composer will be found and trained among us here in New England. It is no more improbable here than anywhere else, and even if you do not find genius to encourage, you still may find comfort, consolation, pleasure and profit in practicing singing or playing when you can. Homemade matters are, after all, very interesting ones, much nearer to us than what we can buy.

In Father's Diary is a note as follows: "Dinner at Dexter's, Club paper by Porter on the Soul—origin and destiny." This organization is mentioned with regularity in the Diaries. It was known to us, by way of Mother (who so referred to it) as the "Old Gentlemen's Club"; why *old* I have never exactly understood, though I believe she imagined most of the gentlemen older than Father. Suffice it to say that that its proper name was simply, "The Club." I recall their coming to our house. Mr. William Howard Taft lived in New Haven then, and was among the guests, other members being Professors Lounsbury, Perrin, Seymour, Dean Weir of the Art School, and others whose names I did not perhaps then know. Father never invited his friends to come to our house, if he could help it, except, of course, the many artists from out of town. He had neither interest nor patience for so-called social life, though he always loved and welcomed *our* friends—my sisters' and my own—being particularly fond of young people. Therefore, "The Club" was an important occasion. While the gentlemen's minds soared to realms of intellectual rarity, we were actually and actively scurrying behind the scenes. What a bustle there was—everything must be perfect (though they would never have noticed!), their menu over a period of at least twenty years had a charming simplicity; it was always exactly the same and went as follows: chicken, peas, rice, ice cream and *plenty* of coffee.

When Father had time he would read aloud to us the tales of W. W. Jacobs, amidst gales of laughter, mostly on the part of the reader. Then, after his late supper of a sandwich, and whiskey and soda, taken at the dining room table by the light of a small green student lamp—a routine matter when he was at home, this habit being the subject of great distress and disapproval to my younger sister and me during a period of intense temperance—he would stay up late into the night working or reading, always in the process of writing something. A great deal of music was written for an occasion or a prize, and, therefore, always under pressure, such as an ode for the inauguration of President Theodore Roosevelt in 1904 entitled "Union and Liberty," facetiously called "Onion and Liberty" by him; an ode for the dedication of the Albright Art Gallery in Buffalo entitled "Spirit of Beauty" * and an ode for Commencement at Yale, and so on. Mr. David Smith says: "Parker rarely lacked a tangible stimulus for composition. Almost all the music from his pen was written for a commission, prize, or special occasion. His fame as a composer of choral music brought him orders from many societies in England and America. At least five prizes were won by him. No other American composer has been so sought out. He was of the type of artist who works better if there is a definite end in view, a definite date set for the completion of a work."

In the afternoons whenever possible he made time for a bicycle trip or a game of golf. He always rode his bicycle from his home to his classes until the time came when he had a miserable Ford, which he drove very badly to the actual terror of his friends and family. Many a November day we were forced to play golf with him the wind whistling over the hills of the New Haven Country Club. Exercise was necessary and agreeable. He would say to us firmly, "Come along! Fresh air and exercise are good for you."

How to do justice to Mother's contribution to Father's life and work, I hardly know. They seemed as one in their completely harmonious, almost intuitive

* This was broadcast last year by a chorus under Alfred Wallenstein in a program of American choral works including both old and new.

understanding where music was concerned; there were
no words—they would have been superfluous. Music
always was, and remains, an essential part of Mother's
nature. Years later traveling with her in Europe, at a
deserted French watering place out of season (than
which nothing can be more gloomy), in Paris, or in a
small German village, her suggestion, "Let's go where
there is music" reiterated her first instinctive desire.
Mother was gay, cheerful and patient always. She
shielded Father jealously from unnecessary details (with
which, again, he had no patience) and from worry. *His*
work was all-important. How often we would come
flying into the house, full of enthusiasm over something,
to be greeted by Mother standing guard. "Hush," she
would say, "your father is working." Her absolute
selflessness, devotion and understanding never wavered
for an instant. Father and his work came first, last and
always.

Letters of this period take up their part of the story:

[*Aunt Alice Jennings to Father.*]
#151 Charlesbank Road
Newton, May 22nd, 1905.
My dear "Will":
I hope it will be some consolation to you, in your
present condition of "grass widowerhood," to know that
your better half and the two darling little girls are a very
great help and comfort to me.

For several days before their arrival, I was much de-
pressed in body and mind, but since they came, I have
rapidly recovered. It was a case of unconscious hyp-
notism.

Anna was so evidently pleased at my improved appearance that I was much encouraged, for I *have* tried to make some return for your goodness, in giving me the means of such a comfortable life, by keeping as well and happy as I could.

You may be interested to know that my antediluvian "Connecticut in Literature" went to the compositor last Saturday. Proofs and payment will soon be forthcoming. At least, that is what the editor tells me.

I am getting my little "American Literature" ready for Ginn and Company, to bring out in the fall, and I shall try other things also. It takes a long time to get started, but I think that I really have literary power which may prove marketable, if the right channel can be found for it. At all events, it gives me healthful occupation.

When Anna, Grace, Isabel, Mrs. Chadwick and Noel surprised me a week ago Friday I felt as though five very bright sunbeams had suddenly made my path radiant. I spent the next Monday with them, and Anna helped me, most generously, about my shopping, while the children were devotion itself. Best of all was our "meet" yesterday, at the dear old home.* Eight of us were there, and it was far more cheerful—far less sad—than I had dared to hope. The garden is so glorious in its spring-tide beauty, and I had all the windows open so that Anna said it seemed natural and attractive. Is it not sweet that nothing but *Life* is associated with that house? From six to eight have been born there, but all the deaths have been somewhere else. I cannot help hoping as Anna suggested, that it may be possible, in time, for some of you to live here. Months and years will transform painful associations to those which are sacred and pleasant, and there can be no spot in the world so dear to us all.

I am delighted at the prospect of seeing you, if only for a little while, and hope nothing will prevent it. I

* Auburndale.

am invited to Nantucket for the summer, but prefer the cultivated beauty and the cultivated *comfort* of Newton.

Hoping you are much better, and that I may see you,
Very affectionately yours,
Alice.

[*Father was taking a cure.*]
White Sulphur Springs Bathing Establishment
Pavilion Hotel and Cottages
John H. Gardner & Son
Sharon Springs, N.Y.
Sept. 6, 1904

My dear Isabel:

Instead of writing to Mamma I think I will write to you tonight and to Grace tomorrow night.

I wish you could see what a jolly place this is. There are not many people here but there are lots of mountains and valleys and I don't mind being lonesome because I am having the rheumatism nicely boiled out of me. This afternoon I took a long bicycle ride to Cherry Valley—isn't that a pretty name for a village? You and Grace would not have liked it much because it was all hills, but that is just what I do like. I got to a place which was 3000 feet above the sea and the view was magnificent.

It was a good deal like the view from the Petersburg. I could see the Catskill mountains in one direction and the Adirondacks in the other with a beautiful broad valley just in front. This is a great hop growing country and the people are all harvesting hops as fast as they can for it is very cold and likely to freeze soon.

They pull down the long green strings of vines and strip the hops off with thick white gloves into a big box, then they are stuffed into bags and taken to the barns to be dried. There are all sorts of pickers, boys and girls and some very old men and women as well, and they seem to like the work for I heard many of them singing and whistling as if they felt well pleased with things.

Just as I was riding down hill into Cherry Valley a great black and white dog ran out of a yard barking furiously. He kept just in front of me and scared me quite a good deal, not because I thought he would bite but because I thought I would run into him. So I put on my brake and got slower and slower and saw that he was only a puppy, but a big one. He kept in front, going round like a cat in a fit, and I got off and spoke to him and he came rushing up to me wagging his tail and licked my hands and pawed me over as if he had known me all his life. I told him how dangerous it was to get in front of a bicycle going down hill, and I hope he won't do it again, but I have my doubts.

Tomorrow I will write to Grace. Give my love to her and to Mamma and to Aunt Alice, and be a good child.

With lots of love and kisses,
Your affectionate
Papa.

Sunday, Feb. 6, 1905.

My dear little Isabel:

After writing a lot of other things it seems natural and nice to write to my absent daughter. There is not much news except that we all miss you at home. The three gold fishes are well, but even they remain hidden except when they are fed. I don't really think that they know you are away, but we can't be sure. Fishes always look as if they were asking questions, I think.

Grace went to Peggy's to luncheon yesterday. I suppose she had a good time, but I didn't see her afterwards. Lottie slept till half past ten and at half past eleven sat down to read, but it was a beautiful day, so I told her to go out of doors and run around in the sun. She brought home a good appetite.

Mr. Rabold took me to the theater in New York last night. It was a German theater and a German play. All the actors and actresses spoke in German. The play was in Vienna where they speak just such German as we used to hear in Munich. Two of the actors came out and sat in a box, and two others were in the audience. They spoke to the ones on the stage and made fun of them. It was quite a new idea, and very amusing, but the audience did not know just what it was all about at first and looked puzzled. I think you would have liked it.

Give my love to Mrs. Camp and Janet, and to Mr. Camp if he is there. Be a good child and don't trouble them, but I know that you won't do that. With love and kisses to you.

Always your affectionate

Papa.

[Father was in Buffalo for the dedication of the Albright Art Gallery.]

THE BUFFALO CLUB

May 27, 1905.

My dear Isabel:

It is a long time since I have written to you and quite bad of me, but you know I have had so many things to do and places to go that I really couldn't.

Today I went to Niagara Falls with a friend and saw the Falls and the Rapids and the Gorge. I will send postal cards to you and to Grace, and when I see you next week shall have some large pictures of these places to show you. It is very beautiful and the weather fine. The wind was from the west and blew the spray from the Falls all over us in the trolley car. It was just as though it was raining and I saw people putting up their umbrellas with bright sunshine. The men who were working on a building near the Falls all wore rubber coats and hats such as the sailors wear in bad weather at sea.

Tomorrow I must have a rehearsal with a big band and a chorus of men, and tomorrow night I must go to Scranton for the Welsh festival.

Mr. Detmers, who went with me to Niagara, said he wished he had you there; so did I, and that Mamma and Grace were there, too. I hope you will all see it someday.

With love and kisses to you all,
Your affectionate
Papa.

[*Visiting Earl Grey at Government House, Ottawa.*]

GOVERNMENT HOUSE
Ottawa
Tuesday morning,
Feb. 1908.

Dear Isabel:

The first of the six performances was last night. At first there was a concert by a local chorus. After this followed a play in three acts. The concert began at 8:15 and the play ended at 11:15. The chorus was rather good. They sang a very long piece and two short ones. I made notes of the way in which it was done and shall tell them about it later in the week.

This morning it is not so cold—already eight degrees above zero—cold enough but quite comfortable. I am glad I took Mr. Sanford's coat. Last night the thermometer was far below zero, and we had to drive in an open sleigh from here to the theatre, about two miles, perhaps more. Without the fur I should have frozen tight.

I now have nothing at all to do till tomorrow night and am going to skate—ski—toboggan—snowshoe—curl, etc., till I am tired, and then go to bed and sleep it off.

I hope that you and Grace are well and *good*. Canadian children of your age are very good—always coming home from the Lawn Club much before dark.*

With love to all,

Ever your affectionate

Papa.

[*To Lottie.*]

GOVERNMENT HOUSE
Ottawa

Feb. 26, 1908.

Dear Ducky:

It is your turn to have a letter. There is just now so little to do here that I wish the days were much longer, for I thoroughly enjoy it—the less the better.

Monday night's concert was very interesting. There was a chorus of 75 which sang very well, but the thermometer was at six degrees below zero, and they sang a little askew—now sharp, now flat. The enunciation was excellent. They had been carefully prepared and followed well, but the accompaniment was only a piano and rather incongruous in the long piece they sang first. The two unaccompanied pieces were much better. Tonight I am to hear an orchestra from Quebec which received the trophy last year and is expected to do so again.

I wish you could be here to enjoy the pleasures and amenities of the noble rich. The house is enormous—I should guess about a hundred rooms. There is an army of servants and everything the heart could wish for. Lewis, the man appointed to look out for me brings

* We often skated in the afternoons, coming home after dark, wherefore the admonition.

— 184 —

in tea and bread and butter at 8:15, which I take kneeling on my elbow, and then dress. Breakfast is from 8 till 10. Nearly everyone comes to breakfast, after which the officers go to work of various kinds. Luncheon is at 1:30 and the afternoon is largely spent in the open air. I tried curling yesterday. There is a fine rink for it about 200 ft. long by 10 ft. wide. The game is a little like shuffle board but is played with weights of from 30 to 60 lbs which slide on the smooth ice the whole length of the court. There are two rinks for skating. I skated yesterday, but the shoes I borrowed were too big. I could go straight ahead well enough but couldn't turn the corners without turning my ankle, and gave it up to umpire at a very exciting hockey game between the officers at Government House and some people from Ottawa, which is about two miles away. They smashed a lot of sticks and two goal-posts, and had a fine time generally. This afternoon I hope to try skis and snowshoes for it is snowing hard. There is an immense toboggan slide with a fine view from the top. I shall not try that alone.

I hope that you are well and *good*. Please send me a line to N.Y. if you can't send it here. I leave on Saturday morning and must go to Philadelphia Sunday night. I hoped to get away Friday but it is quite impossible to do it.

Lord Grey is very pleasant and as courteous as possible. He is Viceroy and has an overpowering (for an ordinary man) amount of state to maintain. Her excellency I have not yet seen for she is not quite well. Lady Sybil and Lady Evelyn are both very nice indeed and kind and courteous.

More next time. Love to all.

Papa.

HORATIO PARKER

Sharon Springs,
Saturday, June 5, 1909.

My dear Isabel:

I had a letter from Lottie yesterday but as I had already written to her I answer it to you for it is your turn next.

It has rained since noon yesterday and the prospect is not yet in sight of clearing, but it will stop sometime. The hotel has six guests so far, but the grub is excellent and plentiful, and I have a fine room with two windows which would be very sunny if there were any sun to sun oneself in. Dora, who brings my shaving water and feeds me at table and gives me my baths, is a duck. She is not very pretty, but that will wear off, and she is very good and good-natured and very efficient. She is German of the most pronounced kind. The *Wirth* * is Mr. Fred Manhs, who is very well nourished, particularly in the region of the equator. There is a *Wirthin,* but I have not seen her yet.

There are two children—six and seven, a boy and a girl. Of course, the boy is the good one. There are some advantages in being a boy after all. *He* speaks German very nicely, but the girl can and will not do it, which is very sad. My life is that of a bath-taking vegetable. I do not work and do not intend to do anything more troublesome than eating, sleeping and bathing till I come home. It is very lonesome and monotonous, but I hope to rest a lot and feel fresh when I come back.

Be a good child and do your own work always. Understand your Latin and your Algebra. Keep Gracie at her work, too. Don't let her forget to improve her mind—it needs it.

With lots of love and kisses to you all

Your affectionate

Papa.

* Hotelkeeper.

FAMILY LIFE—NORFOLK—SUMMERS

Sharon Springs, N.Y.
Sunday
June 14, 1909.

My dear Isabel:

Your letter came yesterday inside of Mamma's and gave me much pleasure. It was nicely written and everything was spelled correctly. Now you must put your shoulders to the school collar and pull hard through the few days still remaining. No matter if you don't have any fun—it will taste all the better afterwards.

It is happily and heavily raining again here after a drought which has lasted nearly twenty-four hours. Although the weather would bring out rheumatism in the joints of a clothes-horse I have no trace of it in mine. Today I had my eleventh bath and have only three more to look forward to. I am now thinking of taking my Wednesday bath before I get up so that I can get home Wednesday night late. How I shall miss the baths and the drain water I drink! Dora is just as nice as ever—gives me the biggest piece of pie, the heart of the lettuce, the most ice-cream, the very dirtiest baths, and all other things which she has control of. If this rain keeps on I doubt if I shall stay even till Wednesday, but probably shall be ashamed to go home before. So tell Mamma to get all the skeletons locked up and all the other secrets hidden for I surely will be with you D.V. on Lottie's birthday.

I shall want a letter Wednesday morning which must be sent away not later than Tuesday at 4 P.M. That will come here with the first mail and I can read it going down to Albany. The first mail gets here at eleven and I leave at 11:35.

With love and kisses to you and all the others.

Ever your affectionate

Papa.

HORATIO PARKER

[Mother was in Germany with her parents, her father being ill.]

THE CENTURY ASSOCIATION
7 West Forty-third Street

Sunday, March 20, 1910.

My very dear Anna:

As usual there is almost no time for me to write to you, but you mustn't think that it is because I don't want to. On Thursday I reached home as usual and found everything in the best of order. There were many letters to dictate and my class and the other school duties. Wednesday was a full day. Lecture 11:30, class 2, letters between, then Phoebe and Millicent came and the concert for Sam * was at four; meantime I had to find stands and music for them, see Walter, etc. Then we had dinner and went to the Kneisels who afterward came home with us. Doubtless Lottie has written to you about them.

Thursday was orchestra rehearsal at 9:45, letters at twelve, class at two and The Club in the evening at Henry Farnam's because you were not here. I read my paper and played parts of "Salome" and "Pelleas" for them. They seemed pleased and talked till 10:30, which is unduly late for us.

Friday I wrote 16 pages, had my class, wrote some more and went to Grace's confirmation. It was a beautiful service, and I felt very kindly toward our fascinating, irregular youngest. She said she had holes "on her stockings"—just like her! If they had been at toe or heel it would have been "in."

Saturday I wrote 12 pages of score and rode bicycle in the afternoon; train to Stratford at 3 and 27 miles home by way of Derby arriving at 6:40. Then I came

* Memorial for Samuel S. Sanford.

down here on the 9 P.M. train, went to Toedts and slept till 9. Today is jammed full of things. Preparation for Easter; three hours sitting with Brian Hooker, and now I am pretty well played out and going to church again. F.S. was in church this morning looking very well and rather languishing, also H. who went to walk during the sermon.

I missed you most going away last night and said to Lottie something about having no one to care whether I went or came. She said she cared a lot, which is a great deal for her. Tonight I go to Philadelphia. Lottie is doing her part splendidly. It is good for her to be responsible for things and I think will benefit her permanently. The children are as good as our children can be, and everything is in excellent order.

I can't write any more now, but send much love and many kisses to you. Give my love to all at home, and don't worry a bit about anything. We are all right and well.

I am your faithful and loving
Husband.

UNIVERSITY CLUB
1510 Walnut Street

Monday, March 21, 1910

My dear Anna:

There is no particular reason why I should write again today after yesterday's letter, except that I have had a good breakfast and am waiting for it to settle. On Monday my breakfast consists of a good deal, being at 10:45 (stops at 11), combination of breakfast and luncheon. It is likely to last till dinner today—oranges, oatmeal (I didn't eat it), sausages, scrapple, fried potatoes and three cups of coffee, besides toast, rolls, butter, jam, marmalade, etc. You see there will be plenty of time to finish this letter before it settles finally.

Yesterday's letter, as I remember, was mostly a time-table of my doings. You know that pretty well already so it can hardly have been surprising. I am too busy to notice what the news is usually.

Converse's opera "Pipe of Desire" was given on Friday. It was badly received by the critics. Each in his own peculiar way jumped on the libretto first, hard, and then lightly on the music. B.H. says the story is deadly. He also says that our piece has more dramatic action by far than any opera he has seen. This alarms me a little for it may be true, and there is always the possibility of getting too much butter on one's potato. After all there ought to be more of the latter than of the former. But it will be time enough to worry about that when more pressing necessity arises.

I hope to write Thursday, Friday and Saturday this week. David will play for me Good Friday so that I can be free. I have asked the Toedts to take a bite with me Saturday night at Terrace Gardens. It is a long time since I was there.

Next Sunday I come hither for the whole week. There is a dinner at the Musical Art Club on Friday, April 1, for Chad, Foote, Sousa and me, so I can't possibly get home till Tuesday, April 5, on which day I have the last Symphony Concert.

A letter from Chad says he is getting well very, very slowly and goes everywhere on three legs and in a cab. I am sorry for him and rather fear he may start up his gout again with the rich victuals of the B. S. Hotel. He will not go to the McCollins with me. I don't yet know whether Ida will be with him or not.

With love and kisses,

Your loving

H.P.

FAMILY LIFE—NORFOLK—SUMMERS

Monday night, April 11, 1910.

My very dear Anna:

There is no news. I have been following my regular timetable, except that Lottie came down with me to N.Y. yesterday morning and went with me to Krehbiels to dinner, after which we played bridge till train time.

I had my last regular Eurydice rehearsal today, thank God! Tomorrow I rehearse with them and the instruments in Witherspoon Hall—concert tomorrow night.

Mrs. Z. asked me to show her some of my opera and I think I shall go out there for a little while tomorrow afternoon, but am not sure. She and Gertrude are very sorry that our church work together is to stop. It is a feeling which I do not share, except in its mildest form, but we must live for much less next year than this. I need rest for I am mentally exhausted. If I could only get myself to take physical exercise regularly, I know I should be better in every way, but with a mental task just screaming for me every time I turn over in bed or out of it, it is not amusing.

One week from tonight is the last Orpheus concert; one week from tomorrow my organ recital, and then my season's work can begin in earnest. I lack only eight pages of score for the end of Act I, and hope to be able to finish them Thursday or Friday.

I must be here again April 28th to conduct parts of a Gilchrist celebration—his 25th anniversary. It is a bore but I must do it, apparently. David Bispham is to sing.

The children were well and good yesterday. Lottie will have written to you about them and their doings.

It is delightful to learn of your father's improvement. I hope it and your exercise will continue with great regularity.

I have just dined with the Haupts who send you their love and kind good wishes.

With love and kisses to you, and greetings to all the others,

Your faithful and affectionate

Husband.

Sharon

Monday

June 6th, 1911.

My dear Isabel:

It is your turn to have a letter but it will be a short one because the sun is shining and I must go out. I have had four baths, one with massage by an operator who speaks German, English, French, Italian and Wendrish, as well as Platt Deutsch. I stick to German for I suspect he has only samples of the others. He says I am too fat, but I have lost seven pounds and hope to find that my evening dress will hook without more resistance than Mamma's when I come home again. I expect to get home Tuesday, June 14th. That will give me twelve baths. I would rather have more but cannot stand the strain any longer, if as long as that. It is desperately dismal and dull. I thought I was to have a letter today. The first came from Mamma this morning dated June 4th and post-marked June 5th—5 P.M.

It was a surprise to know that G.R. had stayed till today. I hope Lottie has not felt the usual effects from her. She generally makes Lottie appear like a cross between a porcupine and a tiger-cat. I know that is not a good-natured thing to say, and I hope it isn't quite so.

Don't you bother Lottie anyway, or Mamma or Grace, but do your work honestly and regularly. You owe it to yourself as well as to Mamma and me. I hope you will have no examination at the end of next year. I expect it in fact.

With love and kisses to all and in the hope that the family will catch up in the matter of letters, I am,

Ever your affectionate

Papa.

Sharon
Tuesday night
June 27, 1911

My dear Isabel:

The black pen refuses to give down any more milk so I perforce must write red. I cannot buy Higgen's Eternal and prefer to go without rather than compromise. Your letter was brought to me just as I was about to write to you anyway. With yours was a long characteristic letter from your younger sister which was so generously devoted to quotations from your older one that I feel I have heard from all of you. I was not surprised about the bicycle (just remember cycle).

It was a pleasure to learn about the boy who has escaped death x times. That is one use to which you can put your slender algebra. By the way, one of my pet caddies in Derby is named William IX. He says his father is German and I rather think he may have chosen the name in token that he prefers to remain an unknown quantity. There isn't much news that I can impart except that my holes are closing up rapidly. Only about eleven of them are left open and they are growing smaller at a greater rate than hitherto. I am reminded of old Mrs. Salisbury on Church Street, who is said to have pronounced her husband "The most perfect gentlemen she had ever known. He never crossed his legs, even in the privacy of his own bed chamber." I am now in the proud position of being able to meet her views in this respect. But it isn't from pure gentleness, but because one knee is skinned and the other lame from Thursday's whacks.

I am perfectly well though, except for being a little stiff and a great deal tired of reading my own orchestral score in other people's handwriting. You will have to read Lottie's letter and talk to Mamma to understand my allusions. I expect to write to Grace tomorrow. Be a good child and give my love to Mr. and Mrs. Strobel and to Springer. It is very kind of them to be so hospitable and nice to you, but I feel sure that if you were at your best it is both easy and pleasant.

With much love and many kisses, I am,

Your loving

Father.

[*We were visiting friends waiting for the completion of the Blue Hill house.*]

Sharon
Saturday night
July 2, 1911.

My dear Isabel:

There was a short sociable letter from Grace this morning with a picture of the house. Please keep it for me because I shall want to look at it when I get to Blue Hill. There was nothing else of interest excepting several pounds of proof—second proof of Act II, which I have now read and must return. I hope it will be possible for me to get to Blue Hill on the 11th. It is a late beginning for my summer vacation but I have an unusually hard winter's work before me next year and must get some of the things done now so as to save money later. I expect to get to New Haven Thursday to spend Friday. Saturday in New York, and leave Monday for Blue Hill. I am rather glad to avoid the confusion of the new house and should feel distressed at having children at so many points of the compass, but hope we can all have a long vacation together next summer.

FAMILY LIFE—NORFOLK—SUMMERS

There isn't much to write about really, and I am tired and sleepy, so will just stop and add a little in the morning perhaps. Good-night!

Sunday morning:

This is a nice hot day but there is a S.W. breeze blowing in at my window, and I am no longer too sleepy to finish my letter. There was a nice little episode yesterday in an ice-cream parlor where I was drinking a bottle of Saratoga Vichy. A black-eyed little girl came in and said to the proprietress, "My mamma says this nickel is bad and you must change it." It was an old one worn smooth but perfectly good, so it was changed. "Now I want an ice-cream cone with a cherry on it," said the same little girl, and paid with the same nickel. She sat side of me and asked, "How much does that cost?" meaning my Vichy. I asked if she wanted some, but she didn't, so I said the cost wasn't important. Also she wanted to know my name, my business and where I lived. Just to be polite I asked her name. She said, "Lilienthal." I said, "I meant your Christian name." Her nose turned up in the air and she said, "I ain't got no Christian name, my forename's Rebecca." She was about seven and very characteristic. I went to the theater again in spite of the fact that the price had been raised to 15¢. It was "Ten Nights in a Bar-room," a tragic play which would have delighted your prohibition heart, and Grace's, too. Perhaps I will tell her the plot—but I must stop now to catch the post.

Give my love to the colony, particularly your host and hostesses. With love and kisses to you and the rest of our family, I am,

Your affectionate

Father.

・　・　・　・　・　・　・

HORATIO PARKER

NORFOLK

The Festivals of the Litchfield County Choral Union were indeed rare and wonderful events. They remain to me among the happiest and most vivid recollections of my youth. Mr. and Mrs. Carl Stoeckel were generous and devoted friends of Father and Mother, and it was through their kindness that we children were invited to participate in these annual musical feasts.

It may be of interest to go back to the simple origin of these festivals. It was apparently due to the initiative and inspiration of Mr. Robbins Battell, born in Norfolk in 1799, that the art of fine music had so long been cultivated in this corner of New England. Mrs. Carl Stoeckel (the only child of Robbins Battell) is mentioned in 1899 as "having invited to her house a few neighbors for weekly musical practice of English Glees under her direction." To her belongs the sole honor of founding the Norfolk Glee Club in 1899, which, in combination with choral groups from four nearby towns, eventually made up the Choral Union, a chorus of seven hundred voices—"founded to honor the memory of Robbins Battell." From so small and simple a beginning the Festivals had, by 1905, when we came to know them, assumed great proportions. They were firmly established and a true contribution to the art of music.

Every aspect of these events was unique. A composer was chosen to write a work. He was offered an honorarium, and assured the performance of his work under ideal conditions. Members of the New York

Philharmonic were imported for rehearsals and performances. The best soloists were engaged, and the chorus admirably trained preparatory to the Festival, always held in the month of June. Tickets were not put on sale but were dispensed by members of the chorus, or sent by way of invitation to honorary guests. The audience numbered about two thousand people. Thus there could be no trace of commercialism in the entire project; and it remains today as it was then, a true, altruistic and loving tribute to art for art's sake. Many well-known musicians contributed to the Festivals, among them being Hadley, Converse, Chadwick, Elgar, Coleridge, Taylor, Sir Hubert Parry, to mention but a few.

Passing through Norfolk again the other day, after many years, I was happily reassured to find that my memory had in no way exaggerated the verdant beauty of that town. The great elms are at least as straight and grand as ever, flanking and over-arching the quiet main street. There stands "Whitehouse," the Stoeckel home, originally the home of Robbins Battell and now of a summer music department of the Yale School of Music.

To arrive in Norfolk in June is, in itself, an experience. The whole countryside in its fresh, springtime radiance, gardens aflame with azaleas, the gentle clop-clopping of horses on the road, remind one of the nostalgic peace of that time of living. In the evenings, the concerts were held in the simple wooden Music Shed, to which one made one's way on foot along a path lit by long rows of flaring torches—charmingly gay and festive. All of the artists were there—a small and intimate group in those days, who enjoyed seeing each other in these lovely surroundings, far removed from the strain of their usual responsibilities. It was a kind of spree; a festive holiday spirit prevailed.

In the spring of 1914 Jean Sibelius wrote "Oceanides" for the Norfolk Festival. He came from Finland to conduct his work—and also to receive the degree of Doctor of Music at Yale University.

Our entire family was invited to stay at "Whitehouse" that June with Mr. Sibelius—the guests of Mr. and Mrs. Stoeckel, both of whom combined an old-world quality of dignity and elegance with simple kindliness. That they were the sole benefactors of these great festivals was difficult to imagine—so modest and unassuming was their manner. By now we were old enough to attend the gala banquets held after each concert—to hear the speeches and enjoy intimately the generous hospitality of our most gracious host and hostess.

Quoting Father at Norfolk:

I have been asked to give my impressions of the meetings of the Litchfield County Choral Union, June 3 and 4. They were very deep but uniformly pleasant. It is, perhaps, not quite polite for me to dwell upon the surprise that I felt in finding so admirable a chorus in Litchfield County. My delight at having my work so well done is a more appropriate subject for comment. I enjoyed the occasion thoroughly, and felt highly honored and gratified at being privileged to take part in so distinguished a function. The perfection of the performance on my work "King Gorm" was a particular source of pleasure. If there were any slips they were my fault, and I did not notice any so my conscience is clear.

Among the deepest of my impressions was the possible significance of such a gathering. There was much beautiful music, beautifully performed. It gave great pleasure to the Chorus and to the audience, but the significance and benefits are deeper than would seem merely from the pleasure given and received.

In the making of music there are three functions, equally indispensable; that of the composer who conceives and creates the music; that of the performer who reproduces the composer's idea and gives it to the hearer; the third function is that of the listener which is equally indispensable with the other two, for music needs to be heard as well as composed and performed to fulfill its mission.

Now the composer is the only real producer of music. All performers are reproducers, and although we hear of a singer creating a new role, it may be doubted if it ever transcends the mental picture of the original creator. The work of the performer is a great and indispensable function with wide opportunity for originality, and it is as necessary as that of the composer. Heaven forbid that composers should reproduce their own works, especially their vocal works!

The duties of listeners are also well defined and indispensable. Unheard music is like unpainted pictures. An intelligent attitude toward performer and composer stimulates both—in fact, is the only incentive for continued effort. I emphasize the need of intelligence in listeners. Passive suffering of music is not the way to acquire merit or understanding. Merely to let music trickle in and out of one's ears is not a more permanently profitable pleasure than that of drinking soda-water, or having one's back scratched. Nothing remains, for effort is needed.

The mind is colored by what passes through it, but most of all by what is retained. It is the intellect rather than the senses or the emotions which stops up leaky minds, and helps them to understand and retain what they hear. For this reason listeners must be cultivated to perform their duties—the composer and the performer can do only half the work.

To suggest the study of the great masterpieces of music to the people of Litchfield County twenty years ago would be like advising the study of justice among Russian bureaucrats, or the study of snakes in Ireland. There were no models—in fact, I believe there was more music in Litchfield County a hundred years ago in the old "singing schools" than there was twenty years ago.

To return a moment to the composers. They are the only real producers of music, but what produces composers? This is a conundrum, but not a hard one. It is like the old question of which came first, the hen or the egg. Hens are undoubtedly the only producers of hens. We may skip the preliminary steps of biological development, and need not trace the evolution of the hen from chaos, but at the present time my statement is true. The same is true of composers. They produce music and music produces them. There is no other way. You cannot produce composers out of desert air, but only from a musical atmosphere. One can produce music without live composers, but not live composers without music.

The need of live composers, when there are so many good ones of the other kind, is not perhaps obvious to all. Every civilized nation must have art of its own, and must do its share toward developing its own art in its own way. Every nation's life really centers in and radiates from its composers, unless it is content to import everything bodily.

Now I wish to charge the founders with having established in Norfolk a fine musical incubator. It is all very well to say that hens are the only producers of eggs, but the one who feeds the hens, gathers the eggs, counts the chickens and distributes them, occupies a place in our social structure which calls for enthusiastic appreciation and approval.

It would be more poetic to speak of the founders as cultivators of a beautiful garden of music from which the present and succeeding generations may cull rich, fragrant and beautiful flowers, but the more homely simile seems to me the more forcible.

Music is the most democratic of the arts. It is hard to overestimate the educational advantage of a revival of the old general practice of choral music, under present-day conditions and advantages, with a complete, excellent orchestra, in a beautiful building, with all sympathetic surroundings and a respectful attitude toward art and artists. This is the atmosphere in which music must grow, and this seems to me to confer a more lasting benefit than the mere pleasure can, great as it is, of hearing and performing beautiful music.

I am sure no one is inclined to underestimate this pleasure, for it is the primary condition under which only the higher development is possible. Cultivated listeners from the field in which such finely competent performers are gathered, and if the result of their labors does not produce composers, I do not know what will. I believe that it will produce in time someone who shall speak in music to the heart of our own people, in a voice which they will recognize as coming from out of their own feelings and aspirations.

God speed the founders in their noble work! May it continue long and bring forth abundant fruit for us and for those who shall come after us!

HORATIO PARKER

While it is difficult to think of Norfolk without the actual presence of Mr. and Mrs. Stoeckel, their home has become the Norfolk Music School of Yale University, where a summer session is established under the able direction of Professor Bruce Simonds. Thus, their spirit shall live long, and serve as a true incentive to future students to "bring forth abundant fruit."

.   .   .   .

SUMMERS

Fortunately, there were long, lovely, in fact blessed summer holidays—surely a boon to all teachers with their arduous task of imparting knowledge to often unwilling subjects. Through the ages the same type of comment seems to apply to professors—perhaps Socrates in ancient Athens encountered the same difficulties. I know that in Father's case part of his History of Music lectures he illustrated by playing the piano to his students in order literally to illustrate the music. Far from his playing having the desired effect of stimulating interest, it produced instead a comfortably lethargic state of mind in his pupils. The students became sponges, sinking back into their seats and permitting the melody to seep, if it might, into their souls, or to soar above, around and past their now completely passive minds. This apathetic atmosphere invariably called forth the comment (in Father's best-modulated voice): "Will those of you in the last rows try *not* to rustle your newspapers?"

To revert, however, to the domestic side of our existence. The early summers were spent in West Chop, Massachusetts, with the Chadwick family as near neighbors. From here Father made several journeys to England continuing the friendships and associations formed in previous years. As many summers as possible were spent in Europe near Mother's family, partly in fulfillment of an agreement entered into by Father with them at the time of his marriage and to which he always carefully adhered. The first summers were spent in Brannenburg, where Grandfather Ploessl had a small farm. My recollection of this time is rather nebulous, though some impressions remain—particularly an aroma of apricots, delicate but pervasive, from the espalier trees that flanked the front door. The house was made of stone, like many others in the region. "Flora" was the family horse, and there were cows, chickens and, of course, a rooster, of whom I am regularly reminded, for he left his mark upon my forehead and was promptly made into soup.

Within a short distance of our farm lived the Griesenbeck family on their wide lands. They were true farmers, hard-working and thrifty. We were sent to buy butter from them and loved to play in their great barn out of which gazed the gentle cows. The family consisted of four boys and six girls, the latter in their sweet, bovine freshness and close proximity somehow really resembling their own cows. A custom of the country was the annual departure each spring of the eldest daughter of the family with the herd to pasturage up in the mountains. There she lived entirely alone in an *almshütte* through the summer tending her flock. We stopped to see her on an occasional mountain trip. In August her return to the lowlands was a cause for celebration. Many villagers went up the mountain to accompany her home. The cows were fittingly adorned with greens and flowers—the girls and boys wore their Sunday finery, making a cheerful sight, coming down the mountain and through the village, amid yodeling, singing and the soft tinkle of many cowbells.

It was Lottie who was Father's most constant companion in those early years, and she also has an old journal, kept at the age of fifteen, of "common and uncommon events," a good deal of which is written in the most delicate German script. She speaks of their quiet life in Germany; of reading Caesar with Father, also "Hermann and Dorothea" of Goethe—and goes on: "Went up the Petersburg (mountain) with Papa, Isabel and Grace. Had lots of fun, although we had a hard time with Grace—she was so very tired. On top of the mountain we found everything blue with forget-me-nots and other flowers. Isabel and Grace put theirs into the Church (there was generally a small Catholic shrine on top of each mountain). As we were going out I gave them each a *pfennig* for the *Opferstock* (almsbasin), and Grace asked solemnly: '*Wass Bekommt mann denn da?*' (What does one get now?) . . . Had lots of bread, honey and springerl (pop). . . . Papa went up the Neuberg. . . . I *won't* go up any more mountains in the rain! D. S. (David Smith)

stayed for tea and afterward *'on jouait' au piano*—
Brahms symphonies."

Without equal in its sphere of influence in their
lives was the *bicycle*. Today one can hardly imagine
the importance of this indispensable object. Daily in
Lottie's journal there is a reference to it. "Those *in-
fernal* watering carts (with which the clean German
streets were constantly being washed) dirty my shoes
and my bicycle beyond words—I can never avoid them.
. . ." Lottie and Father took a long and lovely trip
from Munich to Bozen, Innsbruck and Cortina over the
Brenner Pass, during which they rode or pushed their
bicycles one hundred and ninety-six miles in about five
days, or an average of almost forty miles a day. The
record of this trip is vividly punctuated by calamitous
ejaculations of dismay over the vicissitudes attendant
upon so vulnerable an object as "the bicycle." Such
comments as "These *stupid* Germans—can't even mend
a plain puncture!" abound. Each day's trip was carefully recorded on the cyclometer recently acquired.

Again David Smith recalls:

"You were too young, perhaps, to remember the summer in Brannenburg, Bavaria. While all of you stayed
at the Ploessl house, I put up at the Wirtshaus opposite
the R.R. Station—lodging, one *mark* a day. A weekly
treat for you girls was a trip to the Wirtshaus Sunday
mornings for *Weisswirst*. We used to climb mountains every day, rain or shine. Lottie was very speedy
and got to the top ahead of us. Your father was very
strong, and bounded up—and especially *down* over loose

stones—at a pace that kept me running. I myself got to be good at it. My wind no longer holds out under similar conditions, alas!

"When Mr. and Mrs. Arthur Whiting turned up at Brannenburg they failed to have as good a time as the rest of us. Mr. W. once said to me, 'I am not happy climbing a mountain, and I am not happy at the top.' Mrs. W. had a touch of asthma or hay fever (I believe) and had difficulty in finding lodgings where she was not troubled by the hay stored everywhere. You little girls talked German only, and almost forgot English. Your father and Mr. Whiting used occasionally to play Brahms Symphonies, four hands. Your father used to enjoy irritating his old Brahmsophile friend by making picayune criticisms of passages in the Symphonies, though he was hardly less enthusiastic than Mr. W. at heart."

Later summers in Europe, which I remember clearly, were spent in a small Bavarian village named Rottach-on-the-Tegernsee. This was a tiny village on a lake in the midst of beautiful mountains. I remember Father always had to go first to the "Post" to inform the authorities, even in those days, where he lived, the names of his family, his occupation, how long he intended to stay, and so forth. How truly sweet and peaceful life was in that quiet South German country. Each farmhouse and yard was spotlessly clean and neat; window-boxes with bright flowers at the window; a carefully tended garden, and well-nurtured livestock gave evidence of the pride of these people in their homes.

In every village a tiny Catholic church and graveyard bore witness to the fact that these fine agrarian people had never deserted their land nor their Church over hundreds of years. There stood the family names, many of which we still knew, graven upon the well-worn tombstones, the ancient dates still faintly visible. We knew the many handsome peasants in their gay dress, and were charmed by that most kindly of greetings, their native *"Grüss Gott"* whenever we met on mountain trail, on entering a shop, or on the road. The brightly painted "Postillon" or stagecoach (in the blue and yellow of Bavaria) carried mail and passengers from one hamlet to another, two men in faded blue livery and black plush top hats on the box. The bugler played the "Siegfried" motif, which floated, silvery, into the air, echoing and re-echoing through the still valley. Father took a room in an adjacent farmhouse where he could work undisturbed, except for the mooing of cows and other gentle farmyard sounds. We took trips with him, bicycling or mountain-climbing. I remember particularly one *Ausflug*. We left in the afternoon to climb the Bodenschneid, reaching the top about dusk. There we had our supper of black bread, cheese, honey and milk to the delicate accompaniment of tinkling cowbells—after which, to bed, to wrestle with those elusive featherbeds. The following morning we were awakened with the sun, dew still glistening on the meadow, the Edelweiss and other mountain flowers growing underfoot, to make our descent in the clear mountain air of early morning. Nearly every afternoon we went on an expedition of some sort—on foot, by bicycle, or stagecoach—to meet for tea or *kaffee* at an Inn or farmhouse by the edge of a lake. Mother's sister and her children were often near us, making a large group. Father enjoyed every moment—and why not? He could work well, he could bicycle, and he could climb a different mountain every day if he wished.

Mr. and Mrs. Arthur Whiting spent some time in Rottach and Mr. and Mrs. Ossip Gabrilowitsch, dear friends, were at Kreut, within easy bicycling distance.

We often went into Munich to concerts and to the opera at the Residenz, or the intimate, charming Prinz Regenten Theater. The opera started at four o'clock and ended at ten. There was a real *Pause* during which one might stroll in the small garden or have something to eat, all the while admiring the elegance and splendor of the Royal Families and the very beautiful Princesses, dressed in their crown jewels—the officers in gaily colored uniforms. Here was a romantic and truly unrivalled setting for opera. One sensed the deep and sincere appreciation of these people for music. It was in Munich that Father took us to hear Richard Strauss's "Don Quixote," and I remember his laughing so heartily at the extraordinary and funny sounds of the orchestra. This was in 1914 when the "wind machine," the sound of bleating sheep and other irrelevant noises had not yet become an expected part of orchestra. Needless to say the more serious Germans about us seemed shocked, not to say grieved, by his merriment.

ARTHUR WHITING—OSSIP GABRILOWITSCH—HORATIO
PARKER—BAVARIA, 1911

FAMILY LIFE—NORFOLK—SUMMERS

The following letters apply to life in Rottach.

*[Written from Rottach, Bavaria. Grace and
I were taking a trip through the Dolomites
with friends.]*

Rottach, Bavaria
July 9, 1912.

My dear Isabel:

My letters have been to Miss Isabel Perkins—who has
had yards of them in the way of work so that I have had
to neglect the easier and sweeter duty of writing to you.
And I wouldn't write now but that your letter seems
rather lonesome. Probably you will get letters at Bozen
for several have been written. I don't wonder at your
being lonesome among the gorgeous, gloomy mountains,
but I hope you try to be cheerful with your hosts and your
sister. Did you notice Monte Cristallo? It is my particular
pet Dolomite and I think the highest of all, at least it is the
most stunning and oppressive. I doubt if you can see
it from Cortina, but surely you can on the road to
Pordoiby looking back. The great beauty of big mountains is they don't spoil one's appetite for Tegernsee and
the humble Wallberg and Riederstein.

I can remember all sorts of glaciers and snow-caps, and
look out of our back door at the little white chapel up-
stairs with just as much pleasure as ever, and I should
have walked up there this afternoon only it poured instead. Tomorrow I want to ride into Munich. Clarence and Carl were there yesterday, but Mamma was
away and they couldn't understand grandmother or make
her understand them.

Mamma came here to spend Sunday with me. It
poured. She left me two or three skinfulls of fruit which
I am still working on. The whole place seems as home-
like as ever, and I think you will like the Wohnung.
You and Grace can have a room each, or you can sleep
together in one with two beds.

Yesterday I rode around the lake on my bicycle and was delighted to see how little changed everything is. Only on the other side there are about ten petroleum wells—there were two six years ago, but I doubt if they get much oil. The Riederstein is visible almost all the way and looks very pretty indeed. I can't write to Grace separately so you can let her read this letter. I was very much pleased with the long one from her which came today from Cortina. Her spirits do not seem low nor does she suffer from any dull consecutiveness of mental processes. Her mind skips like a bee from flower to flower—perhaps I ought to find a tenderer comparison but there is no more space.

With love to your hosts and love and kisses to you both, I am,

Your loving
Father.

[*Grace and I were at school at Les Fougères
in Lausanne, Switzerland.*]

Rottach, Bavaria,
September, 1912.

My dear Isabel:

Thank you for your very sweet birthday letter which gave me great pleasure. I was very glad to get your former letter, which was very clear and told me plainly just what I wanted to know. I think 15 *francs* plenty for an allowance and would like to have you each keep an account of what you spend. If you can save, I shall be pleased, of course. You can probably tell by the end of this month how much you need to spend incidentally and, of course, I hope you won't spend much more, although I don't want you to be without anything you need or want within reason.

I had a fine birthday. Mamma gave me a piano arrangement of Strauss' latest opera "Der Rosenkavalier" which interests me much. I had a fine new pail for coffee from you and a charming ash-can for cigarettes from Grace. The next letter I write will be to her. You don't either of you need to write to us separately unless you want to and have time, and I suggest that you write Sunday and Grace Wednesday, or vice-versa. In that way we get two letters weekly and, of course, you must share each other's letters from us. I went in to Munich to "Meistersinger" with Lottie for my birthday present from *Onkel* Ludwig. . . .

With love and kisses to you both,

Your loving

Father.

Rottach, Bavaria,
November, 1912.

My dear Isabel:

I think I wrote to Grace last. If not please apologize to her. Your long letter, which came this morning, was a comfort to us all. It is pleasant to learn that you like to be busy and that you have so interesting a new companion. I hope both conditions will last throughout the year. I hope also that Grace is in the same frame of mind. She never says a word about her room-mate. I suppose Violet is only a tolerable example and influence and that the German girl is too good to be within hailing distance of Grace. Just ask her to say a word or two about them, if she can concentrate and coordinate her ideas—always supposing that she has any.

I have not been very good about writing, but am likely to be worse rather than better because my work is very absorbing just now and seems important, to me, at least.

My studio is a splendid place for work now. Of the first eight days I spent there it was not possible to work on seven because someone was playing piano every few minutes. I called the landlord up and explained to him how I was prevented from thinking by the silly stuff I had to hear, and he had an interview with the people. They were very nice about it indeed, and for more than a week I have heard no sound of piano at all. If it keeps on like this I hope I can make good progress. I am there from 10 till 1, and usually work a little in the evening besides. While I am doing pure composing, that is as much as I can possibly stand. When it comes to writing things out, I can work several hours more each day.

There isn't very much to say about our life. I rode to Starnberg Tuesday with L. and home with Lottie. They both complained about the saddle and I shall try to find a better one for them but don't feel sure that I can. L. fell and sat on her ankle yesterday and it is swollen and tender today. If it isn't much better tomorrow, I shall take her somewhere and have it examined. She is a comfortable person to have here—"not as deep as a well nor as broad as a barn door," but good-hearted, kind, even-tempered and easy to please, as well as eager to please. Her German is slight, rudimentary and bad—like Grace's French. Grace spells her left hand "gosh"—*gauche,* and speaks of "guins" meaning *gaurmes.* I hope her spelling was intended to be facetious, but fear it was in solemn earnest. Mamma is very well and Lottie is physically in far better condition than when she came. Temperamentally she varies as much as any one person can. It would take two, perhaps more, to vary more widely.

Mamma went to a service for Grandfather today—All Souls—and went with her mother and *Tante* Sophie to the cemetery afterwards. This afternoon at five there was a performance of Berlioz' "Requiem" in a big church in Manhaven not far from here. Mamma and I went, and I astonished myself by standing up all through two hours. Mamma went home after one and I didn't blame her at all. I had not heard the work for thirty years and was much interested in it. There is a terrific earful of sound in the "Dies Irae"—three brass bands besides the orchestra, chorus and organ. They are all there and were pretty good—taken from regimental bands in the city. The whole work is orchestrally full of surprises—mostly pleasant ones. One chord is like this—

It is a very famous freak place which every musician likes to hear sometimes. I doubt if I should like it if it lived in the same flat with us. We had to stand because there were no seats to be bought. There were between two thousand and three thousand people in the church, which pleased me immensely.

I will write to Grace next week, I hope, and in the meantime send much love and many kisses to you both.

Your loving
Papa.

Rottach, Bavaria,
October, 1912.

My dear Isabel:

I was very glad to get your nice letter written on Wednesday. It came Friday just as I was leaving for a bicycle ride or I would have answered it before. I went to Mittenwald by way of Partenkirchen the first day and back to Munich by way of Rottach the second, 240 Km.

in all. (144 miles) On the way to Partenkirchen I stopped a few minutes to see Mariele in her convent in Polling. She sends her love to you both and wanted to know if your school was like hers at all. It isn't, except in that the French language offers a considerable hurdle in each. Your chief task is to learn French, of course, at least that plays a larger part in your scheme of work than anything else, but, of course, the other things are very important, too. Using French as a medium of learning and of expression gives it the first place anyway. If you can learn to work better, i.e., not just to sit and muddle and think or hope that you are getting on rapidly, it will be of great benefit. Of course, everybody sits and muddles. I do far too much—but the less the better, and I have improved in the last thirty years somewhat. At least I do not often confound the two and prefer work to the other when I can manage it.

Your picture of Grace's roommate is clearer than that of Byrd Wallis. I sympathize with Violet * and hope she will improve, also that her ways are not contagious. She doesn't seem just the ideal example for Grace, but I am sure she has many good qualities—most girls have.

I know "Le Ruisseau" †—had my chorus in Philadelphia sing it once. Perhaps it is by Gabriel Faure, but I don't quite remember. How does Grace's singing get on? She hasn't mentioned it yet, in fact she confines her letters to generalities for the most part and to her subjective experiences. I expect to send your allowance on the 15th and would like to have you keep an account of your expenses. Send it to me every month so that I shall get it before the 15th. Make it up to the 10th each month and tell Grace to do the same. It is no wonder the concert didn't quite meet your views. Don't dwell upon it to others but just remember that for years you

* Gracie's roommate.
† Grace and I were singing a duet "Le Ruisseau."

have been hearing the best music there is in New Haven, and that it has often been as well performed as possible. Europeans are all and always skeptical about our own musical civilization in America. No matter—we know theirs and they cannot know ours except from more or less colored hearsay. Lottie reaches Gibraltar today and ought to be with you Friday night. I wrote her some weeks ago that she ought to stop in Lausanne on her way from Genoa.

We had a rather breathless letter from her today and expect a telegram Wednesday when she reaches Naples. Mamma wrote to Madam asking if Lottie can be stowed in the school. If not she can go to a hotel or a pension. I wrote her about such things at some length.

If you get a chance, try to hold her attention long enough to tell anything you may want to say and not to write. I hope you keep a diary and write at least a line every day. Try to get used to the exercise—that is a lot better for you than wishing you didn't have it.

Your mountains will have to work hard to look any better than the Wetterstein and the Karwendel did yesterday. Of course, the Lake is glorious—so is the whole place. I hope I may get there in January.

With love and kisses to you both,

Your loving
Papa.

When not in Europe, the later summers were spent in Blue Hill, Maine. It was quite by accident that Father was offered the house of Mr. Franz Kneisel in 1907.

In those days a journey was a journey! We left New Haven by train for Boston with the necessary appurtenances—being such animate objects as goldfish and dogs and, of course, the bicycles which always had to be *wheeled* so ignominiously across lower Boston over bumpy cobblestones to Foster's Wharf. Once on the boat, one sighed happily—we all loved boats—but there was still at least one dog tugging at a leash to be taken bounding around the deck and then fed. We generally had large, friendly dogs who managed to get tangled among the lifeboats—not to mention the more dignified passengers' legs. Finally, however, after the lovely sail out of Boston harbor and supper, we went early to bed in order to be able to arise to the rude and fierce awakening at Rockland the following morning at *five* A.M. Only one who has taken the trip can know the vigor with which our doors were rapped.

I shall always remember the wharf at Rockland—the irresistible emanation of salt, sea and fish. In Rockland, after transferring the baggage, animals and bicycles, we boarded *The Catherine* and sailed a leisurely, round-about course through the many beautiful islands surrounded by glistening blue sea, to arrive in Blue Hill about noon, at Parker Point. This name had been a matter of particular pleasure to Mother on her first arrival in a strange place—I'm sure she must have felt we belonged there, strangers or no.

Father found himself able to do an enormous amount of work in the exhilarating Maine air, and it was there in his studio in the woods, to which each year a team of oxen hauled the piano, that most of the colossal scores for his operas were written.

Those early years in Blue Hill were spent in the company of a happy lot of congenial musical friends, made up

STUDIO—BLUE HILL, MAINE

of the Kneisel Quartette, comprising Mr. Louis Svecenski, Mr. Otto Roth, and Mr. Alvin Schroeder. Added
to this group were Mr. and Mrs. Henry E. Krehbiel,
lovely Mrs. Thomas Tapper, and a small summer colony,
many of whom are still warm friends—the Teagle,
Strobel, and Nevin families.

During the building of our house we stayed for some
time at The Homestead, an Inn, where we all met with
regularity for meals. Sunday supper was a matter of
particular delight consisting as it did of "Skilly—Tea—
Cocoa." We never discovered what "Skilly" was—I remember it as a gray, rather watery mess. There was an
old institution known as "The Bridge Tournament," an
almost diabolically conceived idea for pleasure, but actually calling for the reaches of higher mathematics in
order to arrange that twelve or sixteen people should
each play against a different person every time. I can
still see Father and Mr. Krehbiel holding their heads
(and tempers) for a solution of this intricate puzzle,
neither being mathematically minded. We were fond
of our many village friends most of whom we continue
to meet again each summer. Our gardener, aged eighty,
who has a special place in our affections, has recently
reminded me of a prize of five dollars given to his youngest child at the graduation exercises of the Blue Hill
Academy. Members of the summer colony gave gladly
of their time and wisdom with foresight in the encouragement of diligence in school matters.

The mornings were spent in work, and the afternoons in golf, bicycle trips or frequent "buckboard"

picnics. There was even Blue Hill itself which, with the addition of a pile of rocks on its summit, bears the title of "mountain," measuring exactly one thousand feet.

There were clambakes and many gay parties given by the Kneisel family, lovely Victoria and Willem Willeke, Olga, and Maidie. The clambakes were the sole responsibility of Mr. Krehbiel, a large portly gentleman, full of kindness and fun. He was a perfect major domo. Days in advance he prepared for them. The stone oven was made, the driftwood collected, and finally seaweed placed on top of flat stones, for clams must be steamed. At last, after a time of meticulous and leisurely preparation—for time was not at a premium then—a thin cloud of gray smoke would curl into the air by way of signalling to us that the moment was nearly at hand. Our own house, being just across the cove from the Kneisel place, was a point of vantage from which to follow these careful proceedings. Colored lanterns were hung all over the Kneisel lawns; rare and most delectable Viennese dishes were prepared long days in advance; many available pupils (now famous artists) made music; and every language was spoken. The spirit of Bohemia prevailed. September 15th, Father's birthday, was often the occasion for one of these festive gatherings. The Frank Damrosches would sail over in the *Polly* from Seal Harbor; Dr. and Mrs. Karl Muck were in Blue Hill; Mr. and Mrs. Harold Bauer and Mr. and Mrs. Fritz Kreisler came. I can see Mr. Kreisler now, playing Viennese waltzes on the piano. Occasionally he and Father played, four hands, for a Virginia Reel. We did try so hard to teach Father to dance, but without success. Instead he would play his favorite popular tune, "Oh, Bedelia," for our amusement. There was often a Kinder Symphonie, the more serious musicians playing the silliest instruments.

It was early one clear summer's morning, August 10th to be exact, that Mr. and Mrs. Kneisel, with two students, their fiddles tucked under their arms, came secretly across the fields and sneaked into our pantry, to serenade Mother and Father at breakfast on the occasion of their twenty-fifth wedding anniversary. These were lovely, untroubled times. One is glad to think of them now.

VII

TWO PRIZE OPERAS

"Mona" and "Fairyland"

EXACTLY WHAT MADE Father want to write, or actually *write,* an opera has always been a matter of conjecture in my own mind. Certainly he always said of opera that it was a "beautiful mess"—combining, as it must, drama and music to fit each other. This necessity of itself, precludes in most operas truly spontaneous or natural expression in either of the arts—poetry or music. I can easily imagine that it may have seemed a challenge to him to try this field in which he had never worked, since he was always undaunted by the magnitude of any task, but believed, rather, in the unlimited possibilities of all true art. To quote Father's own statement:

> About five years ago, I asked Mr. Hooker * if he would be willing to make an opera text for me. He was perfectly polite but rather vague in his answer as I believe any good poet ought to be when asked to make a text for music. But when I was able to describe the proposed competition to him, he soon showed me a plan, a list of characters, with their attributes, and with what was likely to happen to them.

* Brian Hooker.

— 224 —

FIRST READING OF THE AMERICAN PRIZE OPERA "MONA"—1911

This first description was about as fascinating as the ground plan of a sub-cellar, and, although my interest was aroused, it was not burning at first.   But when Mr. Hooker sent me the first verses; my interest was at once wide awake, and I forthwith proceeded to make life a burden to him by clamoring for more, and he sent me more, and still more; beautiful verses, which stimulated the imagination, warmed the heart, and seemed to cry out for a setting in music.

Most probably it was again because it offered an opportunity to win a huge and most lavish prize of ten thousand dollars. This form of generous sponsorship of art had long helped in the establishment of great artists, not only in this country, but in Europe.   The actual beginning of the opera, "Mona," is recorded in a note in Father's Diary, dated July 14th, 1909, at Blue Hill, Maine:

"Received text of Act I"
July 27—Finished sketch of Act I. . . .
Sept. 14—Finished sketch of Act II—To New Haven— Orchestra rehearsals begin—Philadelphia & New York Church—Rode bicycle from Stratford to Derby, and home—Beautiful ride—Oratorio begins.

I leave these notes to convey the fact that regular duties continued as usual.

1910
March 1st—"Hora Novissima" in New York—Anna sails for Germany—Memorial Concert for Sam Sanford— Kneisel's in evening—*Sent opera to Brian Hooker*— Sembrich concert.
June 3rd—To Sharon—Baths I . . . X.   Norfolk—rain— rain!   Blue Hill—rode to Bangor—Rode to Bar Harbor concert (about 40 miles).   *Finished score Act III.*

During this time we knew Father was working with exceptional intensity. Mr. Brian Hooker often came to stay, and they would then discuss their work together for hours at a time.

The first intimation of the winning of the prize came to Mother in New Haven. It was a telegram, very terse, with no mention of the prize itself, but saying only:

New York May 2nd, 1911
    Meet Chadwick and Loeffler without fail at station at 6:40. Very important.

Chadwick—Loeffler

Father happened to be out of town, and Mother went down to the station alone,—the old, grimy New Haven railway station. One can imagine her pleasure and excitement at hearing the news they had to give her, and her eagerness and hurry to convey it to Father. Mother was always capable of pleasure and excitement even over small and simple family matters. But this was a really big one!

Mr. Chadwick and Mr. Loeffler, both naturally a little disappointed not to find Father there, were consoled by Mother's presence at the train, and wrote to him the following day. It seems appropriate to quote their letters here:

[*Chadwick to Father.*]
New England Conservatory
G. W. Chadwick
Director

May 3, 1911

My dear Parker:
    Loeffler and I were sorry not to be the first to grasp

— 228 —

your hand and give you our hearty congratulations, somewhat mitigated by Anna's really touching welcome. Be sure that nobody rejoices at your success any more than we do—I hope we may find a time before the work on the production begins for you to play it all through to me which I am sure will reveal even more beauties than I have already discovered. You will find Mr. Hertz * a most interested and conscientious artist to work with and I hope the other artists will be equally so.

If you do not forget that many of Mr. Hooker's beautiful lines cannot possibly be heard even with the best intentions, you will probably find many places to be improved, especially in the last act.

Above all I rejoice that this prize has been won and most fairly by a genuine American composer and a genuine American author. It will go far toward the encouragement of the others, and toward the respectful consideration of their works.

With every good wish.

Faithfully yours,

Chad.

[*Charles Martin Loeffler to Horatio Parker.*]

My dear Parker:

The rather gigantic job of reading through 24 opera scores is done! Ouff! And one breathes easier again. The work was all the more wearisome to me, as I was the one that had "Mona" *first* and then 23 more or less indifferently interesting ones (in grade down to very punk!) *after*. Therefore, my pleasure and fun was over after the first score was perused, and the rest was one long, wearisome, tragi-comical *corvée*, with very few rays of sunshine in it. All this confidentially! Let me tell you, my dear Parker, how happy I am that you should have written this score, and how easy you have made it

* Alfred Hertz, a conductor of the Metropolitan Opera Company.

to me—to us—to strew palms and laurel at your feet. It was fine of you to quietly work away at your task without much heralding and trumpeting it abroad. Your work seems to me what Edgar Poe calls a "fine sustained effort." Your orchestral score surpasses also everything you have done hitherto. Will you be amenable to a few short cuts in the First and Last Act, where recitations seem somewhat spun out? I hope so. Well, to have awarded you the moneyed prize was the least, the easiest thing to do; the greatest fun is to sincerely applaud your performance, Long live America, long live the gifted of this land, you and admirable Brian Hooker, the great painters and architects and the *tutti quanti* that make this land one of the wonders of the world!

Let us now all pray for a fine performance next winter. Hertz is honest and means to do his best for you and the post.

God bless you, dear Parker, take your well earned rest this summer and surprise us again before long with a new work.

Kind messages to Mrs. Parker, whose presence at the Railway Station consoled us for your *unexpected* absence.

Faithfully yours,
Charles Loeffler.

And here we have the following notes in Father's unresponsive Diary:

May 2nd. News of prize—*Golf*. . . .
May 3rd. Prize paid in New York
May 5th. See Hertz

At home telegrams and letters poured in from friends, fellow-artists, colleagues at Yale University and former students all over this country, Europe and even Japan.

Father, as usual, was entirely calm and detached, seeming quite unconscious of the praise and honor bestowed upon him. He must, however, have been very pleased with this reward of great labor, though his mind was already turned to the future, thinking and planning for the coming production.

The excitement in New Haven reached a high pitch, and here are several of the letters from New Haven friends and colleagues. The letter of Mr. Morris Steinert is especially revealing of the sense of personal gratification felt by him and of the friendly and sympathetic relationship between the New Haven Orchestra and its leader.

[*William Lyon Phelps to Father.*]

Yale College,
New Haven

Dear Horatio:

Glorious! *Wunderschön! grossartig und fabelhaft!* You have brought tremendous honour to Yale! I told my classes all about it.

God bless you all.

Yours,

W.L.P.

[*Professor Lounsberry to Father.*]

New Haven, May 19

Dear Professor Parker:

I made up my mind at the outset that I should let others—especially the others who really know something about music—exhaust themselves in congratulations, before I, who am as ignorant of it as a grunting porker, should descend upon you with anything of like tenor. But I don't believe that among the many who can appreciate and understand music there is a single person who felt any keener gratification at your success in securing the prize than did I: though I intentionally deferred the communication of the pleasure I experienced when I heard of it, none the less did I intend to inflict upon you in my own good time my congratulations. I am more delighted with the recognition of your talents that you have received than with the money that came along with it, though I am perfectly willing to concede that the latter is something that can be endured with Christian resignation. I am sure that this is but the beginning of many similar things in this new field which you will accomplish successfully. With the best wishes of an aged veteran, soon to be played out entirely, I remain,

Sincerely yours,

T. R. Lounsberry.

[*Morris Steinert to Father.*]
Dr. Horatio Parker,
420 Temple Street
New Haven, Conn.

My dear Friend:

Our quiet New England town was thrown into a state of musical enthusiasm last week, when it became known that Horatio Parker, of Yale, had captured the prize in the composition of grand opera.

We, the members of the New Haven Orchestra, well know that Dr. Parker has been our conductor since the starting of the Symphony, and that he is with us yet. Therefore we can conscientiously and rightly call him our own, and his successes are felt by us. Consequently I, as President of the New Haven Symphony Orchestra, am engaged in the pleasant duty of extending to you our true and affectionate congratulations upon this important event, and adding one more leaflet to the laurel wreath that crowns your brow. . . . Will you kindly accept the assurance that we share with you in part the honors accorded you by the musical world, and will you kindly recognize that we are the old guard, assembled around our leader? May your health, also your enthusiasm for the divine art of music ever be fresh and fruitful with you. . . .

With many kinds regards, I am

Sincerely yours,

Morris Steinert

President of the New Haven Symphony Orch.

Naturally the excitement felt by the members of Father's own household was not less, though the first expression of it by Grace, who frequently spoke without thinking, delighted and amused Father for years by its frank difference from the reactions of nearly everybody else. "My!", she exclaimed at breakfast, "the *others* (operas) must have been bad!" I cannot pass over this phase of the opera without a mention of another person whose first reaction was somewhat the same. His unaffected remark seemed to Father so delightful that, under the name of "The story of the *Caddy*," he quoted it again and again. The news of the winning of the opera award finally reached Blue Hill, Maine, by way of the "Bangor Daily News," the local newspaper, about the same time that we arrived for the summer. Upon reaching the golf course, Father's pet caddy was waiting for him and greeted him simply and aptly—"Gee, Mr. Parker, but you was lucky!"

More interesting than my own recollections of this time when I was quite unaware of the many artistic and practical problems with which Father and Mr. Hooker had already had to cope, and of the difficulties yet to be met before the Opera could reach production, are Father's own words on the subject in two talks at about this time. Speaking at Norfolk, Connecticut, Father said:

> I have been asked to speak to you about American opera and am forcibly reminded of Sir Thomas Browne's essay, "Owls in Norway" which begins as follows: "There be no owls in Norway." The rest of the essay is devoted to a description of the kind of owls which are not to be found there.
>
> Just at present there are only three American operas in sight: Converse's "The Pipe of Desire," Victor Herbert's "Natoma," and Converse's last opera "The Sacrifice." In the language of to-day these are grand operas, and excepting Mr. Walter Damrosch's "Scarlet Letter" I think they are the only ones which have been heard here for forty years or more. . . . I have no wish to be either historical or hysterical, as some enthusiasts for American music seem, and there is not time to give a complete account of the history of this form of art in this country. . . . I shall therefore dwell only upon certain phases which seem important at the moment.
>
> There is a certain vagueness about the term "American opera" and in some minds this term seems applicable only to works which have an American subject or place of action, but this is surely incorrect. No one save an Italian can think of "The Girl of the Golden West" as an American opera. One touch of local color ought to settle this point forever: that is where the red-shirted miner in California bursts into tears and asks "What

would my Mamma say if she knew where I am now?"
Local color, important as it may be, is always incidental
in art and especially in music. No amount of local
color can make an opera American—and no lack of it
can prevent an opera from being American if it is conceived here by our own people and executed in the
spirit which must inform all creative artists of whatever
nationality. The popular idea, therefore, that an American opera must have red Indians in it or darkies or cow-
boys is obviously incorrect. . . .

And here are the words, referred to earlier, giving
Father's opinion of opera as an art-form, a view I know
he had long held:

Opera is a heterogeneous mixture of utterly irreconci-
cilable arts. A beautiful mess, delicious, desirable and
fascinating. Nothing anyone can say against it or about
it can interfere with others' or even with the sayer's enjoyment of it. It can, therefore, do no harm to speak
the truth as one sees it. The dream of mixing music
and drama is as iridescent and hopeless as that of
squaring the circle. Still the best mathematical minds
have worked over it and come close to it, and I believe
a perpetually insoluble problem is a boon forever.

There are perhaps some reasons why material American elements are incompatible with the opera as an art
form. Mr. Hooker says we need remoteness and familiarity as well as appropriate subject matter for the
more impersonal arts. Such familiarity comes by way
of the drama and painting and perhaps sculpture into
poetry and then later into music. For instance
dramatists can use the telephone, painters can paint it,
we might perhaps see it in marble without being much
shocked, but any reference to it in poetry is pretty sure
to seem funny, and to sing about it would be a little

like putting Queen Elizabeth into bloomers. Perhaps you can recall the effect of hearing the word "Whisky" sung in opera.* It is just a little delirious and of course it is not necessary to have the real thing in the theater ever. A French theatrical principle declares that verisimilitude is more important than variety itself. This, possibly, may account in part for the extreme lightness of French light opera, which is as light as a perfect soufflée, or the soda-water of our childhood, which used to be nine-tenths sweetness and air. But we must recognize that one cannot get a good grip with one's teeth in such substances. Nobody can chew atmosphere, however charming, so that alone is not enough.

As illustrating verisimilitude, I recall the church music in "The Jongleur" of Massenet. It might be called modern French Gothic imitation stucco Gregorian, and it bears the same relation to the real thing that canvas pillars do to marble ones. That is, it creates an illusion of solidity. There is this difference, however, marble will not do in the theater on the stage, it is too heavy, but music is so ethereal that it weighs, even when genuine, no more in the theater than elsewhere. "Fidelio," for instance, is like marble, yet it is theater also.

There is a society for the promotion of opera in English. I think this ought to be preceded by a society for the protection of our mother tongue from singers. Even those born to it sin grievously, and foreigners still more. Some operas lend themselves to translation, but hearing "Siegfried" in French, "Louise" in German, and "Il Trovatore" in English will go far to reconcile lovers of opera to leaving operatic texts in the language in which they were born. Opera in English ought to be made in that tongue.

It is hard to speak about "Mona" because, as Mr. Hooker says, "It hasn't happened yet," but it seems

* In "Madame Butterfly."

pretty sure to happen next year, and after that we shall
know more than we do now. Certainly no opera house
in the world has such resources for producing this particular work as the Metropolitan, and I believe that no
pains and that nothing else will be spared to make the
production all we hope for, so that if the work does
not appeal to the public, I think it will be our fault,
and not that of the forces of the opera house, every department of which I believe will do all it can to make
the production successful.

These beautiful rural surroundings tempt me again
to use the homely barnyard simile of three years ago
when I accused Mr. Stoeckel of maintaining a musical
incubator at Norfolk. Mr. Hooker and I have been
industriously producing eggs which will surely and duly
be hatched next winter. We think we know what kind
of fowl will emerge but we cannot be sure. A cross between the eagle to look at and the nightingale to listen
to would please everyone, but there is no such thing in
nature and perhaps it is too much to expect in art. . . .

Speaking before the MacDowell Club of New York at
about this time, Father goes a little more deeply into
the technical problems of the opera and its music:

My one excuse for addressing you to-day on the subject of a yet unborn opera is that the MacDowell Club
stands for the interchange of ideas between artists who
work with different media of expression: between poets,
painters and musicians, people who are trying to get
things out of their heads—new things—if they have the
power of finding them and giving them forth.

I shall make no attempt to foreshadow or forestall a
performance of the opera under consideration. But
painful as the process must be to a parent, I shall have to
dissect and analyze the child who cannot speak as yet

for itself. And to such a gathering as this it is surely not necessary to apologize for using technical language. A description of artistic processes in words of one syllable would hardly satisfy you or me and it will be plain that I must speak to a more sympathetic and enlightened intelligence than the man in the street.

I shall describe the story and the music. As a matter of literary construction they ought, no doubt, to be dealt with separately but I shall venture to go from one to the other. Either salt pork or molasses taken singly would prove cloying, or at least uninteresting, but taken together I have been told that they form a palatable dish.

Here Father takes up the story of the play itself. Since he considers it scene by scene, illustrated by passages at the piano, it is too long to quote. It would, moreover, be less interesting than it was to his hearers who were able to listen to his playing of the accompanying themes. Briefly stated, the play deals with the conflict between Romans and Britons after Caesar's conquest of the island. It tells of the tragic love of Mona, who believes herself destined to liberate her fellow tribesmen, and Gwynn, the pacifier and youthful optimist, in whose blood both strains mingle, and who seeks the solution of their difficulties in finding the best for both factions. Mona does not know of his Roman birth, nor of his real name, Quintus, made into "Gwynn" by the British tribesmen. Discovering this, she kills him, only to realize when he is dead that she has not only lost her *love but also all hope of fair treatment for her countrymen.*

Some of Father's phrases, describing these early

Britons, have a tragically ironic appropriateness in this year of writing, when England is again besieged:

> The conquest of Britain by Rome, complete as it seems to have been now at this distance, was at no time so successful as to secure the acquiescence of the conquered nation. Foreign domination has always been a natural and constant incentive to revolt. The British tribes never failed to recognize this nor to act in accordance with the principle just laid down. . . . I may not take time to describe the social and moral condition of Britain under Roman rule. It is enough to say that the British as a race were brave, intelligent and faithful, with ethical and religious principles as high and admirable as those of their conquerors, superior in fact in many details if we may venture an opinion. The story is not an archeological study but a tale of very human passions and happenings.

Of the relative merits of the play and the music there is room for, and there has been, some difference of opinion, though I should not venture to express one myself. I do know, however, how very highly each of the two collaborators—Father and Mr. Brian Hooker— regarded the work of the other. Mr. Hooker's admiration of Father's music is eloquently expressed in a letter which he sent to Father on the morning following the first performance. As to Father's opinions of the poetry, over and over expressed, I cannot do better than quote the concluding phrases of the talk at Norfolk:

> The poem is a strong, clean story told in beautiful English verse. It has been an unfailing, unflagging incentive and inspiration to make good music. It seems to me *the* poem for which English speaking composers have

longed and waited, hitherto in vain. We all know that
things, like persons, may be very good indeed without
inspiring affection. Mr. Hooker and I both believe that
our work may be respectable and we hope sincerely that
it will prove likeable as well. When it does "happen,"
we are willing everyone should know that it is quite the
best work we knew how to produce at the time, also
that if it is successful, we hope we can profit by the
hearing sufficiently to do better another time.

Of course, the opera *did* eventually "happen," after
weeks and months of work and preparation. We went
to an occasional rehearsal; it was a strange experience to
sit in that great, empty opera house and exciting later to
go behind the scenes to the dressing room of Mme.
Louise Homer, and to watch the management of innumerable details necessary for an operatic production on
that tremendous stage.

In the Diary notes of 1912, are recorded, in succession—

"Mona" rehearsal—Bach "Passion" rehearsal—Eurydice Concert—"Mona" rehearsal—Concert, Derby; and
finally,—Act I—Act II—Act III—Formal Dress Rehearsal;
then,—

March 14, 1912
First "Mona" performance—Anna sick—Wrote letters—
Golf—Supper.

Thus barely and tersely recorded, the long-awaited performance actually took place on the night of March
14, 1912. Poor Mother was ill at the home of Mr.
and Mrs. Krehbiel. I'm sure it must have been the
result of sympathetic anxiety and excitement. We chil-

dren, with friends and relations, sat in the middle Parterre box, and I recall scattered impressions: that first hush as the Conductor makes his way through the orchestra to his stand;—the graceful sweep of those great, yellow-gold curtains going up on the First Scene;—much familiar music (we had heard it all in the making);—the Intermission, with Father and Mr. Hooker looking like pygmies on that great stage;—the ovation to them both, wreaths, flowers, billows of applause; and from then on, huddling in the back of the box, overcome with emotion. It was a spectacular occasion, and a moving one.

The opera, despite the enthusiastic response of the first-night audience, was not well received by most critics. I include the letter from Mr. Hooker which I have mentioned.

[*Brian Hooker to Father.*]

36 Convent Avenue
New York City
March 15, 1912

Dear Mr. Parker:

The papers to-day look rather like a headache after the intoxication of last night. How far their disapproval can affect our future audiences remains to be seen. But while the fate of *Mona* is still in the balance I want to say to you that neither criticism nor the popular verdict can alter my feeling about your part of the work. I have lived with the score all winter; and I have never heard or remembered a page of it without finding some new beauty or fitness in it that I had not noticed before. After a hundred hearings it has but more and nobler things to say. That is what I care about in music; and that, in any art, is what is really worth while. Once fairly launched into deep water of understanding, that is what will endure.

To work with you has been from the first a growing honor and pleasure. I feel that now more strongly than when you came to me at first, more strongly than when you won me the prize and my first real chance of success. And I wish for nothing more than the opportunity to make another opera with you, and to show people what we have learned from this.

With best remembrance to Mrs. Parker and the rest, believe me,

Very sincerely yours,
Brian Hooker.

A most friendly and cheerful reminder has recently come to me from Mr. and Mrs. Sidney Homer. Mr. Homer says:

> I do not believe it is possible for you to realize what an inspiration your Father was to all who knew him and, also, to all who heard his works.
>
> I remember the first performance of "Hora Novissima" and what a vista it opened up to the American people, and of course I remember all the rehearsals and performances of "Mona." Those were memorable occasions. They were unforgetable to those who were privileged to know the work well.
>
> I hope to hear a great revival of "Mona." Have you ever thought of giving it in concert form? Many operas and music dramas have been given in that way. It enables the public to become familiar with the music.

And from Madame Louise Homer:

> I sang your father's songs and the big contralto aria from "Hora Novissima" for a long time before I met him. After I met him I understood his works even better, and

of course when I studied and sang MONA I became still more conscious of his ideals and the depth of his convictions.

His patience and encouragement during the rehearsals of "Mona" I shall never forget. We were all working under pressure, studying this important work and singing performances of other operas at the same time. Usually I had all summer in which to prepare new roles, but this time I had to learn a great role in the middle of the season. It was a tremendous thing to do, and because I knew your father and longed for great success for him I felt a great responsibility.

But he was calm and cheering through it all, and inspired us with confidence and determination.

How exciting the first night was! How proud we were!

But you were there and shared in it all.

Despite criticism, it must have been an exciting and thrilling time. Father notes in his Diary another performance of "Mona" at the Metropolitan on March 23rd. On this occasion he dined at Sherry's as the guest of the directors of the Metropolitan Opera House with Mr. Hooker, the librettist. A newspaper account says that:

The guests were seated at a table arranged as a hollow square, inside of which were banked roses in the form of a garden. After the dinner speeches were made . . . Otto H. Kahn and Henry Rogers Winthrop presided. There were about 80 guests.

Father was one of those called on to speak, and said:

I count it a pleasure and privilege as well as an honor . . . to enjoy the generous hospitality of the Directors of the Metropolitan Opera House. I am particularly glad of an opportunity to acknowledge the uniform kindness we have met in every department of your great organization. From one end to the other of the building, and from top to bottom, everyone has been interested, zealous and helpful in a degree which made us very grateful indeed. There has been no smallest opportunity for kindness or courtesy which has not been met unhesitatingly. . . . With regard to the work itself we are in some measure indebted to the Directors of the Metropolitan Opera for the original impulse to make it.

I have lived with the poetry now for nearly three years and like it far better than at first. Perhaps it is not quite perfect, most of us are human, but it is good enough for me. I feel that it has called forth the best music of which I am capable. Quite the best in our language.

The result of our labors is not Italian opera or French opera or German opera. I believe it is American opera, for it certainly is nothing else and whether one likes it or not is a matter of taste concerning which others may dispute. . . . I am told that I have been quoted as having expressed a poor opinion of Verdi's work. Without any desire to seem to give importance or weight to my opinion, I should like for the sake of the simple truth to tell you what I really do think of that great composer. For me his work is one of the most inspiring of examples. He was a man who like Gluck, Haydn, Wagner, Handel, went onward and upward throughout the whole of a long life, whose last work was his very best.

He was one of those men who, like the others mentioned, in the very evening of a long life still created convincing, abiding master works of music. And these are the gentlemen who give to a musician of my age courage to compose, courage to hope that something of freshness, something of beauty may yet be found among the ideas which come into the mind and ask for utterance. These writers of music give comfort and courage. . . .

But this sounds like an obituary and I am not dead—far from it; very well and all the better for the hospitality and kindness you have shown.

I have always believed that every country which must have art must bear its own share of the burden of producing such art. And I look forward to the time when a musician like a painter shall take his place among the art-producers of the world, shall find a voice which will be heeded not merely by his own compatriots, but wherever high music is loved.

Father and Mr. Hooker wrote one more work in this form,—the opera "Fairyland," which won the $10,000 prize offered by the National Federation of Music Clubs. Not generally considered so unified, vigorous or important a work as "Mona," it was extremely well received at its performance on the West Coast. Most of the music of this opera was written during the Sabbatical year spent in Germany, while my sister and I were at school in Lausanne, Switzerland. We were, therefore, not near the work in the making. The opera was produced in Los Angeles on July 1, 1915. Mother and Father journeyed West for the performance, but we children did not go; and the occasion can be most vividly conveyed in the words of Aunt Nellie, who was present with Father at the first performance and described it later in a talk before her Tuesday Musical Club in Salt Lake City, Utah.

Part of what she says I shall not quote, since it covers a road we have already travelled: telling of Father's boyhood, studies with his Mother who, "began to play the organ at the age of sixteen, and continued to do this almost without intermission till a month before her death at the age of 67." She also mentions a most picturesque circumstance, viz., that in Munich her:

> brother made many musical acquaintances, and friends, among whom was a fascinating old man, Franz Lachner, who was a personal friend of Schubert, and who had walked side by side with him, both carrying torches at the funeral of Beethoven! . . .
>
> . . . The mere mechanical labor of writing music is tremendous, since no aid of typewriter or stenographer can be called in. In one change of key in a chorus for voice and accompaniment, I remember counting, in curiosity, to find 174 flats, and that was just a mere small detail of the real writing. The orchestral parts and score of "Fairyland" made a package four feet square and eighteen inches high, every note of which was written by my brother's own hand.
>
> So, also, when a book is finished a good proof-reader is a vast help to a writer, but no proof-reader can read for a musician his original composition! He must read every note himself, personally, often many times over. Then after that come many months of study and separate and ensemble rehearsing, with direction and correction. . . .
>
> As I came away with my brother after the première, I asked him if it had gone as well as he had expected. He replied emphatically: "Ten thousand times better than I ever dreamed it could. . . . Really, I was immensely pleased by the way in which the work was done in Los Angeles. I was astonished at the wealth of musical resources which the city showed. The performance made a profoundly satisfactory impression on me. The light-

TWO PRIZE OPERAS

ing was not all that might be hoped for, but, otherwise, things were excellent, and especially from a musical point of view. I have never seen more earnest unselfish co-operation on the part of a chorus and orchestra. They and Mr. Hertz seemed indefatigable in their efforts toward the success of the performance. And the warm welcome and generous hospitality of the people was delightful."

[To Isabel and Grace. Father and Mother were on their way West for the performance of "Fairyland" at the World's Fair in Los Angeles.]

The California Limited
    Santa Fe   Enroute.   Wednesday, June 10, 1915

Miss I. G. Parker,
Dear Miss Parker:

In spite of the affection I feel for your dual person-ality it joggles too much for me to bring it to adequate expression and I shall wait until we are on dry land to continue. Since writing as above we have been tearing through the desert lands of New Mexico—Indiana, cow-boys and their simple residences—once in a while a wind-mill to furnish water (all the rivers run underground here) and a patch of growing things, chiefly horses, hens and fruit trees.

Just now we are stopping at Albuquerque where Mamma sent post-cards to her three offsprings. We saw Schumann-Heink on the platform and had a few words with her. The train starts and stops. We are now at the edge of the Grand Canyon and are solemnly stunned by it. The distances are enormous but one cannot real-ize them. The colors are crude, as artificial as those of Tegernsee in the dewy evening, but I have my joy in them and wish that I were less civilized, i.e., European-ized, so that I might howl in response without posing.

Someday a Western-born musician will do it and the rest of the world will sit up. We came through the most inviting (to me) country (Mamma was not invited) yesterday and last night. Just after I had gone to bed Mamma lifted her curtain and made me climb down again to see the station at Flagstaff, Arizona. There was a board like the one at Enterrottach only it said different things:

Petrified Forest   9 miles
Painted Desert   12 miles
Natural Bridge   60 miles
Moqui Reservation 75 miles.

This is the nearest railroad point to all of them, and the 60 etc. miles are performed by mule or horse if at all. I should like to try it, but only when I am sure of time to recover. Just now I have too many operas, lectures and other engagements. The thing I particularly want to see and shall not is the way the cliff dwellers lived—like swallows building against the rocky eaves of mountains.

There are models and photographs and other consolations, but one always hopes the real thing is more, and it always is if one has the imagination. More next time; don't go out in the canoe at all if the weather is not perfectly smooth and *never be in it after 6:30 P.M.* till we both get home.

With love and kisses,

Your affectionate

Father.

Berkeley, Cal., June 23, 1915

My dear Kids:

Two letters from Isabel and one from Grace have reached me so far. All were highly satisfactory including and especially Isabel's accountings. *Continuez!*

TWO PRIZE OPERAS

I enclose Isabel's allowance which can be endorsed and mailed to the bank.

I have been here since Monday and in a state of constant eruption. The work has now begun in earnest but it is not hard, only rather absorbing and confining. I came up from Los Angeles Sunday night on the *Yale,* which used to run from Boston to New York.

The Pacific was anything but quiet in spite of its name, but I was hungry and comfortable tho' many were the opposite.

The climate here is quite different from Los Angeles, far cooler. Nearly all the journey was hazy—not just foggy but rough and cold. It was like a rather unpleasant trip to Rockland except it didn't rain and isn't going to till October.

Coming through the Golden Gate the sun broke through the clouds and the bay with its islands and San Francisco looked most attractive. Berkeley is up in the foot hills with beautiful views and pleasant, nearby climbs which I have only sampled as yet but hope to enjoy next month. There is a wild lot of students—5000 with more girls than boys—all after condensed information in a hurry. Some of the signs are rather characteristic for a restaurant.

DO YOU

EAT

Sure you do

There is a Chocolatorium for girls, etc. Newsboys are louder and have less to sell than in any other place I know. But naturally the place is full of fascination, sunshine and flowers everywhere and all the time. The hills are beautiful and scenes most inviting. The nights are cold and the days cool. The groves of eucalyptus and sequoia are most romantic and beautiful. I shall try to get some photographs which will give you an idea of them. I haven't been to the Exposition yet but expect to go Thursday evening to a concert by Saint-Saëns. Perhaps also on Friday on my way back to Mamma and Los Angeles. Three days of the week I have a class in the morning—the other two at four in the afternoon.* More next time.

With love and kisses,
Ever your affectionate
Father.

Berkeley, July 11, 1915

My dear little Isabel:

Grace writes that your nose is slightly out of joint. You must guard against that since it is your only one. I have been much pleased by your letters and your regular accounting for what you spend.

Mamma will be with you shortly after this letter and I hope all the tension will relax then if not before. I understand perfectly well that housekeeping is not soothing unless one is used to it, but it must be done, and I feel sure that you have done it well and profited by the doing. One of the crying needs of our age is a few new animals to eat. Beef, Pork, Mutton, Mutton, Pork, Beef, *da capo* and *ad inquisition*. Still you would not like dog, cat, iguana, armadillo, goat or crocodile. We are hard to suit I fear. I hope Mamma has told you all about "Fairyland." It seems very distant now, rather like a feverish but not unpleasant dream. I will talk about it when I get home, but can't write just now with much ease.

Yesterday we all went to the Fair. There were nine of

* Lecturing at the summer session of the University of California in Berkeley.

us. Nellie with her pair, and Lottie (Ted's) with hers as well as Stephen. We began in the morning and got home by midnight so that I am feeling somewhat worn today. We sent you postal cards without much news on them or sense either.

I wish you and Grace could see all the things here which would interest you. Perhaps you will some day. With it all, i.e., the interest, it isn't quite comfortable. East or West, home's best, and I would rather be there now than have so long to wait and far to travel.

With love and kisses.

Your affectionate father

H.P.

San Mateo, California
July 25, 1915

My dear little Isabel:

No doubt I ought rather to be writing to your Mother. Please apologize to her and let her read this if you approve.

Your last financial statement was quite convincing and satisfactory. I am pleased that you should do it so carefully. Do form the habit. It is easily done, and it is invaluable for later use.

I am now taking a little country air—millionaire to be accurate. A pleasant San Francisco merchant who has a piano-playing wife of great charm did me the honor to ask me to stay over Sunday.

We had Margaret Anglin last night for dinner, together with many other good things to eat. Then we had three entire string quartets, two violin sonatas and a long French piece for violin and piano.

They have a private quartet on the grounds with nothing else to do. I will tell you about it when I get home. One week from tomorrow I hope to see the last of Berkeley for a time.

I have had quite enough of it and although I enjoy it and have been very well treated, the best thing I can find about the Pacific Coast is the fact that I live elsewhere.

Be kind to Mamma and Grace and the others, and expect me about ten days after this letter.

I shall be glad to see you.

With love and kisses,

I am your affectionate

Papa.

It is, however, the earlier opera "Mona," rather than "Fairyland" which after the years looms as the bigger work, and I should like to conclude this chapter with an estimate of its worth written by Mr. Walter Kramer * ten years after Father's death:

> The tenth anniversary of the death of Horatio Parker occurred on Wednesday, December 18, 1929. In the bustle of a busy musical season, the completion of a decade since the death of one of America's outstanding composers passed with comparatively little notice. It is, therefore, a privilege for me to call attention on this occasion to the work of an artist who labored long and ardently in behalf of the highest standards in American creative music.
>
> As dean of the music department at Yale University, Horatio Parker contributed a more than significant chapter to music in academic institutions in the United States. His pupils, several of whom I have known personally, and with one of whom I studied, revered him as a master, most exacting and at the same time truly inspiring.

* Quoted from: "Horatio Parker—Ten Years After—An Appreciation," by A. Walter Kramer. *Musical America*, Dec. 25, 1929.

TWO PRIZE OPERAS

He is best remembered for his oratorio, "Hora Novissima," a work which won him honors in 1902 from the English University at Cambridge and which today occupies a unique position in contemporary Oratorio literature. His other oratorio, "Saint Christopher," is also important, despite the fact that it has never achieved similar popularity. In memory of the Yale men who died in the war, Dr. Parker composed a choral work entitled "A.D. 1919," performed at Yale University under his direction, his swan song, and which is, in many ways, one of his most personal expressions. . . .

He came into the greatest general prominence in 1912 when his opera, "Mona," won the $10,000 prize offered by the Metropolitan Opera Company for an American opera. When it was produced under the direction of Alfred Hertz considerable fault was found with the musical idiom.

Reviewers declared that the work was lacking in melody, that the music did not have genuine operatic feeling. I recall having attended the dress rehearsal and all the performances given that year. From the beginning I was impressed with the unusual beauty of this music, which, to be sure, was advanced in utterance at that day and a far cry from some of the operatic novelties which the Metropolitan Opera House was offering twenty years ago. . . . That the music of "Mona" was far in advance of its day and that it is perfectly understandable today, I have proved on more than one occasion, when I have played parts of the score for friends of mine without any information as to what music I was performing. In every case, without a single exception, my friends who have listened have been enthusiastic about the music, some of them who heard the opera when it was performed at the Metropolitan being dumbfounded at the different impression gained on hearing it today, even in its less favorable presentation on the piano.

HORATIO PARKER

I have always felt that a revival of this opera properly cast would be a great success. It is sincerely to be hoped that this work will be tried again some day, just as other works which have not been successful at their première have been reheard with entirely different results.

In addition to his important contributions to oratorio and opera, Dr. Parker composed a wealth of dignified church music, a delightful Suite for trio of piano, violin and violoncello, an organ Sonata and Concert Piece for the same instrument, as well as numerous shorter organ compositions. He belongs to the unsensational composers, those whose output is characterized by seriousness of purpose, dignity of style and masterly workmanship.

To the rising generation of composers in this country, whose art, I regret to say, is founded on qualities almost diametrically opposed to these attributes, the achievement of Horatio Parker should be made known. I am not deluded into thinking that they will find his music particularly sympathetic to their highly seasoned harmonic senses. It would be an excellent thing, however, for them to be acquainted with it for its sobering effect and as an example of distinguished musical endeavor.

VIII

NINETEEN-TWELVE TO
"A. D. 1919"

IN THE SPRING of 1912 we sailed again for Europe, this
time by the Southern route. Father's Diary recalls the
voyage thus:

> *June 15*—Sailed at one o'clock—fair, cool, smooth—Fair,
> rather rough—Grace slightly seasick—nothing else to
> record.
> *June 17th*—Bad fourth toe—bed all day with toe—mile-
> age 420. (He records the mileage daily)
> *June 21st*—Fair, cool—stopped at Azores—landed and saw
> church—Gibraltar—Landed, Algiers.

This was merely a pause in our journey, but how
well I remember Algiers, the Mosques, the Arab women
in their veils, men in dirty white robes, the flat-roofed
houses where they knelt to pray—poverty and filth all
about!

> *June 28th*—Landed Naples—Straits of Messina—stopped
> at Patras—Corfu—Coast of Albania and Dalmatia.

This voyage took us five days to the Azores, thirteen
days to Trieste, our destination. Now, as I write, the

"Transatlantic Clipper," droning eastward in the afternoon sky, passes over the house at four o'clock to reach the Azores in twenty-four hours and Lisbon, Portugal, in thirty-two.

From Trieste we traveled to Munich, and thence to Rottach, Bavaria, where the next entry is:

Diary
   Miethete Wohnung—bought bicycle and ordered piano. (The bicycle and piano were really more important than our abode.)

This *Wohnung* cost about two hundred marks, or fifty dollars for the summer—and the maid, "Peppi," received sixteen marks, or four dollars monthly. She was a superb cook, or could it have been our appetites in that clear mountain air?

And so the summer proceeded. We had a pleasant *Wohnung* that summer on the top floor of a typical Bavarian chalet, through which ran a long hall with rooms on either side, from a high balcony at the front to a balcony at the back of the house. From the rear balcony we looked down on wide meadows where flowed a rambling brook. Looking up one felt one could almost reach out and touch the miniature chapel on top of a small, but very steep, mountain, the Riederstein. This tiny white jewel, silhouetted against the blue sky, seemed to reach its spire to Heaven, as it glistened in the sun. Here, again, we lived the simple life of the people of that country—the only Americans within many miles.

The Diary varies little in these ensuing months:

—Started writing "Fairyland"—work—rode bicycle—
walked with children. . . .

—Rain—rain . . . poured. . . .

And how it did rain that summer—almost without
ceasing—so that we were soon forced to disregard the
weather, bicycling and climbing mountains in spite of it,
and in the midst of it, coming home drenched to the skin.

We stayed in Europe from June of 1912 until the
autumn of 1913, Father taking his Sabbatical leave of
absence from Yale University, and Grace and I, when
summer was over, being sent to school in Lausanne,
Switzerland. Father, as editor-in-chief of a new series
of school books entitled "The Progressive Music Series,"
traveled about the Continent and to England gathering
material from many musicians: Reger, Max Bruch,
Wolf-Ferrari, and Richard Strauss in Germany; Roent-
gen and van der Stucken in Holland; Debussy, Pierné,
Vincent d'Indy in Paris; Sir Edward Elgar, Sir Charles
Villiers Stanford, Delius and others in England; Sibelius
in Finland.

There were a number of friends living in Munich
and the sympathetic atmosphere of that city (loved
for so long) served as the pleasantest possible environment for them all. Mr. and Mrs. Ossip Gabrilowitsch, of whom Father was very fond, were there as
well as Professor Henry D. Fine of Princeton, with his
family; Mrs. H. H. A. Beach and Mrs. Gustave Schirmer, also Mr. William Milligan Sloan of the Academy
of Arts and Letters.

I can imagine the jolly times they had together that
winter while we were in Switzerland at school. Who

could have believed then that hardly more than twelve
months later, in the hot August of 1914, the incident
of Sarajevo would mark the beginning of the first
World War. This winter was really the end of a
period; the next, with the summer that followed,
marked the beginning of another, of which no one now
can see the outcome.

The following are letters to my sister Grace and me
at school in Switzerland:

Munich
November 27, 1912.

My very dear little Isabel:

I was too sleepy to go out and am now nicely left
alone. Mamma and the kids have gone to Mrs. Preston's to tea. I have been working till tired and can re-
sume our long interrupted correspondence.

Your decision and Grace's to stay in Lausanne through
the holidays is wise I am sure. You will have had far
more French than Lottie had. Of course, you both
needed more, but then you will get it. Then, I was
always sorry for the distraction of Lottie's Christmas
irregularities here, and you will avoid them. Although
they were amusing in her case and would be very pleasant in yours, as well as delightful and welcome to us,
they were exhausting and very disturbing, and I believe
they would be twice as much so in the case of two as in
hers, i.e., two of you would get twice as far off the track as
one. But that dog is hung and we can go on cheerfully.

Mamma wrote to Gracie today and told her, probably, that we have been entertaining New Haveners.
Henry Farnam and Dr. Summersgill, who was superintendent of the New Haven Hospital while Lottie lived
there, wrote to us last Sunday from Nürnberg. I found

them at the Vier Jahreszeiten and told them where to go
for grub and what to look at. They don't speak any German at all and, although they are old travellers, they
seemed rather helpless. Yesterday I met them in a café
with Mother. They took me to supper and I took them
to the Hofbräuhaus where there was a band concert, and
Mother and the children went too. The room was as hot
and smoky as it is big—and it is tremendous, but we were
cheerful; sent postal cards to Dr. Arnold and others, and
generally amused ourselves quite well, except that we
nearly missed the last car and Lottie and Leila both
have chilblains and were scared lest they might have to
walk from Neuhausen. I haven't any such things but
was quite content to ride.

Last Sunday we made an *Ausflug*—Leila was not here,
she went to see the royal palaces at Linderhof, Hohen-
schwaugan, etc. with the Graydons and had not returned
to us. Mamma and I agreed to meet in Ebenhausen,
which is about fifteen miles away, up the Isar valley.
One o'clock was the time, so I left at 11:15 and was on
hand; saved two chairs for them with much difficulty for
the place was over full. I ordered something (*Kalbs-
kopf*) reserved until they came and began to wait. At
two I had eaten four strudel and saw no signs of them,
so I ordered my dinner served. Just as I was half-way
through it a little farmer boy came in with his cap and
told me that Mamma and Lottie were at Kloster Schaftlarn, about ten minutes' walk down hill. I paid my bill
and went down just to find them giving a last lick to
their plates. They had taken the car to Grünewald and
walked up on the wrong side of the river a great *um-
swing*—and arriving at Kloster they read on a signboard
that it was Km. 4.7 to Ebenhausen (which is by the road,
but only ten minutes straight up hill); they became dis-
couraged and sat down to feed and refresh themselves.
We didn't stay together very long, for it was three

o'clock, and the sun sets at four, but we all had a lot of fresh air. They walked to Baierbrun and I rode around on my bicycle to Wolfratshausen, which we went through with the Stoeckels, and then home. Schaftlarn is where *Grossmamma* lived as a girl, and we tried to get her to go with us but she was afraid of the walking and stayed at home.

There isn't much news, except that we are to have Thanksgiving dinner tomorrow with the Americans living here at the invitation of the American Consul.

I hope you are both good and well and happy. Particularly also that Gracie's tragic work basket has profited by the catastrophe of last week. I suppose yours was in applepie order—like your ribbon box—at least I hope so. Have you recovered from your cold? And can you sew your buttons on? And does your Russian roommate still continue to seem all you hoped at first?

With much love and many kisses for both of you

Ever your affectionate

Papa.

Munich,
December 26, 1912.

My dear Children:

Christmas has come and gone—we are all alive still and trust that you too have survived the pleasures and perils of this happy season.

This is the first of my "thank you" letters, and I was really more than pleased by the characteristic photographs. I should have known them by the poses even if the faces had been rubbed out.

I at once fished them out and wrote "Rottach, Summer of 1912" on the backs of them, putting Gracie's back upside down which seems, queerly enough, to heighten the illusion. Now they stand on my writing table and I shall take them to my work-room and put them under the postal-card of Lake Leman with the two-winged sail boat which adorns my wall—the one I stare at most.

We have had peaceful celebrations complicated with many things to eat.

Tuesday at five we had a little private tree four feet high which *Grossmamma* had prepared for the servants, and at seven we went to *Tante* Sophie's where we found one beautifully decorated with artificial snow and ice and reaching from the bottom of the floor to the ceiling. It was there that I found the case and photographs of my favorite daughters, together with many other objects of usefulness and beauty. Two very fine handkerchiefs with H.P. engraved upon them in suitable colors by and from Lottie—a beautiful plush hat—a warm brownish waistcoat and a marvelous sweater of camels-hair from Mamma—a nice red necktie from Leila in case of sore-throat—a green English one and a letter case from Uncle Ludwig—a case for my house-keys (of leather) with *"Bitte nicht so spät"* from Mariele—tokens from *Tante* Sophie and *Kleine* Lottie, with other things of which others will send you a catalogue. Then we had a long and very good meal with a little music and a larger champagne punch afterward. Christmas Day the whole Ruck-deschel * tribe came here for dinner—also a good one. We all sat down in our *Wohnzimmer* at a long table. Everything else had been moved out so there was room enough and grub enough—even ice cream enough for once. Otto had received a fountain pen which he wears outside as a decoration. He had evidently been anxious to use it, but had been hampered by a shortage of paper, for his left hand was adorned with O.B.R. unmistakably painted by the pen in question. After dinner we took a much needed walk through the mud and then went to a coffee-house—not on my account but rather on *Gross-mamma's,* although there were no growls from the others.

* Mother's sister's family.

After coming home Mamma and I and Uncle Ludwig and *Tante* Sophie went to a Symphony Concert and to another coffee house before going to bed. You see it was rather a full day.

Of course, we all missed you sadly and thought and spoke of you often, besides drinking your health at intervals. We shall expect an account of your own doings before long and hope you were very happy.

I think your decision to stay in Lausanne was a wise one, and in spite of missing you, I think we all are glad you had the additional benefit and advantage of continuous French, as well as the new experiences which you would have missed here where there was little that would have been new to you. I was much pleased with your letters, and liked Gracie's poem in which no one was neglected. The German sentences with a correct use of the subjunctive after *dass* came as a pleasant shock. I could understand Isabel's using such a construction—after having seen it in school—but for Grace to use it right except by accident—many things may happen in the course of much persevering volubility—is delightful.

It made just a little the impression one might receive from a large and elegant cravat on a man's bosom who is otherwise presumably imperfectly equipped—one involuntarily wonders whether there is a proper shirt beneath it. But I hope Gracie's German is warmly and properly clad and that there is more to it than merely what meets the eye. An occasional German sentence or two in future letters would be reassuring and would confirm a very favorable impression.

Probably no one has told you that we took advantage of Mother's absence in Lausanne to go out into the hills.

We got to Tegernsee at eleven and went up on the Neurath, Leila and Lottie and I. It was muddy in Tegernsee but about half way up everything was covered with snow, and although it rained a little, we were happy

and made the whole distance in an hour and a half.
Clarence had sent me by Lottie an enlargement of a
snap-shot which he took from the Gindelalm Schneid
where he and Steuart played leap-frog. It is a beautiful
picture and I wanted to show them the place, so after
our luncheon we walked over to the Gindelalm. The
Senverhütten was closed and we couldn't get up on the
Schneid—the snow was four feet deep so we kept on
down to Schliersee. The girl at the Neurath told us
we would need at least four hours, but we took just
about three. Lottie had a bad cold so we came home,
although we had hoped to stay away another day or two.
We want to go back and go up on the Wendelstein and
down to Brannenburg. The villages are disappointing in
winter. They look cold and bald and the lakes look
just like plain water—no blue color to them, but the mountains are magnificent and look their very best in their white
clothes and their great bold outlines. They seem far bigger as the towns seem smaller, but we enjoyed it all and are
eager to go on and do some more of it. If I were alone
I should go to some new place, but with the children I
like to go to the places I know they will enjoy seeing. For
our next trip I have in mind the Wendelstein, Tatzlwurn,
Brunerstein and Brennenburg. You know these all well
if you can't remember them now. I hope next summer
will be fine and that we can go up a lot more as we would
have done last summer but for the weather. Make the
most of your own mountain chances and write to us about
them. It will make our mouths water.

With many thanks for your thoughtful and welcome
gift, and with very much love to you both, I am,

Your loving
Father.

In the Autumn of 1913 we returned to America—
leaving Grace at Les Fougères in Switzerland.

HORATIO PARKER

Philadelphia,
Feb. 2nd, 1914.

My dear Gracie:

I was glad to get your letter and am beginning to answer it just before my Eurydice rehearsal. The book of songs came and was what I wanted. Thank you for the trouble. I am very sorry you feel lonesome but not surprised, because it is often a matter of the weather. I would get that feeling myself if I were less busy. Don't pay much attention to it. Don't use your eyes in dark weather.

Probably you read and write too much. Do it less if you must on account of your eyes. Your report was a joyful surprise, but I should be sorry if it had been at the expense of any of your eyesight. About the hospital course, I cannot decide finally as yet.

I am glad you feel like shying at some of the gaieties which are imminent next winter, and I quite agree with you that a knowledge of nursing is most valuable. But you must read Emerson's "Essay on Compensation" and you will learn that you can't get anything worth having without sacrificing something else. Constant contact with sick people is not pleasant, and nurses, to be skillful and efficient, have to become hard. You see they lose their softness and sympathy in return for the skill and usefulness they gain. But, of course, there is a middle stage and a middle course.

If we can find the right opportunity I shall be glad to have you gain the knowledge of "first aid," etc., which you want. Perhaps they have a course in sore toes, which I should dearly love to have someone in our family take.

With love and kisses,

Your loving
Papa.

Mrs. Zimmermann wanted me to enclose this poem for you. She thinks you will like it.

YALE UNIVERSITY

New Haven, Conn.
March 20, 1914.

Department of Music
126 College St.

My dearest Youngest:

It just happens that I can write to you. Mamma is in New York with Mollie Sawyer. Isabel is there visiting the Stoeckels and Lottie is in Baltimore still, so I am luxuriating in the whole empty house. I have given the servants leave of absence and am quite alone but for the occasional hoof-taps of our S.S.S. furnace-boy. I hope they teach other things better than they do furnace.

Really I ought to be in N. Y. having been invited by Mollie Sawyer to go with her to the première of Wolf-Ferrari's new opera—the one of which he played me parts last year—but that was postponed till Wednesday next, and I am fortunately and happily here nursing a game leg, which would hardly have been improved by Mollie's hospitality or the midnight train.

There is little to record, except that we had our last Symphony Concert on Tuesday so that there is a large and welcome gulf fixed before any more of them can happen. Mr. Stockel was here and was pleased. Everything went very well indeed, excepting one place for our harp in the "Valse des Fleurs" by Tschaikowsky. It was a solo place and was too hard for her. I was to blame for not knowing it, but I didn't till it was too late. She ended well, however, with some sweeping chords and perhaps distressed no one but me.

I have resigned from the leadership of my two Philadelphia choruses and shall have very little money next year. Perhaps I can take in washing, or do some other useful thing—I hope so.

It is a grisly cold day, or rather night, freezing hard.

HORATIO PARKER

I stumped over the golf course this afternoon. If I had been in equal control of both legs I could have made a fine score, but it is hard driving while you stand chiefly on one leg and try to save the other. I feel better for the oxygen and exercise and hope tomorrow will offer a less bleak and windy condition of affairs.

Give my love to Mollie and Janet and take for yourself all you can care for.

Your loving
Papa.

YALE UNIVERSITY
Department of Music

New Haven, Conn.
April 3, 1915.

Office of the Dean
126 College Street

My dear Isabel:

You seem to crave information about Peter.* I regret to announce that he is a cocoanut-fibred ruffian, although he is improving. His attitude toward his elder colleague † is deplorable. He insists on playing with him vigorously and roughly whether or not the elder wishes it. He bites his ears, nose and legs, which for awhile is pleasantly stimulating but becomes irksome in time. Also, he taught Bob to dig under the fence. This they have done three times and in each case they both got out. Bob invariably ran away, but Peter, who is conservative, curled up on the front door mat. I filled in the hole with a spade, and the last time several days ago, I took them out and held their noses to the hole and licked them carefully with your whip, which produces more noise

---

* A very stupid Airedale.
† A collie.

than pain. Since then the earth has remained undisturbed.

There is little else to report, excepting a snowstorm at present which interferes seriously with my golf, and seems likely to jeopardize my new Easter necktie tomorrow.

I expect to leave for Boston next week Wednesday and Mamma expects to go Thursday, so I think you ought to come home on Wednesday. Your existence seems a dizzy round of gayeties. I hope that both you and Lottie will not over-estimate the value of unessential things, but admit that my hope is based upon no very solid foundation. Give my love to Lottie and Howard and cordial remembrances to all the Matthai family.

Ever your affectionate father,

Horatio Parker.

In the year 1914 the Diary continues:

Finished score Act I of "Fairyland."

Kneisel quartette concert. . . .

Eclipse—supper party for twelve. (A meeting of "The Club")

Golluf (golf) —Eurydice—Orpheus Concert—last—rather good (loving cup).

Wrote asking honorary degree for Sibelius.

Lunch with Corporation of Yale—Forgot to go.

Phelps *Kaffee Klatsch.*

This was an old New Haven institution to which Mother belonged. A group of ladies met regularly to sew, converse in German and drink *"Kaffee."* It, of course, disbanded with the entry of this country into the war.

June
   Norfolk—performance of Sibelius' new piece.
   Commencement—Blue Hill.
July 4th
   Finished scoring opera.
July 29th
   Sent off opera!! *

The use of two exclamation points again marks the satisfaction of work finished, a sense of achievement, I hope. Then came a period of release from the driving, almost fierce determination to finish a given work by a specific date. With the completion of this second opera and the return to college in the fall, he took up once more the sober and often humdrum tread of academic life at Yale.

And here, because they fit so appropriately into the picture of Father's life at the Music School, of which I saw very little, I am delighted to be able to quote some of the pleasant recollections of two of his students of those years. They were two of whom Father was very fond, and whom we knew well ourselves, for they were often at our house: Douglas Moore and Bruce Simonds.

Douglas Moore (now Professor Moore, a distinguished composer, and head of the music departments of Barnard College and Columbia University) was, at college, as well known for his dramatic as for his musical gifts. It seems fitting that his first meeting with Father should have come about, indirectly, by way of the Dramatic Club.

* "Fairyland."

I had been writing some music, for the Yale Dramatic Association, and was playing it one day in the Music School for David Stanley Smith. Dr. Parker came into the room just as I had finished a march for the soldiers of Louis XIV. Mr. Smith introduced me as a student who was writing some music for the performance. "Did you write this?" Dr. Parker inquired, sitting down at the piano and playing by ear the entire piece which I had just finished.

Father had evidently heard it, in passing, through the open door. Douglas has told me how impressed he was by this feat of musical memory, as well as by Father's kindness later. "He came to the performance, and was very encouraging about the music." But, as many have testified, Father was not always so kindly. Douglas continues:

> In class the next year he was distinctly formidable. I remember one day he came upon a similarity between two fugues submitted by different students. "Was there collusion?" he asked sternly. "Yes sir," replied one of the students. "Do you mean to say that you copied each other's work?" "Oh, no sir." "Well then, there wasn't collusion!" . . . Some of his instructions were surprising. "Composing is the art of eliminating reminiscence. Don't write double-stops for the violin—one note sounds bad enough at a time." . . .
>
> One evening at his home he sat down at the piano and played a piece of popular dance music and asked me what it was. I replied loftily that I was not prepared to know since I was unfamiliar with much popular music of the day. "Strange," he murmured, "I find so many traces of it in your music." He also played through my football march, "Goodnight, Harvard," one evening.

I had kept it a dark secret because I thought he would not like it and was much embarrassed. "I could forgive you for it except for this (a cheap chromatic turn of the melody between the second and·third phrases). It isn't bad at all." . . .

After I had been demobilized in 1919, I was very unhappy and undecided whether I should go on in music or join my brother in business. David Smith was discouraging and told me I was aiming too high, trying to write the Ninth Symphony when I should confine myself to songs. Dr. Parker remarked that that was easy to say, and that I should go on. "You will write music," he told me, "I don't know just what kind it will be but I am sure you will write it."

He also sent me a delightful steamer letter as I left to study with D'Indy. . . . In it he said that I was a little inclined to confound solemnity with seriousness.

Dr. Parker was one of the most distinguished and attractive men I have ever met. I believe I was the first student who was not afraid of him and he liked me for it. Bruce Simonds was another. We had a conducting class, Bruce, Roger Sessions, several others and myself. Bruce was the only one who dared to be orchestra. The others were polished off in short order when they tried to read scores at the piano.

*　*　*

Bruce Simonds, whose brilliant abilities (already evident at this time) as a concert pianist have since pushed partly into the background his considerable gifts for composition, is now Dean of the Yale School of Music. A person of wide intellectual tastes and interest in all the arts—his reminiscences are so delightful that I should like to quote them entire; they bring so vividly to life, as no words of mine could, these years at The Music School, the last under Father's guidance.

Horatio Parker was even in his lifetime something of a legendary figure. Dean of the Yale School of Music, conductor of the New Haven Symphony Orchestra and also of choral societies, the first American composer to be recognized in England, the winner of two ten-thousand dollar prizes for American operas, he commanded a feeling of respect which was increased almost to awe by whispered stories of his severity as a critic, his ability to detect consecutive fifths "around two corners," and by the terrifying and fascinating accounts of his Damascan wit. His courses in composition at Yale were a magnet to musical students, and, in my own case, the deciding factor in sending me there for study in spite of the fact that at that time no credit was given for a course in music taken before Junior year. When I registered at the School of Music, he was not to be seen, nor was I sufficiently advanced to be enrolled in his courses that first year; but I remember very well a certain afternoon a few weeks after college had begun. During a class in counterpoint I happened to look through a half-open door into the adjoining library. Very quietly someone had come in and was standing before the shelves looking for a book; a rather tall, dignified person, with graying hair. Distinguished he certainly was, distinguished enough to be slightly informal in his dress, and the carriage of his head came from an inner dignity rather than from military drill; at that precise moment it was thrown back so that he could read the titles through his glasses as he scanned the shelves deliberately. Of his face, half turned from me, I could see only that the complexion was ruddy. Months later, watching him for signs of approval or disapproval, I was to learn the line of that arched, aristocratic nose, the humorous droop of the eye-

lids, benign and quizzical by turns. It was precisely this
mixture of surprise, tenderness and amusement that I
caught the first time he looked at me directly. Near the
close of that first year, during which I had never met
him, I happened to win a competition in organ-playing,
awarded by judges sitting behind a screen. I looked
absurdly young at the time, so much so that stepping up
to receive the prize from Dr. Parker's hands I was greeted
with, "What, *you!*" A few moments later, always careful
to keep the balance, he was telling me that it had been
a close decision, and that my improvization had been
inferior to one of the others.

The improvization at these competitions was always
an agony. Three of us entered the contest that year for
the Lockwood Scholarship in organ-playing, and we were
all on pins and needles over the possibility of being
asked to improvise. The exact time, too, was left hanging in the air until the last possible moment, when we
heard that the playing would take place at the extraordinary hour of half-past six in the evening, the hour of
dinner for most college students. Somewhat hungry, we
presented ourselves at Woolsey Hall at the end of a
torrid afternoon and were heard in turn. To our relief,
improvization was not mentioned. I was last to play
and had chosen the Bach Toccata in F. Now this is a
most comfortable piece to play if one is nervous, for it
begins with a conveniently stationary organ-point in the
pedals which lasts for two pages before the music bursts
into a difficult pedal solo. Then there is another respite
before a second more difficult pedal solo. By the time
this is reached the performer is in fine fettle, or should
be. . . . I placed the music on the rack. "Oh," said Dr.
Parker, looking over my shoulder, "this is a very long
piece. Just begin here," and to my consternation he
pointed to the second pedal solo! There was nothing to
do but begin. I plunged in. Faster and faster the notes

whirled by, as I wondered whether he would let me play to the end. He did. There was a short pause, and through the whirl still ringing in my ears I heard him say something about . . . dinner? What was it? I stared at him. "You must have thought," he repeated very distinctly—and was there a twinkle in his eye? . . . "that I am in a hurry for my dinner." Then seeing that I was still bewildered, and with that curious mixture of tenderness and irony, "It doesn't go as fast as that." Needless to say, I did not win that competition.

No sketch of Dr. Parker would be complete which did not call to mind his beautiful speaking voice and the purity of his diction, even in moments of stress. These, by the way, were not infrequent. One never knew when a flushed and tearful secretary, clutching innumerable papers, would rush out of his office and attack her typewriter furiously. That large pleasant room with its sunny windows giving on the feathery willow tree outside was no place for the faint-hearted. In general, however, his most provocative remarks were delivered with a deliberate precision which lent them an air of almost Olympian impersonality. Almost invariably they were designed to test your mettle. "You are not very good at following out your own ideas," he said to me one day toward the close of my association with him, "and,"—a slight pause—"you're even worse at following out anyone else's." If such a remark were received in a healthy spirit of humor, all the better. Egotism was so foreign to his own nature that he could not tolerate conceit in his pupils. Any suspicion of bombast was pricked. The first time I called at his house I very stupidly sent in my card. When I was admitted to the Parkers' large, comfortable living room, I found that I had broken up a bridge game, and my embarrassment was immediately tripled as Dr. Parker advanced holding my card gingerly with the tips of his fingers and greeted me cordially

with, "Here, take this, you might need it again sometime."
Could there have been a neater rebuke to undue formality? Having administered it, with the ease of the perfect host he proceeded to make me feel completely at home.

His own modesty was invincible. Students who hoped
to get an acquaintance with his works from attending
his classes were disappointed. They were never mentioned. Any other topic to be sure, might be introduced,
sometimes to the astonishment of literal minds who had
expected to hear about fugues and found themselves
listening to a discourse on the early church. But these
digressions were, in a sense, part of his scheme. His own
culture was so broad that he was appalled at the average
music student's narrowness of mind, and he set himself
the task of stretching it. He also liked to expand our
vocabulary. I can well remember his delight one afternoon at finding that one of his pupils, at least, thought
the words 'collision' and 'collusion' synonymous.* He
saw unerringly through excuses for doing insufficient
work. He himself was often called upon to write music
for a special occasion, usually too close at hand; not an
inconsiderable part of his music was written at high
pressure. This fact was never invoked as a reason for
slovenliness. If he were setting a Latin or Greek text,
every nicety of meaning and pronunciation was studied
before the music was allowed to take shape. His orches-
tration was polished to the same degree. But of these
processes we as students were unaware, and the ease with
which he sketched passages as models on the classroom
blackboard was deceptive. We got an inkling of his
scrupulous attitude toward his own work one day when
he submitted two alternative hymn-tunes for our inspection and opinion, as humbly as Molière read his
plays to his cook. As he took infinite pains with his own
music, he expected his pupils to do the same with theirs,

* The same occasion that amused Douglas Moore.

and it was quite a common thing to have him demand changes in student overtures after the parts had been copied, even after the first rehearsal. To weeping expostulations he was serenely indifferent. And if in his opinion certain students were not capable of doing original work such as was demanded by the Bachelor of Music degree, he was ruthless in dismissing them. His eye was above personalities, on standards.

Though a martinet, he was no pedant. "That man ought to go out and get drunk!" he would say of a student whose work was dry. Nor did he encourage self-deprecation. "If you don't like your own things, nobody else will," he remarked. His own taste was not narrow; he adored the purity of Palestrina, and he admired the color and complexity of Strauss; Franck and the French Impressionists he cared less for. Whether deliberately or not, he did not mention Stravinsky or Schönberg as far as I can remember, though that may mean simply that he thought them too advanced for his students.

The vein of naughtiness in him was delightful. One of the favorite stories which went the rounds of the Music School while I was there ran that, during the intermission of a long and very worthy concert of chamber music, Dr. Parker was observed leaving the building very unobtrusively. He was followed across the New Haven Green to the door of a moving picture theatre, where he presumably spent the rest of the evening in sweet content. Such was his charm that the orchestral players against whom he raged at rehearsals—and with justice for sometimes they played very badly—adored him. The kettledrummer in particular was a faithful ally though he came in for a large share of denunciation, being constitutionally unable to keep the place. Crash would go the baton! "Louis, Louis!" Dr. Parker would cry, adding a torrent of German, unintelligible to student ears, and Louis would draw himself up and glower at Dr. Parker, like a turkey cock. But an hour later Louis would be found cheerfully executing any task Dr. Parker deemed necessary for the orchestra.

It was this human, unexpected, thoroughly lovable side that I saw more and more clearly as those few precious years of my association with him slipped by. I even reached the point, incredible as I would have thought it earlier, of serving back to him some of his favorite little catchwords, on occasion. The last time I saw him, our conversation began with one of those absurdities. Working in the library (not the one in which I had first seen him, for since that time, through his efforts, the School had a splendid new building) I saw him standing in the library. "Whose cat's dead?" I enquired, using one of his phrases in my sauciest manner. "I don't know," he replied, "but you look as if you had just eaten the canary." Then we said goodbye quite properly, for two years, since I was going abroad. He never knew that I watched him from the window until he turned the corner out of my sight—forever.

* * *

It was in this period at Yale that he wrote various articles and papers and delivered many addresses. Speaking of this aspect of Father's career George W. Chadwick says:

After he went to Yale he developed a decided literary ability. To a close and discriminating observation he added an individuality of expression, illuminated by gleams of pungent humor which caused him to be sought after as a speaker and contributor to various periodicals. His essay on contemporary music, delivered before the American Academy of Arts and Letters, is a good example of his ability in this direction. The individuality of his style was no less evident in his literary work than in his music.

He was fond of making paradoxical observations, sometimes rather difficult for less subtle minds to follow. Of a certain piece for organ and orchestra he said, "That has no business to sound so well." This was really a retroverted compliment to the composer for making a successful mixture for organ and orchestral tone, a problem which requires an expert musical chemist.

* * *

David Stanley Smith was first a pupil and later intimately associated with Father, succeeding him as Dean of the Department of Music at Yale University. I include his summary:

> It only remains to tell what manner of person Parker was. One may read between the lines that only a man of great energy and electric temperament could endure through such a career. One will not be surprised to learn of bursts of temper followed by a complete calm. Parker's devotion to his family was notable; indeed, the principal motive that kept his energies so steadily in action was the desire to provide for his wife and three daughters.
>
> Men of learning who set great store by diplomas and degrees should note the case of Parker. Though he deserted his scholastic studies at an early age for the pursuit of music, and though his degrees of M.A. and Mus. D. were honorary and not the reward for work done "in course," few of his colleagues in the University showed more general acquaintance with things at large than he. He was a worthy member of the American Academy of Arts and Letters. His diction and use of words were remarkable for beauty and unexpectedness. After the cares of work had quieted, and a game of golf had refreshed him, he would converse delightfully and humorously with his friends. Not everyone understood him. Not everyone knew how sensitive and friendly a

spirit lay behind the reserved address. But everyone was fascinated by the original twists of his talk and his handsome dignified appearance.

Parker was modest and never went in for self-advertisement. He enjoyed his successes quietly, and, one doubts not, grieved over his failures poignantly, yet without complaint. He had a high sense of artistic righteousness; he always insisted on the dignity of music. To give an instance: year after year he would refuse to start the orchestral overture at the Yale Commencement Exercises until everyone in the hall had been seated. Beethoven should be listened to and not be regarded as a signal for conversation. He hated music as an accompaniment for eating, and all the cheap uses to which the art is put.

As a congenial companion, a loyal comrade, and a steadfast friend, Parker has left a blessed memory. His conversation, punctuated with keen wit, was stimulating, and not of the prima donna variety. Devoted as he was to his own art, he found time to be interested in politics, in literature, and in other arts. His mind was stored with a variety of information, and his memory was as remarkable for facts as it was for music.

His judgment was sound, and based on a comprehensive knowledge of the musical art. While his musical creed was founded on beauty of design, melodic breadth, and logical structure, he was interested in all modern developments in harmony and instrumentation. He had a singularly open mind in regard to modern compositions, and often expressed himself enthusiastically about some of the most "advanced" of them. But with pretense or shams of any kind he had no patience, and he was quick to detect them in some of the modern fads of polyharmony and polycacophony.*

*   *   *

* "A Study of Horatio Parker" published in the Musical Quarterly, April, 1930.

In the Diary, again are two bare entries:

August 2, 1914
  War in Europe.
April 6, 1917
  War declared on Germany.

The ensuing war years were years of heartsickness, of poignant mental and physical suffering for Father. I can see him so well, that look of infinite sadness, of disillusion. Here, after a lifetime of high endeavor, of faith in all things beautiful and good, of hope for a future finer and still nobler world, were these two great nations at war. In both countries he had lived. He had grown up in the tradition of the old-world Germany of culture, of great music, of art. He had studied there, worked, and enjoyed the happy life of simple people. In England, his second home (was he not always thought to be an Englishman by strangers?) he had many dear and close friends. There he had tasted the fruits of success in the honors accorded his earliest big work. He had been warmly received by these people whom he understood, and with whom he had but recently renewed old friendships.

In this first World War one became at once painfully conscious of national affiliations. All things German were looked upon with suspicion. Eventually, with our own entry into the war, there was the unhappy incident of Dr. Karl Muck, conductor of the Boston Symphony Orchestra (a friend of Mother and Father); German music, German opera, were discriminated against; the language could not be used. (I remember with what devilish glee Father delighted in speaking German to Mother at the *movies*—to her intense discomfort.) All of these small and inescapable prejudices must have hurt Father terribly. It was a bitter time when passions were easily aroused, more bitter even, for one who knew at first hand the intrinsic worth of each people. Father was fond of saying, "Not all Germans have horns and hoofs." Mother's only sister, *Tante* Sophie, died in Munich in the early days of the war, supposedly due in part to privations resulting from war.

Naturally these trying years, combined with hard work, were to take their toll of a nature sensitive, tender and compassionate. In the years 1915 and 1916, respectively, my sister Charlotte and I were married. These, to us, rather important events, are quite casually noted in his Diary: "Lottie's wedding" . . . "Isabel's wedding."

The following letters are written after my marriage.

March 27, 1916.

My dear Isabel:

We were glad to get your letter today and to learn that you are in a state of complete preservation so far.

I am sending your golf clubs, five in number, by express in the leather bag, and hope sincerely that you will make good use of them.

I have not forgotten the pieces for 'cello and piano. Please keep on expecting them until they come. They have already been ordered but I have not yet seen them. Also, your complete edition of Schumann is delayed. Breitkopf and Haertel sent me two bound volumes but they were in different bindings—one covered plentifully with thumb and finger marks, and the other considerably shopworn. I thought it best to send them back, but that, too, will come in time.

Also, separately, I am sending you a copy of a wedding hymn * which you will, perhaps, recognize.

Grace is going to Baltimore about the tenth of April to stay over Easter. If you can have her as a visitor for two weeks, beginning about the twenty-seventh of April, I should like to have her go. I rather want her to have the experience and there is a show full of undergraduates on the eighth of May which I am quite willing she should miss. We all feel your absence very much, and I should be glad to have Grace with you, if it is not inconvenient. Of course, you must see to it that she is not a burden, and I will see that she is not an expense.

We have no golf here as yet because there are snow-drifts still left of considerable depth, but with the temperature between 60 and 70 in the shade, they cannot last very long.

Next time I will write some gossip, but this must do for the present.

With love to Ralph and to you,

Ever your affectionate
Father.

April 11, 1916.

My dear Isabel:

I went to the Mahler Symphony on Sunday night; also I sent two tickets to Mrs. Semler but they didn't reach her until Monday. I am extremely sorry because the performance was one of the most imposing that I have ever seen. The chorus from Philadelphia was nearly one thousand in numbers. They were all dressed in black and white and filled the stage to the top of the proscenium arch. The work is a choral rather than an orchestral one, and as I say, the performance was a stupendous achievement on the part of Stokowski. I

* Epithalamium for Isabel's wedding. Feb. 12, 1916.

doubt if anyone else in this country could have done the work.

I saw Mrs. Benson yesterday in Philadelphia and hope to see her again tomorrow, also B. ———— M. sang in the chorus in New York and I shall expect a detailed account of her doings tomorrow at dinner time.

Unluckily there are many other things to do so I must stop. Grace goes to visit Lottie tomorrow. No doubt she will write to you there.

With much love to you and Ralph in which we all join, I am,

Ever your affectionate
Father.

In the spring of 1916 the masque "Cupid and Psyche" was presented in commemoration of the 200th Anniversary of the founding of the Yale School of Fine Arts. The text, in verse, was by Mr. John Jay Chapman, and Father wrote the music. Later came the formal opening of the Music School in its fine new building on College Street, given through the generosity of Mrs. Elizabeth Sprague Coolidge in memory of her father, and now known as Sprague Hall.

"The Red Cross Spirit Speaks" with words by Mr. John Finley, was sung in Carnegie Hall by Madame Louise Homer who wore a red satin gown, arms outstretched, making a Red Cross, Mr. Walter Damrosch conducting. It is with a sense of almost fearful foreboding that I hear again, after more than twenty years, of the forthcoming performance of this song to be sung at the American Academy of Arts and Letters' annual meeting, in memory of John Finley.

"A Dream of Mary, a Morality," again with a text by

Mr. John Jay Chapman, was written for the Norfolk
Festival that spring.

New Haven
June 1, 1917.

My dear little Isabel:

I am sorry that through no fault of yours and through
no fault of my own I was not able to enjoy the hospitality
of your home last night and the night before, but I am
at least as much indebted to you; perhaps a little more
even. I got down quite late Wednesday night and went
to the Century Club smilingly asking for mail. Behold,
there wasn't any mail! The mail clerk in a spasm of
conscientiousness or precaution, or some other unnecessary and unpleasant emotion, sent your letter to me on
to New Haven, so that I received it this afternoon when
I came home.

The fact is that the Century Club is such a collection
of paleozoical curiosities we can never be certain that
anything will happen except the unexpected. Any self-
respecting club would blow up by the roots if its mail
clerk dared to forward any correspondence of any member without instructions, especially if the correspondence
were in a lady's handwriting. That is one of the pur-
poses of clubs. Years ago I recall finding many letters
with various Italian, angular, upright and otherwise interesting handwritings, and scented in various degrees
from musk to yellow soap, addressed to a venerable
professor of Columbia, whose name begins with the same
letter as mine. Lurid developments followed in the
daily press. One lady threw herself into the sound,
another expired in a bathtub, a third hung herself from
a telegraph wire, a fourth was found wandering in the
White Mountains,—but I spare you further details.

This is merely to show that the action of the mail clerk
is entirely without reason or precedent. Nobody but he
is to blame, and since I don't know what instructions he

has, or whether any secret by-laws guide his action, I shall not dare to give him rats about it until next autumn, by which time we all shall have forgotten.

I went to a neighboring caravansary and was very comfortable. Thursday there was organ music beginning at 9:15 and ending at 6:47, with one hour for luncheon. Thursday evening I dined with the Toedts, who asked very cordially after you and sent you their love. At 8:30 I went to a committee meeting at Reggie deKoven's highly expensive residence, and at 9:30 went and chewed rags for an hour with Dan Mason. This morning I listened to the rehearsal for Norfolk; saw Mr. Stoeckel, who sent his love to you, Percy Grainger, Frederick Stock and many others. They were rehearsing Carpenter's new symphony, which is to be done next Tuesday when I hope to hear it. Also, they rehearsed a new piece of Percy Grainger's with more and queerer percussion instruments than I have ever heard in one spot in a state of captivity. I went beaming to Mrs. Grainger and said it was "very good Fun"; whereat she was highly indignant, pointing out that it wasn't meant to be fun at all but very serious. I quoted the inscription on the University of Verona, *res severa verum gaudium;* in other words, true pleasure is to be found in serious things. But she didn't seem altogether consoled, and I had to say that I could not possibly take such youthful, driving stuff with a long face. She says she hopes it will prove to be very great; at least it is most interesting. By the way, Berlioz' translation of the inscription has always pleased me, *L'ennui est le vrai plaisir.*

With much love to you and Lottie and Howard,

Ever your affectionate

Papa.

YALE UNIVERSITY
Department of Music

New Haven, Conn.
Office of the Dean   June 19, 1917.
126 College St.

My dear little Isabel:

Thank you for your invitation. Perhaps I ought to say unluckily I am quite mended again. Commencement is tomorrow with Paderewski and Arthur Whiting both receiving degrees. The next day is Thursday when I have to move finally out of our present building, and Friday we go to Bluehill, so you see, much as I should like it, there isn't time for me to visit you. The railroad train would have no terrors, for lo! these many years we have lived within far less than one hundred and fifty feet of a railroad.

I hope you will be happy and comfortable, and I hope you will be able to come to Bluehill. You cannot come too soon or stay too long, and you can tell Lottie the same.

I wish you were going to be here for many reasons, particularly, however, because I should like to see you; and the same applies to Lottie to whom I wrote at length on her birthday. If you should feel moved and able to come here before the summer really begins you would both be tremendously welcome, but I suppose it is too much to hope for, and we shall be gone by Friday morning, including Alexander.*

With love and kisses to you both

Ever your affectionate

Father.

Love to Ralph.

* Alexander Freckles, Llewellyn Setter.

HORATIO PARKER

(Postal Card)

Blue Hill
July 16, 1917.

Dear I.:

At Grace's suggestion I am writing to say that you will be sorry to learn she has measles and think a present would relieve the monotony of her imprisonment. She is eager to get well and hopes that you will feel moved to help her to that extent.

We send love and hope that Ralph's equator has quieted down. We have no mimeograph in Bluehill so please let us know. With love to both.

Ever your affectionate

H.P.

July 31, 1917

My dear little Isabel:

My pen is at home and I have a few minutes before the horn blows—hence the pencil. Grace has lost the last of her measles but tipped over with Betty in a Ford and is lame, particolored and partially skinless in consequence.

Betty yelled "Grace! are you hurt?" Grace said, "I think I am dead and that my leg is broken." Whereupon Betty—"Walk on it," and it wasn't. The skin will grow again, but her clothes will not, and the sunset color will fade from her legs and arms. No matter, as Schiller remarks *Auch das Schöne muss Sterben.* How is Ralph's interior? Speaking of sunset colors—if he is to have his addendum extracted let them take the index and do such other pruning as may be called for. I hope he is better, if not, perhaps he can have it done at Uncle Sam's expense in return for military training. I wish you both would or could come up here. It is not cool today, but will be hereafter or when there is a wind.

BLUE HILL GROUP—1915

Last night Mrs. Q., N. and R. came to play bridge in the longest thunderstorm I ever lived through. Mamma told them how Vannie put "raw rice right round the roast" with complete success, but I couldn't get Grace to repeat it. Dempsey (Nevin's dog) and Roger (Dolme's dog) had a joint interview with a porcupine at the height of the storm. They came in with all the signs of discomfort their deadliest foe could have hoped to have them exhibit. To add to the interest the telephone was out of order—dangerous besides in such a storm.

Sue walked over to the P.P. wharf for Dr. Dolme, who took them both to the village for Dr. Littlefield's ministration. They were under ether, given by Dick Quay, for a long time, and today are feeling terribly pale. Neither got up for breakfast. Mamma says it is nice to have such a good dog as Sandy, large enough to ignore porcupines and wise enough to go home when it pours.

With love and all good wishes to both of you,

Ever your

Father.

Blue Hill
Tuesday, Sept. 19, 1917.

My dear little Isabel:

We miss you very much. Being quite childless is a rather new and not altogether pleasant feeling. You were wise in deciding to go by the little boat, it was bumpy going sometimes to Bucksport. We took fifty minutes one way and forty-five the other, both too short for me because I enjoyed the view and would gladly have had more of it. The spaciousness of things on top of the ridge is fine in just the way the Kreutzalin is, and the boldness and beauty of the river reminded me of the Danube at Passau. I am sorry you missed these things, but they will not move or change and you can still have them another time.

— 289 —

Saturday night was a bridge party at Krehbiels—four tables and in the end Vannie brought in a beautiful birthday cake, white to match my hair, and with burning candles. Of course, no cake has room for the proper number so she resorted to a decimal system which had to be explained, and even then the cake was crowded. Marianne Kneisel also sent me a *Sandtorte* which I admire more than I love, but Mamma appreciates it fully and promises that it shall not go to waste, even if she cannot call in Sandy's help.

He seems quite well now with perfectly clear eyes. Nixie * has just called on him and all his springs seemed to stiffen up at once. I never saw a dog stand more erect. She was decent for a minute, but then began to snarl, swear and bite. If all girls were like that it would be a weary world. I hope you had a comfortable journey and feel none the worse for it; certainly the sea was smooth. You certainly gained up here, but still you were not very brown when going away. You were always the darkest puppy in our basket and we hate to see you looking or feeling pale. But one must make sacrifices for such blessed expectations.

With love to Ralph and kisses to you,
Ever your affectionate
Papa.

October 11, 1917
My dear little Isabel:

It will be some time before I can make a party call, but it is none too soon to say how much I enjoyed seeing you and Ralph and the nice house in which you are to spend the coming months. I could see no reason why you shouldn't be exceedingly comfortable. Except, as

* Nixie was a mean, tiny black Pomeranian, and Sandy a large, gangling Setter.

a vegetarian, you probably will not enjoy the ham as much as I did, but it is good, nutritious grub, and there are many Germans, poor, and I hope rich as well, who would give their shoes for it, and perhaps their other garments.

Grace's face has resumed its normal outlines which were instantly improved by the bag, even before I had unpacked it. I got home quite tired at eleven, found the front steps had been painted so that I couldn't reach the bell, the kitchen door carefully locked and Alexander's door also carefully locked. Through a violent mental effort I had brought back my umbrella and after serenading Mamma as loud as I dared, but without effect, I pounded on the door and the rest of the house with my umbrella until Grace came down and let me in. She was really in fine spirits and made me a niggle * but charged a dime for it. The shock was the same which I felt at the end of the tunnel when they charged me two cents to get out again, but I laid it to the war and have almost forgotten it.

During my absence Alexander ran away, but returned this morning in an expensive automobile so that his absence cost us nothing. Now that he is back, and when the paper-hangers are out of the house, Mamma feels that she will have to go away to visit you. Of course, nothing that I say has the wildest sort of Old Testament prophecy, but I think you can expect her next week.

Ralph enjoys living in the country and I am sure your situation is as comfortable as fancy could make it. Eat enough and drink enough, and don't get excited. Drink plenty of milk no matter what it costs, and if you happen to feel like exercise, do take it. I have just been reading a nice, old-fashioned book on therapeutics. The author, who is a modern physician, says that "good health

* "Niggle"—fried egg sandwich—price 5c.

is the result of effort" and I think unless you have too much natural resistance to overcome, that exercise would be good for you. At least I hope so, especially if you take it.

Grace will write and Mamma will write and so will I, if there is anything to say.

With many affectionate thanks for the loving care I had from you and from Ralph,

Always your devoted

Father.

P.S. Of course, we want you to come and see us whenever you feel so inclined, and we don't need any notice or preliminary questioning. At any time in the present or future there will always be plenty of room and more than plenty of welcome for you any day of the week.

Yale University
School of Music

Office of the Dean
Sprague Memorial Hall
126 College St.

New Haven, Conn.
November 14, 1917

My dear little Isabel:

Thank you sincerely for your nice letter which came this morning. I am glad you like the sound of the piece * and the way it was received. Other people also have written to me expressing interest. It is not printed, and although I tried to give it to the Red Cross, it didn't seem possible to do so, and I am going to see if it can't be printed under other conditions less portentous than the Red Cross itself.

We miss you quite as much as you would like to be

* "Red Cross Spirit Speaks."

missed, but there seems no help for that. We all join
in sending love to you and Ralph.
Ever your affectionate father,
H.P.

YALE UNIVERSITY
School of Music
Office of the Dean
Sprague Memorial Hall
126 College St.

New Haven, Conn.
January 4, 1918.
My dear Isabel:
A good Christian cannot have too much Grace, but I
am not altogether convinced in the case of you and Ralph.
Please tell her she must be very good if she ever expects
to visit you again. Tell her, also, to write to me on
Saturday, soon enough for the letter to leave the same
day, when she expects to come home. If I am free I will
try to meet her, but the trains are so uncertain that I
am not sure it would be possible. These are excellent
times for people to stay home or wherever they may happen to be, if they can. But I should be extremely sorry
to have missed my visit to you, which I shall always remember with pleasure in spite of the difficulties experienced in getting to and fro. . . .

For your amusement I am enclosing a letter just received from Mr. Ruckstuhl. We can all see that it is
not just the name for a Frenchman, but I cannot quite
see that he has improved it.

Our thermometer is still about zero and shows unfor-
tunate tenacity of purpose to stay there, but since there
is no likelihood of its going lower, it may go up. A
geologist told me yesterday that it was to be expected;
that his tribe had been looking forward to a long spell
of cold weather between 1918 and 1920, because such

spells come in cycles of about thirty years, and there is a record of them which he thinks goes back to Roman times. I hope this may comfort you and Ralph as much as it doesn't comfort me, but I can't think of anything we can do about it.

With much love to the whole household,

Ever your affectionate father,

Horatio Parker.

* * *

[*C. Hubert H. Parry to Father*]

(Opened by censor)

Royal College of Music.

Prince Consort Road
South Kensington
London, S. W.
March 30, 1917
(Received April 21, 1917)

My dear Professor Parker:

Our "Music in Wartime" Committee were moved with quite unusual pleasure when it was communicated to them that Messrs. Littleton and Clayton of Novellos had been instructed by you to allot some royalties which were due to you to some Society which was engaged in work connected with the war, and that they had chosen our Society as in their opinion most appropriate to receive your bounty. I was instructed by the said Committee to write and thank you most cordially. There is something so unusually charming in the contribution coming from you in such a way. I hope you will approve. The said Committee is the Music section of the Professional Classes War Relief Council, and in that capacity ministers to the need of the distressed musicians by getting them engagements, and it has a double existence as outside the Council it also supplies concerts to Camps and Hospitals, Red Cross and otherwise. Last year we gave over 770 Concerts and this year I think we shall do

more. We give also midday and midnight Concerts in
the Munition Works, and are told that they turn out
much more munitions in consequence, as it puts spirit
into them. So I hope on the whole you will think us
worthy recipients. And I wonder how you like coming
in together with us. I think Wilson was eminently right
to stand out as long as he could. I admired his management of a very difficult situation throughout, immensely.
I should have liked the States to have kept out of it if
it had been possible, but it has proved not to be.

With most hearty thanks,

Yours most sincerely

C. Hubert H. Parry.

* * *

On March 17, 1918, a beautiful early spring morning
filled with the eternal expectancy and reassurance of
that vernal season, Anne Parker Semler was born.
Father happened to be in New York, so he came for a
moment to see us and wrote the following note:

[*Birthday of Anne Parker Semler.*]

March 17, 1918.

CENTURY CLUB
7 West Forty-third Street
New York City.

My dear little Isabel:

Uncle Ted has just turned up at this place. I have
told him to see you as soon as he can. Meanwhile don't
be excited at all. It is all right; all of your kids are
perfectly reliable. One yelled murderously but very well
just as I came out. It was yours. God bless you, dear.
My congratulations and love to you and to Ralph. Tell
him not to swell up too much, it isn't quite safe.

Ever your loving

Father.

Here, at last, during the sad years of war and rapidly failing health was a new spark of life—another generation being born to serve as a connecting link in the delicate thread of life. Here was tangible evidence of future and enduring hope. This was the only grandchild Father was ever to know and love, though eight more have succeeded her. We went to live with Mother and Father, my husband, Ralph, being in the Navy. The baby was a source of utter joy to all of us. (She happened to be a very good baby.) One vicissitude, however, stands out! Having always been dependent upon and directed by Father, I remember very well asking his advice some months later about leaving my child and going to see my husband, who was stationed in Philadelphia. In response to my problem he replied, and I shall always remember it: "If you take my advice you will do as you think best." This left the responsibility squarely upon my own shoulders and I *went,* only to return home with a bad case of influenza which I then passed on to each member of the family in turn, except Father, who prowled around from one room to another, cheering us up. My utter chagrin can be imagined.

Father had many amusing expressions. One thinks of them often. "Remember," he said, "there is *no* substitute for hard work. You get nothing for nothing and . . . little for sixpence." And of his own work he said so often, "If my work is any good, it will last, if not, it had better die with me—the sooner the better in fact."

Fearing, in fact knowing, that this account may seem eulogistic, I can only reiterate the old thought that time

FATHER AND ANNE PARKER SEMLER—BLUE HILL, 1919

serves to eradicate difficulties, leaving in relief much that is good and true. Father's life was full and overly abundant, in human matters as well as those of the mind and spirit. Yet he always had time and sympathy for the least of our problems. His was a vigorous personality and, therefore, in his lifetime and since it has been a source of inspiration and comfort, becoming always more so in times so troublous as these. Living, as our generation has, in the midst of the grim catastrophe of war, of the brutal stark realism and tragedy of these days can one but wonder? Every worthy ideal hangs trembling in the balance. In the rapid change of all conditions for living it has seemed refreshing to go back to Father's life, to recapture for you those everlasting ideals of courage, fidelity and affection.

It was in the spring of 1919 that Father wrote what others have referred to as his own Requiem, The Ode, in honor of Yale men, killed in action, and those returning from the first World War, set to the wonderfully beautiful poem * by Brian Hooker. This gives the title "A.D. 1919" to this chapter, for the double reason that it was his last large work and in the last year of his own life. Upon the arrival of this inspired text Father turned to Mother, saying, "How *can* I write music for this? It is all there."

Once again in a time of ill health and deep spiritual suffering this work was conceived. "One can safely say that no musical composition by an American ever had moved an audience as did this short composition. Not the least moved was the conductor himself. He knew

* See Appendix.

it was his Swan song. He knew, also, that it was the most deeply felt composition of his, since far back in 1892 when he had written "Hora Novissima." . . .

For some reason "A.D. 1919" has rarely found its way far from New Haven, but there it is given from time to time at official ceremonies and is affectionately known as "The Ode." The outside world is poorer for not being acquainted with this work. There is surely no more poignant episode in American music than the phrase, "And these shall have sweet sleep," the trumpet is heard in the distance sounding taps. Of this work Father remarked: "It was written so that every man Jack in the audience might understand it." He was I believe too tired and perhaps already too ill to do his best work. Yet there was no doubt about the understanding and emotion of those who first heard it, in Woolsey Hall at the Commencement Exercises, the seats filled with many students returning from France or the high seas, my husband among them. I had left home at six o'clock in order to be present at the Memorial Service that Sunday morning in June, and can still hear the lift and fall of the voices at the words "Friends with the hearts of strangers, Boys with the eyes of men."

This was a moment, indeed. Clad in the crimson robes of a Doctor of Music of the University of Cambridge, England, Father conducted the first performance of this tender, stirring work, and I think he may have known it was the last time he was ever to conduct.

It is not, however, with a sense of anything concluded that I wish to leave you, for nothing is lost while there are those who remember, and he has left you what I cannot. You will have this remembrance—you, and those who come after you, and as you learn to know his music a hymn perhaps, or some other work, it may seem more vital to you, knowing how and whence it came.

As I began with Father's own words, quoted from his Diary at eighteen, I shall close with words of his. In the sentences set here at the end from an article "Our Taste in Music," * he was, of course, not speaking of himself. Yet they express him as nothing else could.

* *Yale Review,* July, 1918.

EPILOGUE

"I believe firmly in permanent musical values. I think that those parts of Handel's 'Messiah' which now please us most are exactly the ones which made the greatest impression on the very first audience which heard the work sung. I know not whether they are what Handel himself wrote with greatest pleasure or at highest tension, for a composer is at times a partly unconscious instrument who records beauties thrust upon him, flowing through him from heaven to earth. He does not always know what he writes, however perfect it may be. Seventeen-year-old Schubert writing the 'Erl-King,' cannot have known what he was making, although of course he loved it. But the high aim and simple integrity of great composers are no accidents. Such men have made themselves perfect instruments by their life and work and thought."

—Horatio Parker,
1918.

APPENDIX

GENEALOGICAL SKETCH

The family of Horatio Parker was of English origin. The Parkers came to New England in 1635. Deacon Thomas Parker (1609-1683) sailed from London England on the ship *Susan and Ellin* March 31, 1635 and arrived in New England about six months later. Of his ten children the third son Lieut. Nathaniel Parker (1651-1737) had a son Stephen (1714-1785); his son Captain Stephen (1738-1814), active in military affairs during the Revolution, had eight children. The youngest son was Elijah (1776-1858) and his sixth child was Charles Edward Parker the father of Horatio Parker. Henry Elijah Parker a brother of Charles Edward was a Chaplain in the Civil War of the 2nd New Hampshire Volunteers. He was Professor of Latin at Dartmouth College for 25 years. All of the family were scholars with literary and classical tastes.

The Jennings family came to Virginia in 1683. Samuel Jennings was driven from his home by Indians and settled in Danbury, Conn. His son Samuel married and became the father of nine children, of whom John (1809-1871) the seventh, a clergyman, was the father

of Isabella Graham whose mother Susan Cornelia Keyes
was born in Salisbury, Conn. (1809-1891). Isabella Graham Jennings was the mother of Horatio Parker.

* * *

A MUSICIAN OF THE CHURCH: A SERMON

BY THE REV. WINFRED DOUGLAS

Preached in the Church of the Advent, Boston, at a
Service in Memory of the late Horatio Parker

> In all his works he praised the Holy One most high
> with words of glory; with his whole heart he sung songs,
> and loved him that made him. Ecclesiasticus 47:8.

It is highly significant of a right attitude toward
human thought that when Jesus the son of Sirach gathered "certain particular ancient godly stories of men
that pleased God" into his book of Wisdom, known to
us as Ecclesiasticus, he more than once included leadership in sacred music among the excellences of his
heroes. Such a mental position regarding musical
leadership is not very common among Americans today, nor indeed among Europeans. The conception of
music as a decorative commodity to be bought as ex-
pensively as possible of persons who possess the skill to
make it, is widespread: and the commercial motive ac-
cords but ill with spiritual leadership, even in the
minds of the thoughtless. Hosts of others look upon
music as primarily a sensuous pleasure: and regard its
purveyors as being almost inevitably of a weakened

APPENDIX

moral fibre, and therefore, perhaps, less responsible to
a moral law than their neighbors, perpetually busy in
more godly occupations untainted by beauty. Nor is
the Church herself free from such false views. Among
the very ranks of the clergy will be found men who
seemingly regard the music of their churches merely as
a bait to draw in the unwilling; or as a conventional
tradition of inescapable rigidity; or as a snare of the
devil. And, indeed, in this last particular, they are not
wrong, if music be turned from its rightful spiritual
end to serve an alien purpose. "Lilies that fester smell
far worse than weeds." We must face the facts. Music
is the satisfaction of a universal human need for utterance on a plane which words alone cannot quite reach:
and when that utterance is directed toward God, as it
ought to be in every tone of the Church's music, we
must recognize in it a vehicle for great spiritual leadership. It is the glory of Horatio Parker's life not that
he received eminent and well-deserved honors from his
fellow men at home and abroad, but that from his youth
up his musical career had that quality of spiritual leadership. He was a setter-up of lofty standards, and he
never declined from them himself, nor diminished them
for others in the smallest degree, so long as he lived.
They were not merely standards of esthetic taste and of
technical efficiency in craftsmanship, high as were his
self-imposed requirements in those necessary particu-
lars. They were standards of truth, of sincerity, of
steadfast faithfulness to lofty ideals of nobility and of
intellectual beauty, of loyalty to the Church, and of loving and humble service to God. The training and use

of his rare native talent for these aims were what made Horatio Parker a great Church musician, and the intellectual and spiritual leader of so many of his craft who would fain pursue the same course to the same goal.

A man does not receive such ideals out of the vacant air; and we ought, for a moment, to voice our thankful praise of the mother who so largely formed them in her son, and who filled so unique a place in his artistic career; being not only his first instructor in music, but later his literary collaborator in several of the very works which stamped him as America's first choral composer. Isabella Jennings Parker both trained his delicate and sensitive literary taste, so important a factor in his work, and herself supplied with her own high skill those "Words of glory" to which he sang his first great song of praise. I had the privilege of knowing Mr. Parker at the time he was composing "Hora Novissima"; and I shall never forget his look of filial love when he told me of his mother's difficult feat of translating in the original metre St. Bernard's rhymed leonine hexameters, and of his dedication of the work to the dear memory of his father.

This is not the occasion for a review of Parker's varied and eminent successes in the field of secular music, nor for a critical estimate of his sacred compositions: for them we are all glad and grateful, and because of them, we, and all the world of American music, mourn the loss of a great and well-loved leader. But there are certain aspects of his work as a Church musician on which we may well think for a few moments in this holy place. And first of all, let us remember one of its less mentioned, but not less admirable features—his long activity as a Church organist. He began this duty at the age of sixteen, and continued it with little intermission during the greater part of his life. Many of us here present know how great are the restrictions of time and desire involved in this task; how long a labor must often be the prelude to how small a result, judged by the world's standards. Parker's example should be an inspiration to us: he verily sung the organ's song with his whole heart; sparing himself not at all, that God's temple might sound with fitting praise. Even the honors and manifold occupations of his later days could not withhold him from a humble willingness to volunteer ˙for this duty at many services, little and great, in his parish church. Nor must we forget the very considerable body of organ music, well suited to church use, with which he has enriched the repertory of the parish organist.

In his numerous anthems and choral settings of the service, Parker speaks, and will long speak, to a larger public. And here we may note among the many excellences of fluid melodic invention, fresh and vital harmony, and solid formal construction, a never-failing sense of dignity. The WORTHINESS of God's praise is felt on every page. No lesson could be more needed by the young Church composer of our time. Bishop Huntington once said to me that as a people we lacked the feeling of reverence. And it is reverence—not sensuous beauty, not dramatic effectiveness, above all not vocal display—but just reverence, which is the characteristic stamp of the purest and best in Church music. It was such reverence, aided by his own high fastidiousness, which made Parker the composer so careful in the adjustment of tone and text. When music unites itself to words, it gains its own freedom by becoming the obedient handmaid of the words it voices. It can lift them to an intensity of meaning and of fullness of emotion which they cannot attain alone, but it can do this only when subservient to their own purpose; just as God's service alone gives man his perfect freedom. In his fine restraint and just sense of word values, Parker achieved in his church composition a sincerity and distinction that make them worthy offerings to Almighty God. A word should be said here of his deep interest in the purest type of sacred vocal art— unaccompanied choral singing, now happily on the increase in the American Church. This interest can be shown in the brilliant motet, "Adstant Angelorum chori"; and in the a cappella numbers of "Hora Novissima," and of the "Legend of St. Christopher"; and elsewhere in his works.

A still wider usefulness, one affecting more human lives, and one which may prove more lasting than any other, characterized Parker's work in hymnody, both as a composer of hymn melodies, and as an editor and laborer in the field of raising standards of our hymn singing. None will question his preeminence as the best American writer of hymn tunes. He alone among our composers attained an individual style which was a real contribution to the rich treasures of hymnody. These tunes, while keeping the personal characteristics distinctive of their composer, have achieved great popular success, because they well express the feeling of our time and of our country. Not a few but many of them will live in the hearts and in the voices of men when larger works of their author have fallen into disuse. The vitality of a good hymn is amazing. The old melody of "The royal banners forward go" was written in the autumn of 569 A. D.: but it is still sung throughout the whole world. Horatio Parker's modern setting of the same words is the only one yet made worthy to compare with it, and may well live as long. The last hymn composed by Parker was the Rev. Frederick Edwards' great prayer for Christian unity and for national and international righteousness:

> "God of the nations, who hast led
> Thy children since the world began"

The stanza of ten long lines, culminating in the refrain,

> "Hasten the time of our release,
> Bring in the reign of truth and peace"

presents extraordinary difficulties to the composer. Finding no adequate tune, the Hymnal Commission requested Parker to write one. His granting of the request brought out the quality of the man and his attitude toward hymn-writing very strikingly. He composed not one, but two tunes; and when after careful testing one was chosen as the better, he revised it again and again, even after a final proof had supposedly been read; so that nothing less than his best should be offered for the Church's use. Such was his invariable attitude toward every part of his large share of the work of revising our Hymnal. His unfailing insistence on historic accuracy and on musicianly purity of style were not qualified by his deep sense of the value of hymns for congregational worship. He gave unsparingly of his time and effort and skill to this work: and as a member of the Joint Commission, I desire here publicly to voice for my co-laborers as well as for myself our deep sense of bereavement at his loss, and our gratitude that he lived to perform so large a part of our common task.

Thus Parker's influence for good in hymn-singing extended far beyond his own tunes. Of the seven musical settings of the Church Hymnal authorized by the General Convention in 1892, his was by far the best: and though its commercial success was not great, its influence has increased more and more, and the things for which he contended in it have been more fully set forth in the musical edition of the New Hymnal, in the preparation of which he took so active a part. These things were, primarily, the fullest provision for congregational singing of hymns; a more sober standard of devotion, which would exclude the flippant, the showy, the sentimental, and the fashionable; and the restoration of many rich treasures of sacred melody temporarily fallen into disuse. Parker recognized that, notwithstanding our well known self satisfaction and ecclesiastic pride, a serious decline had taken place in the department of Church music during the last half of the nineteenth century. Let the musician who doubts this compare the better hymnals of Lowell Mason's day with those of the time when Parker compiled his hymnal. The weakening which befell English Hymnody with the adoption of part-song methods of hymn tune writing in the fifties was carried much farther in America; partly due to a lack of a stable musical tradition, and partly due to the frequently unreasonable and ill-judged development of the boy-choir. Tunes began to crowd our books which were solely designed for a theatrical showing off of this often misused agency of song. Most of the old expressive minor and modal tunes, with many of the graver and nobler major ones, fell into disuse. Hymns were speeded up until tunes that should possess majesty and be sung by the whole great body of the faithful were customarily taken so quickly as to lose even dignity, and to be impossible of participation by great masses of people. Against all this Parker steadfastly set his face; and it is due to his wise leadership more than to any other cause that we are having in the Church to-day a remarkable growth of interest in congregational song which is transforming the spirit of our worship far and wide.

As we thankfully remember the songs which Parker sung with his whole heart, we come now at last to those notable choral works with orchestra which have brought him enduring fame in two continents. They do not need my unskilled praise. They were his own anthems of love to God that made him, in which he was free from all save self-imposed limitations, and could indeed sing the full song of his heart. They carried American choral music to lofty eminence before unattained: and they did so because in them a high native talent spoke through the medium of a well schooled mind and a trained character in the utterance of a deep love of God and of all that is high and holy. When I think of "Hora Novissima," of the truth and beauty and celestial joy of it, it may well seem that Horatio Parker made for himself the prayer that St. Bernard of Morlaix breathed before attempting to write the words:

"Lord, to the end that my heart may think, that my pen may write and that my mouth may set forth Thy praise, pour both into my heart and pen and mouth Thy grace."

It was not only his own effort, and human training, and great opportunity well seized which made Parker what he was; but also the grace of God consciously and humbly sought. It is wonderful that we can possess as his last great choral work the tenderly beautiful "Dream of Mary," the last warm outpouring of a gentle, humble human heart close to God, that was also the heart of a genius. The lord grant him rest eternal, and let light perpetual shine upon him.

> "Where saints find full employ,
>   Songs of triumphant joy
>   Ever upraising;
>   They who are most beloved,
>   They who are tried and proved,
>   Together praising."

* * *

[*The Living Church—March 6, 1920.*]

APPENDIX

A. D. 1919

BRIAN HOOKER

There's a clamour of many voices,
  There's a murmur of marching feet,
And a music that rejoices
  Where the ranks move down the street:
Friends with the hearts of strangers,
  Boys with the eyes of men,
Having endured all dangers
  And so returned again.

Therefore with banners burning
  And cheers that rise and roll
Honour to these returning
  Who saved our honour whole.
Kingdoms and Dominations
  Have owned their fighting worth—
This common clay of nations
  Clad in the hue of earth;

These common souls and human
  Who laugh their sins abroad
But hide the love of woman
  And seek the fear of God.
Through poison, fire, and prison
  Unscared, unscathed, they came—
The sons of Man arisen
  Against the sons of Shame.

What of the many others
  Forever over seas—
Lovers and sons and brothers
  Like these, yet not like these?

HORATIO PARKER

For two shall have toiled and striven
  Equal in worst and best,
And to one shall be glory given,
  And to another, rest.

For two shall have trod one measure
  And of one cup drunk deep,
And one shall sweet pleasure
  And one shall have sweet sleep.
Look where the soft clouds blossom
  O'er the green country-side,
And the earth clothes her bosom
  In beauty as a bride

Can any peace delight them
  Whose delights rest undone,
Or any heaven requite them
  For this world wooed and won?
Filled full and flushed with morning
  They sang and took the sword—
The night came without warning,
  And where is their reward?

As a man makes a garden
  Not for the fruits repaid
But only to be warden
  Of life his hands have made;
As a woman bears her children
  Not that their loves atone,
But only to look upon them
  And know them for her own—

O youth foregone, foregoing!
  O dreams unseen, unsought!
God give you joy of knowing
  What life your death has bought.

APPENDIX

For our fathers gone before us,
  That they have not toiled in vain;
For the mother hearts that bore us
  And shall not waste their pain;

For the childhood games and laughter
  And the sorrows that turn their tears
To a song in the heart hereafter
  Unto the end of years—
For these, and what else unspoken
  Live when a soldier dies,
You are the body broken—
  You are the Sacrifice.

For the flower from the clod emerging
  And the fire from the cloud released,
For the wife that is more than virgin
  And the man that is more than beast;
For the spirit in strange communion
  With earth, yet more than earth—
The mystery of union
  The miracle of birth.

For these, and what holier dreaming
  Our dust and its deeds have meant,
You are the blood redeeming,
  You are the Sacrament.
For the pure fear that hovers,
  The sure faith that descends
Between the lips of lovers,
  Between the eyes of friends—

All giving beyond repayment,
  All truth neither bought nor sold,
The body more than raiment
  And the soul more than gold—

HORATIO PARKER

In all that we live believing,
  In all that we might have lost,
You are the spirit living—
  You are the Pentecost.

Your hands confirm our manhood,
  Your hearts hold women true,
And the wide eyes of children
  Are clean because of you.
Thro' desperate wars undaunted
  Our future arms retain
Your gift of fear confronted,
  Your gift of conquered pain.

Stronger when foes dispute you,
  Wiser when fools deny,
We who must live salute you
  Who have found strength to die!
Bring flowers they loved!
  Let trumpets sound, and the feast be spread!
Shall not earth live the fairer
  For their sake who are dead?

Not ashes nor any sorrow
  Be borne for such as they—
Give them the golden morrow
  They dwelt in yesterday!
Seeing our days inherit
  What joys they dared forego.
Surely they see and share it—
  Surely they know—they know!

There's a clamour of many voices,
  There's a murmur of marching feet,
And a music that rejoices
  Where the ranks move down the street:

APPENDIX

Friends with the hearts of strangers,
  Boys with the eyes of men,
And souls that have done with dangers
  And slept, and risen again.

Among them, above them,
  The unseen legions throng,
With the gold of our dreams we have crowned them,
  And their robes are the sound of our song.
Therefore with banners burning
  With lights and garlands dressed
Honour to these returning,
  Honour to those at rest.

HORATIO PARKER

WORKS OF HORATIO W. PARKER

Compiled by W. Oliver Strunk, Washington, D. C.

This bibliography is based upon a list of the works of Horatio W. Parker in the Library of Congress, compiled in 1921 by Walter R. Whittlesey, of the Library staff, and on supplementary information received in 1922 from Andrew Keogh, Librarian of Yale University. The arrangement by opus number adopted in previous lists of Parker's works (in "The Musical Times," September 1902, and in the dictionaries of Grove and Baker) has been retained. Single hymn-tunes have not been included. A number of Parker's compositions remained unpublished; these, and certain published compositions, were not directly accessible to the compiler. For this reason the bibliography is neither ideally accurate nor ideally complete; it is offered rather as a contribution to Parker bibliography than as a final treatment of the subject. Some of the original publishers, listed below, are no longer in business, or their catalogues have been absorbed by other firms.

ABBREVIATIONS

AMCo	The American Music Co., New York.	HWG	The H. W. Gray Co., New York.
ASB	A. S. Barnes & Co., New York.	JBM	J. B. Millet Co., Boston.
		JC	The John Church Co., Cincinnati.
APS	Arthur P. Schmidt & Co., Boston.	ML	M. Leidt & Co., New York.
BMCo	The Boston Music Co., Boston.		
CSE	Charles S. Elliot & Co., New York.	N	Novello & Co., Ltd., London.
CWT	C. W. Thompson Co., Boston.	OD	Oliver Ditson Co., Boston.
ES	Edward Schuberth & Co., New York.	RBr	Russell Brothers, Boston.
		SB	Silver, Burdett & Co., Boston.
GBJ	The George B. Jennings Co., Cincinnati.	TP	Theodore Presser Co., Philadelphia.

APPENDIX

GS	G. Schirmer (Inc.), New York.	WAP	Wm. A. Pond, New York.
H&L	Hall and Locke Co., Boston.	YUP	Yale University Press, New Haven
HBS	H. B. Stevens Co., Boston.	MS	Manuscript

Priv. pr.—Privately printed

acc.—accompaniment; ch.—chorus; orch.—orchestra; org.—organ; pf.—pianoforte

Published and Unpublished Works, Arranged by Opus Number

Op. 1. MOUNTAIN SHEPHERD'S SONG. Part-song for men's ch. [Uhland.] RBR, 1884. [Publ. without opus no.]

Op. 2. 5 PART-SONGS. Ch. MS, 1882.

Op. 3. THE LORD IS MY SHEPHERD. Psalm for soprano solo, women's ch. and org.; violin and harp ad lib. GS, 1904. [Composed in 1883.]

Op. 4. CONCERT OVERTURE IN E-FLAT. MS, 1883.

Op. 5. REGULUS. Overture in A major. MS, 1884.

Op. 6. THE BALLAD OF A KNIGHT AND HIS DAUGHTER. Cantata for ch. and orch. (Leopold, Graf zu Stolberg.) GS, 1891. [Publ. without opus no.; performed in Munich, 1884.]

Op. 7. SYMPHONY IN C MINOR. MS. [Munich, 1885.]

Op. 8. KING TROJAN. Cantata for solo voices, ch. and orch. (Fr. A. Muth.) APS, 1886. [Publ. without opus no.; performed in Munich, 1885.]

Op. 9. 5 MORCEAUX CARACTÉRISTIQUES POUR PIANO. 1. Elégie. 2. Scherzo. 3. Impromptu. 4. Caprice. 5. Gavotte. APS, 1886. [Publ. without opus no.]

Op. 10. 3 LOVE SONGS. Pf. acc. 1. Love's chase. (Thomas Lowell Beddoes.) 2. Night piece to Julia. (Robert Heink[!]) 3. Orsame's song. (Sir John Suckling.) APS, 1886. [Publ. as Op. 14.]

Op. 11. STRING QUARTET IN F MAJOR. MS.

Op. 12. VENETIAN OVERTURE IN B-FLAT. Orch. MS. [Munich, 1884.]

Op. 13. SCHERZO IN G MINOR. Orch. MS. [Munich, 1884.]

Op. 14. BLOW, BLOW, THOU WINTER WIND. Part-song for men's ch., pf. acc. (Wm. Shakespeare.) GS, 1892. [Publ. without opus no.]

Op. 15. IDYLLE. Cantata for solo voices, ch. and orch. (Goethe.) GS, 1891.

Op. 16. THE NORSEMEN'S RAID. (Normannenzug.) Cantata for men's ch. and orch. or pf. (Hermann Lingg.) JC, 1911.

Op. 17. 4 COMPOSITIONS FOR THE ORGAN. 1. Concert piece. 2. Impromptu. 3. Romanza. 4. Andante religioso. GS, 1890.

Op. 18. THE MORNING AND EVENING SERVICE, TOGETHER WITH THE OFFICE FOR THE HOLY COMMUNION. Ch. and org.; in E.N., 1892.

Op. 19. 4 SKETCHES FOR PIANO. 1. Romanza. 2. Scherzino. 3. Étude mélodieuse. 4. Nocturne. APS, 1890.

Op. 20. 4 COMPOSITIONS FOR THE ORGAN. 1. Wedding song. 2. Fughetta. 3. Melody and Intermezzo. 4. Fantasie. GS, 1891.

Op. 21. THE KOBOLDS. Cantata for ch. and orch. (Arlo Bates.) N, 1891. [Springfield Festival, May 7, 1891.]

Op. 22. 3 SACRED SONGS. Pf. acc. 1. Morning. 2. Evening. 3. Heaven's hope. GS, 1891.

Op. 23. 6 LYRICS FOR THE PIANO WITHOUT OCTAVES. 1. Reverie. 2. Ballad. 3. Rondino. 4. Fairy tale. 5. Barcarolle. 6. Novellette. GS, 1891. [Publ. as Op. 25.]

Op. 24. 6 SONGS. Pf. acc. 1. Cavalry song. (Edmund Clarence Stedman.) 2. Egyption serenade. (George W. Curtis.) 3. The light is fading from the sky. (Elizabeth Akers Allen.) 4. O ask me not. (Hans Hopfen.) 5. Pack, clouds, away! (Thomas Heywood.) 6. Spring song. (George W. Curtis.) GS, 1891.

Op. 25. 2 LOVE SONGS. Pf. acc. 1. My love. 2. O waving trees. GS, 1891. [Publ. without opus no. with "Violet" (1891) as "Three songs."]

Op. 26. HAROLD HARFAGER. Part-song for ch. and orch. or pf. GS, 1891. [Publ. without opus no.]

Op. 27. 2 PART-SONGS. Soprano solo, women's ch., pf. acc. 1. The fisher. (Goethe.) 2. The water fay. (Heine.) GS, 1891.

Op. 28. 4 COMPOSITIONS FOR THE ORGAN. 1. Triumphal march. 2. Larghetto. 3. Pastorale. 4. Concert piece No. 2. GS, 1891.

Op. 29. 6 SONGS. 1892. [Apparently unpublished.]

Op. 30. HORA NOVISSIMA. Oratorio for solo voices, ch. and orch. (Bernard de Morlaix.) N, 1893. [New York, Church Choral Society, May 3, 1893.]

Op. 31. DREAM-KING AND HIS LOVE. Cantata for tenor solo, ch. and orch. (Emmanuel Geobel.) GS, 1893. [Awarded a $300 prize offered by the National Conservatory of Music; performed in New York, March 30, 1893.]

Op. 32. 5 SKETCHES. Org. 1. Prelude. 2. Vision. 3. Scherzo. 4. Pastoral. 5. Nocturne. N, 1893.

Op. 33. 6 PART-SONGS. Men's ch. 1. Three words. (William Barclay Dunham.) 2. My love. (Langdon Elwyn Mitchell.) 3. Valentine. (Charles G. Blanden.) GS, 1893. [The 3 remaining numbers apparently unpublished.]

Op. 34. 3 SONGS. Pf. acc. 1. I know a little rose. 2. My lady love. 3. On the lake. (Mortimer Collins.) GS, 1893.

Op. 35. SUITE FOR PIANO, VIOLIN AND VIOLONCELLO. GS, 1904.

Op. 36. 4 COMPOSITIONS FOR ORGAN. 1. Canzonetta. 2. Canon. 3. Fugue in C minor. 4. Eclogue. GS, 1893.

Op. 37. THE HOLY CHILD. Cantata for solo voices, ch., pf. acc. (Isabelle Parker.) GS, 1893.

Op. 38. STRING QUINTET IN D MINOR. MS.

Op. 39. 4 PART-SONGS. Men's ch. 1. Behold, how good and joyful. 2. Softly now the light of day. 3. Lord, dismiss us with Thy blessing. 4. Blest are the departed. GS, 1894.

Op. 40. CÁHAL MÓR OF THE WINE-RED HAND. Rhapsody for baritone and orch. (James Clarence Morgan.) HWG, 1910. [Boston Symphony Orchestra, March 29, 1895.]

Op. 41. SUITE FOR VIOLIN AND PIANOFORTE. MS.

Op. 42. ODE FOR COMMENCEMENT DAY AT YALE UNIVERSITY, 1895. Men's ch., pf. acc. (Edmund Clarence Stedman.) GS, 1895.

Op. 43. THE LEGEND OF ST. CHRISTOPHER. Dramatic oratorio for solo voices, ch., orch. and org. (Isabella Parker.) N, 1898. [New York Oratorio Society, April 15, 1898.]

Op. 44. [Apparently not used.]

Op. 45. ADSTANT ANGELORUM CHORI. Motet for ch. (Thomas á Kempis.) GS, 1899. [Awarded a $250 prize offered by the Musical Art Society of New York; performed by the Society, March 16, 1899.]

Op. 46. A NORTHERN BALLAD. Orch. MS. [Boston Symphony Orchestra, Dec. 29, 1899.]

Op. 47. 6 OLD ENGLISH SONGS. Pf. acc. 1. Love is a sickness full of woes. (Samuel Daniel.) 2. Come, O come, my life's delight. (Thomas Campion.) 3. He that loves a rosy cheek. (Thomas Carew.) 4. Once I loved a maiden fair. (Old English.) 5. The complacent lover. (Sir Charles Selby.) 6. The lark now leaves his watery nest. (Sir William Davenent.) JC, 1899. [No. 3 publ. without opus no. in vol. 2 of "The music of the modern world" (D. Appleton) 1897.]

Op. 48. 3 PART-SONGS. Men's ch. 1. The lamp in the

West. (Ella Higginson.) 2. Awake, my lady sweet-lips. (Ella Higginson.) 3. The night has a thousand eyes. (Francis W. Bourdillon.) JC, 1901.

Op. 49. 3 Morceaux Caractéristiques pour le Piano. 1. Conte sérieux. 2. La sauterelle. 3. Valse gracile. JC, 1899.

Op. 50. A Wanderer's Psalm. Cantata for solo voices, ch. and orch. N, 1900. [Hereford, Three Choirs Festival, Sept. 13, 1900.]

Op. 51. 4 Songs. Pf. acc. 1. Love in May. (Ella Higginson.) 2. June night. (Ella Higginson.) 3. A spinning song. (Isabella G. Parker.) 4. At twilight. (Editha Ashmon Baker.) JC, 1901.

Op. 52. 3 Songs. 1900. [Apparently unpublished.]

Op. 53. [Hymnos andron.] Greek Festival Hymn for Men's Chorus and Orchestra. (Thomas Dwight Goodell.) GS, 1901. [For Yale University on the 200th anniversary of its foundation, Oct. 1901.]

Op. 54. A Star Song. Lyric rhapsody for solo voices, ch. and orch. (Henry Bernard Carpenter.) JC, 1902. [Awarded one of three $500 prize; offered by the Paderewski Fund. Performed at the Norwich Festival, Oct. 23, 1902.]

Op. 55. Concerto for Organ and Orchestra. N, 1903. [Boston Symphony Orchestra, Dec. 26, 1902.]

Op. 56. Symphonic Poem. Orch. MS.

Op. 57. The Office for the Holy Communion. Ch. and org.; in B-flat. N, 1904.

Op. 58. 3 Sacred Songs. Org. acc. 1. Come, Holy Ghost. (St. Ambrose.) 2. Lo, now the shades of night are swiftly fading. (St. Gregory.) 3. Declining now, the sun's bright wheel. (Charles Coffin.) N, 1905.

Op. 59. 4 Songs. Pf. acc. 1. Songs. (Robert Louis Stevenson.) 2. Serenade. (Nathan Haskell Dole.) 3. The blackbird. (Wm. E. Henley.) 4. Good-bye. (Christina Rossetti.) GS, 1904.

Op. 60. Union and Liberty. Part-song for ch., pf. acc.

(Oliver Wendell Holmes.) GS, 1905. [For the inauguration of President Theodore Roosevelt.]

Op. 61. SPIRIT OF BEAUTY. Ode for men's ch. and orch. or
band. (Arthur Detmers.) GS, 1905. [For the
dedication of the Albright Art Gallery, Buffalo.]

Op. 62. CRÉPUSCULE. Aria for mezzo-soprano and orch. or
pf. (Vicomte J. de Beaufort.) GS, 1912. [Publ.
as Op. 64.]

Op. 63. THE SHEPHERDS' VISION. Cantata for solo voices,
ch. and org.; oboe, strings and harp ad lib. (Frank
Van der Stucken.) HWG, 1906. [Publ. without
opus no.]

Op. 64. KING GORM THE GRIM. Ballad for ch. and orch.
(Theodor Fontane.) GS, 1908. [Norfolk, Litchfield County Choral Union, June 4, 1908.]

Op. 65. SONATA IN E-FLAT FOR ORGAN. GS, 1908.

Op. 66. SCHOOL SONGS. Ch., pf. acc. 2. Springtime revel-
ries. (Nixon Waterman.) SB, 1912. 3. The storm.
(Nixon Waterman.) [Publ. in Gertrude B. Parsons' "High School song book" (SB)1919.] 4. Freedom, our queen. (Oliver Wendell Holmes.) SB,
1911. [No. 1 apparently unpublished.]

Op. 67. 4 COMPOSITIONS FOR ORGAN. 1. Festival prelude.
2. Revery. 3. Scherzino. 4. Postlude. [Publ. as
Op. 66 in "Recital pieces; a collection of 21 original compositions for the organ by Horatio Parker"
(GS) 1910.]

Op. 68. 5 SHORT PIECES FOR THE ORGAN. 1. Canon in the
fifth. 2. Slumber-song. 3. Novelette. 4. Arietta.
5. Risoluto. GS, 1908.

Op. 69. [See Op. 16.]

Op. 70. 7 SONGS. Pf. acc. (Brian Hooker.) 1. A man's
song. 2. A robin's song. 3. A woman's song. 4.
I shall come back. 5. Offerings. 6. Only a little
while. 7. Together. JC, 1910.

Op. 71. MONA. Opera in 3 acts. (Brian Hooker.) GS,
1911. [Awarded a $10,000 prize offered by the

APPENDIX

Metropolitan Opera Company; performed in New York at the Metropolitan Opera House, March 4, 1912.]

Op. 72. COLLEGIATE OVERTURE. Men's ch. and orch. Priv. print, 1911. [Without opus no.; performed in Norfolk by the Litchfield County Choral Union, June 7, 1911.]

Op. 73. A SONG OF TIMES. Cantata for ch. and orch. (John Luther Long.) GS, 1911.

Op. 74. 7 GREEK PASTORAL SCENES. Solo voices, women's ch., oboe, harp and strings or pf. (After Meleager and Argentarius.) GS, 1913.

OP. 75. THE LEAP OF ROUSHAN BEG. Ballad for tenor solo, men's cho. and orch. (Henry W. Longfellow.) GS, 1913.

Op. 76. SONGS. [Apparently unpublished.]

Op. 77. FAIRYLAND. Opera in 3 acts. (Brian Hooker.) GS, 1915. [Awarded a $10,000 prize offered by the National Federation of Musical Clubs; performed in Los Angeles at Clune's Auditorium, July 1, 1915.]

Op. 78. THE PROGRESSIVE MUSIC SERIES. 8 vols. (With Osbourne McConathy, Edward Bailey Birge and Otto Miessner.) SB, 1914-16.

Op. 79. MORVEN AND THE GRAIL. Oratorio for solo voices, ch. and orch. (Brian Hooker.) BMCo, 1915. [Boston, Händel and Haydn Society, April 13, 1915; for the 100th anniversary of the founding of the society.]

Op. 80. CUPID AND PSYCHE. Masque in 3 acts. Incidental music for ch., oboe, strings, harpsichord and harp. (John Jay Chapman.) [No. 8 priv. pr. without opus no.; performed in New Haven, June 16, 1916.]

Op. 81. YALE PAGEANT. Incidental music for ch. (Francis Hartman Markoe.) Priv. print, 1916. [Without opus no.]

Op. 82. The Dream of Mary. Morality for solo voices, ch., children's ch., congregation and org. or orch. (John Jay Chapman.) HWG, 1918. [Norfolk, Litchfield County Choral Union, June 4, 1918.]

Op. 83. The Red Cross Spirit Speaks. Song, orch. acc. (John Finley.) HWG, 1918. [Publ. without opus no.]

Op. 84. A. D. 1919. Cantata for soprano solo, ch. and pf. (Brian Hooker.) YUP, 1919. [New Haven, June 1919.]

Published and Unpublished Works Without Opus Number, in Chronological Order

1882. 3 Songs. Pf. acc. 1. Slumber song. 2. Wedding song. 3. Goldilocks. APS.

1886. Devotion. Song, pf. acc. (F. L. Humphreys.) WAP. [Composer's name given as N. W. Parker.]

1890. Bow Down Thine Ear. Anthem for ch., org. acc. GS.

Christ Our Passover. Anthem for ch., org. acc. AMCo (HWG, 1908).

Count Robert of Paris. Overture for orch. MS. [New York, Manuscript Society; Dec. 10.]

The Lord Is My Light. Anthem for ch., org. acc. GS.

Magnificat in E-Flat. Solo voices and ch., org. acc. GS.

Nunc Dimittis in E-Flat. Ch., org. acc. GS.

2 Sacred Songs. Pf. acc. 1. Rest. 2. There is a land of pure delight. APS.

1891. 12 Christmas Carols for Children. Unison ch., pf. acc. GS.

Deus Misereatur in E. Ch., org. acc. GS.

Give Unto the Lord. Anthem for ch., org. acc. N.

I WILL SET HIS DOMINION IN THE SEA. Anthem for
ch., org. acc. N.

THE RIVEN TOMB. Anthem for ch., org. acc. [Publ.
in the New York Herald, March 29.]

1891. TE DEUM IN A. Ch., Org. acc. GS.

VIOLET. Song, pf. acc. GS. [Publ. as Op. 23, No. 3,
with "Two Love Songs" [(Op. 25) as "Three
Songs."]

WHO SHALL ROLL US AWAY THE STONE? Anthem for
soprano solo and ch., org. acc. ML.

1893. BEFORE THE HEAVENS WERE SPREAD ABROAD.
Anthem for tenor solo and ch., org. acc. N.

COME, SEE THE PLACE WHERE JESUS LAY. Song, pf.
acc. GS.

IN GLAD WEATHER. Song, pf. acc. (Charles Buxton
Going.) ES.

MAGNIFICAT AND NUNC DIMITTIS IN E-FLAT. Ch., org.
acc. N. [Publ. as Op. 34.]

A ROSE SONG. Unison ch., pf. acc. (Richard H.
Stoddard.) [Publ. in "The children's souvenir
song book" (N).]

SALVE REGINA. Song, pf. acc. GS.

2 SONGS. Pf. acc. 1. Love is a rover. (Samuel Min-
turn Peck.) 2. A song of three little birds. GBJ.

2 SONGS. Pf. acc. 1. Fickle love. (Louise Chandler
Moulton.) 2. Uncertainly. (Charles Swain.) HBS.

TE DEUM IN B-FLAT. Ch., org. acc. GS.

1894. DIVINE CARE. Song, pf. acc. (Alice C. Jennings.)
HBS.

LIGHT'S GLITTERING MORN BEDECKS THE SKY. Anthem
for bass solo and ch., org. acc. GS.

2 SHAKESPEARE SONGS. Pf. acc. 1. A poor soul sat
sighing. 2. It was a lover and his lass. HBS.

1895. 2 COMPOSITIONS FOR PIANOFORTE. 1. Capricietto. 2.
Dialogue. [Publ. in vol. 13 of "Famous composers
and their works" (JBM).]

1896. 3 COMPOSITIONS FOR ORGAN. 1. Postlude. 2.

Melody. 3. Marcia religiosa. [Publ. in vols. 2-4 of Dudley Buck's "Vox Organi" (JBM); Nos. 1 and 3 reprinted in "The American organist" (TP) 1918.]

FAR FROM THE WORLD, O LORD, I FLEE. Anthem for soprano or tenor solo and ch., org. acc. (William Cowper.) CSE (N, 1901).

SPANISH CAVALIER'S SONG. Pf. acc. (Isabella G. Parker.) HBS.

1897. IN MAY. Part-song for women's ch., orch. and harp. GS.

O LORD, I WILL EXALT THEE. Anthem for ch., org. acc. GS.

1898. CALM ON THE LISTENING EAR OF NIGHT. Anthem for soprano or tenor solo and ch., org. acc. (Rev. E. H. Sears.) [Publ. in the Churchman, Dec. 10 (N, 1900.)]

GRANT, WE BESEECH THEE, MERCIFUL LORD. Part-song for ch. BMCo.

REJOICE IN THE LORD. Anthem for ch., org. acc. CWT.

1899. BEHOLD, YE DESPISERS. Anthem for bass solo and ch., org. acc. N.

1900. IN HEAVENLY LOVE ABIDING. Anthem for soprano solo and ch., org. acc. (Anna L. Waring.) N.

1901. COME AWAY! Part-song for ch. (John Dowland.) N. [Publ. as Op. 54.]

AN EVEN SONG. Part-song for women's ch., pf. acc. (Celia Thaxter.) N.

THE ROBBERS. Part-song for ch., pf. acc. (Joanna Baillie.) [Publ. in W. L. Tomlins' "The laurel song book" (SB).]

THOU SHALT REMEMBER. Anthem for baritone solo and ch., org. acc. N.

1904. BRIGHTEST AND BEST. Anthem for soprano solo and ch., org. acc. GS.

IT CAME UPON THE MIDNIGHT CLEAR. Anthem for

APPENDIX

solo voices, and ch., org. acc.; violin and harp ad lib. OD.

2 Songs from Tennyson's "Queen Mary." Pf. acc. 1. Milkmaid's song. 2. Lute song. GS.

1905. Come, Gentles, Rise! Christmas carol for unison ch., pf. acc. (Rev. Daniel Evans.) GS.

I Shall Not Die, But Live. Anthem for baritone solo and ch., org. acc. OD.

Springtime of Love. Song, pf. acc. (Frank Dempster Sherman.) GS.

1908. Piscatrix. Part-song for men's ch. GS.

The Wandering Knight's Song. Pf. acc. (Spanish ballad, 1555.) JC.

1909. To Whom Then Will Ye Liken God. Anthem for tenor solo and ch., org. acc. HWG.

1911. A Christmas Song. Pf. acc. (Dr. J. G. Holland.) [Publ. in the Century Illustrated Monthly Magazine, Dec.]

1912. Song of a Pilgrim Soul. Part-song for women's ch., pf. acc. (Henry Van Dyke.) Priv. pr.

1913. Alice Brand. Cantata for solo voices and women's ch., pf. acc. (Sir Walter Scott.) GS. [Publ. as Op. 76.]

1914. 2 Songs. Pf. acc. 1. A perfect love. (Alfred H. Hyatt.) 2. Her cheek is like the tinted rose. (Florence Earle Coates.) APS.

3 Songs. Pf. acc. 1. Morning song. (Martin Schütze.) 2. Across the fields. (Walter Crane.) 3. Nightfall. (Martin Schütze.) BMCo.

1918. Hymn for the Victorious Dead. Song, pf. acc. (Hermann Hagedorn.) [Publ. in The Outlook, Dec. 18.]

1919. He Faileth Not. Anthem for soprano or tenor solo and ch., org. acc. HWG.

Triumphal March. Part-song for ch., pf. acc. (David Kilburn Stevens.) [Publ. in Gertrude B. Parsons' "High school song book" (SB).]

1923. I REMEMBER. Part-song for women's ch., pf. acc.
(Henry Wadsworth Longfellow.) [Publ. in "A
book of choruses for high schools and choral societies" (SB).]

Editing and Arranging

1895. THE BATTLE HYMN OF THE REPUBLIC. Part-song for
ch. GS.
A COLLECTION OF ARRANGEMENTS AND TRANSCRIP-
TIONS FOR THE ORGAN. GS.
IN EINEM KÜHLEN GRUNDE. Part-song for men's
ch. GS.
DIE LORELEI. Part-song for men's ch. GS.
MY COUNTRY, 'TIS OF THEE. Part-song for ch. GS.
THE STAR-SPANGLED BANNER. Part-song for ch. GS.

1907. Saint-Saëns, Camille. THE RAINBOW; QUARTET FROM
"THE DELUGE." Ch., org. acc. GS.
UNIVERSITY HYMNS WITH TUNES ARRANGED FOR
MEN'S VOICES. (With Harry B. Jepson.) ASB.

1908. COSSACK WAR-SONG. Part-song for men's ch. GS.
Grandval, Mme. de. 2 CHORUSES FROM STABAT
MATER. Ch., org. acc. GS.
3 IRISH FOLK-SONGS. Part-songs for men's ch. 1.
The Shan Van Voght. 2. At the mid-hour of night.
(Thomas Moore.) 3. Kitty Magee. (Francis A.
Faley.) GS.
2 MINNELIEDER. Part-songs for foresinger and men's
ch. 1. Moonrise. 2. Three roses. GS.
Rheinberger, Josef. THE VALLEY OF THE ESPINGO.
Ballad for men's ch. and orch. Op. 50. (Paul
Heyse.) [Vocal score.] GS.

1911. MUSIC AND DRAMA. H&L.
MUSIC AND PUBLIC ENTERTAINMENT. H&L

1912. GERMAN, FRENCH AND ITALIAN SONG CLASSICS. 4 vols.
JC.